AWAKENING

A Journey
of
Enlightenment

AWAKENING

A Journey *of* Enlightenment

by

Andrée Louise Cuenod

Portal
Center
Press

Awakening, A Journey of Enlightenment

© 2015 by Andrée Louise Cuenod

Second edition.
The first edition was published in 1995 by Northwest Publishing, Inc.

Portal Center Press
Gleneden Beach Oregon
www.portalcenterpress.com

ISBN: 978-1-936902-17-0

Printed in the USA

With a great deal of love, I dedicate this book
to my mother, Polly Cuenod,
for her loving foundation upon which I built
my life and my conscious spiritual growth,
and to Mauri Leonard
for her long-term loving friendship and her help, tolerance,
and support of me in all of my writing endeavors.

AWAKENING
by Christine Thomas

I once asked, Who am I?
And heard no reply.
Years later, lost and afraid,
I cried from the depth of my heart,
"Who am I?"
Suddenly there was no "I"
Only infinite pure white Light.
Now that's what I call a response!
Beyond joy and even love!
I thought, "Do I have to go back?"
Of course with that thought I was back!
A glorious individual individuated
From all that is.
Back in human form
I find the work still has to be done.
But how great is the progress
Now that I know who we all are.
Every day an adventure
Every insight and discovery a delight!
It is. (And all the rest is story.)

CONTENTS

PREFACE 1

PART ONE - A PERSONAL JOURNEY OF ENLIGHTENMENT 11

   1. THE EARLY YEARS: Experiences that Set the Stage for My Spiritual Understanding 13

   2 THE DAWNING OF ENLIGHTENMENT 25

   3 GATHERING, DEVELOPING AND REFINING MY TRUTHS 35

PART TWO - THE ILLUSION OF HUMAN LIFE 47

   4 THERE IS ONLY ONE: GOD 49

   5 OUR ORIGIN, EVOLUTION, AND DESTINY AS HUMANS: MY IDEA OF CREATION 63

   6 HOW IT WORKS 77

   7 WHAT DOES ALL THIS MEAN? 93

   8 THINKING IT THROUGH 103

PART THREE - OUR PERSONAL HUMAN EXPERIENCE 113

   9 EXPERIENCING PHYSICALITY, ESPECIALLY THE LOVE ASPECTS .. 115

   10 ADVERSITY IN OUR EXPERIENCE 127

   11 EXPERIENCE OF PAIN, DISABILITY, DISEASE, & AGING 137

   12 HEALING 151

   13 OUR EXPERIENCE OF DEATH 165

PART FOUR - MAKING THE MOST OF OUR EARTHLY EXPERIENCE 181

   14 AWARENESS *vs.* JUDGMENT 183

   15 GETTING TO KNOW AND LOVE OURSELVES 193

   16 IMPROVING RELATIONSHIPS 201

   17 CREATING OUR REALITY 215

18 CHOICES: HAPPINESS IS AN ATTITUDE & SERENITY CAN BE A HABIT 233
  19 GOING WITHIN TO *KNOW* AND LOVE OUR SELVES 241
PART FIVE - THE SHIFT 257
  20 THE VEIL IS LIFTED 259
  21 LIFE'S CYCLICAL NATURE AND EARTH-CHANGES 269
  22 AWAKENING 281
AFTERWORD 293
APPENDIX 297
BIBLIOGRAPHY 299
ACKNOWLEDGMENTS 301
INDEX 303
ABOUT THE AUTHOR 309

PREFACE

Accept only that which appeals to your Heart, as Truth—let the rest pass you by, for the time being—for to each comes his own; and none can gain his own until he is prepared for it.

~ "The Law of Learning," from *The Upanishads*

Philosophers have considered and debated the issues of our human origin, beginnings, and existence as long as we've had the written word, and probably a lot longer. Our very existence as humans on Earth is the greatest enigma with which thinkers of all ages have grappled, and our ability to question it is considered by many to be the primary difference between us and animals. *Orthodox* fundamentalists, both theologians and scientists, have for centuries dogmatically argued their opposing positions on these issues from their own narrow points of view. Most thinking people the world over have given some thought to these issues, but few have come up with definitive answers.

The Hebrew Scriptures on which the religions of Judaism, Christianity, and Islam are based do not provide a reason for creation. The book of Genesis begins with the acts of creation, without explaining either the who or the why of them. Nor are these explained elsewhere in the Bible. Without answers from which to draw understanding, we wonder why the universe was created and why and how life began. We ask how we humans got to be so different intellectually from our alleged ape-like cousins or our primitive ancient ancestors. We speculate whether there is more to our life than what is obvious, and we question if our life here has purpose and meaning. What is it all about? We'd like to know if there truly is a God, and if so, what its/his/her nature is and what our relationship is to God. We wonder if we have a soul, and whether we've had previous human lives and will continue to reincarnate into future lives.

Was there a first cause? If there is cause for our being, there must be purpose. Why then is there such disparity in our living conditions—why do some of us have a seemingly beautiful life while others endure such hardship? Why do some among us live so briefly? Is this all there is to life? If so, why are some people loaded with talents and others mentally or physically challenged? Why do some people starve to death in poverty and wretchedness as others grow obese in their affluence? Or, are we here by accident, some serendipitous quirk of nature?

We may suspect that there's more to our existence than science's explanation of spontaneous generation by happenstance and our evolution to "modern humans" through natural selection on random mutation. And we may not buy altogether the Genesis story of our beginnings, other than perhaps metaphorically. Science, in trying to answer the hows while denying the existence of a first cause (what and why), has done little to help us understand our life. Religion hasn't done much better with the why questions. The quarreling between them about our origin and beginnings exists because neither has a solid answer for *why* we are here. Neither knows what our existence is about. Philosophies and religions have been built around the issues of our beginnings, life, and destiny, but usually avoid the issue of why we are in this life. And without an answer to that question, how can we know what our life is about? Does anyone know truly what human life is all about?

I believe I do, which is why I've written this book, to share with you my complete picture of life and its resulting wholly positive philosophy. I feel we cannot begin to understand our life here without first having some idea of the *whys* behind it. My picture answers all my questions and gives me great comfort. It makes possible my understanding of life on Earth in a way that helps me see it quite differently than what we've all been taught. And it removes all fear from my experience.

The two key words in the title of this book are Enlightenment and Awakening, and in addition to the big WHY question they are what this book is about. So, before we go further, I'll give you my definitions of those words. Awakening is our ultimate destiny in Earth life. It's a case of waking up to the complete Reality of our spirit life in full conscious awareness. (And that's the Reality I mean when I capitalize it.) I believe we are in a sense in a dream state in this life and that after we've had all the experiences we set out to have through numerous human lives we will find a way to wake up. We will awaken to the truth of our spirituality, divinity, and our Oneness. We will have completed a *circular* journey as humans in Earth life, a journey through which we veiled Reality from us and temporarily replaced our great native intelligence with intellect and our natural spirit abilities with five limited physical senses. After eons of human experiences of a great variety of conditions, we are now on the upward arc of our circular evolution, awakening our conscious awareness to the full Reality of our spirit beingness, our Oneness, and our divinity. We are coming full circle.

To me, enlightenment is a path in the later stages of the upward human evolution journey that many of us use to enable, further, and hasten our awakening. While there are many paths toward awakening, the most effective one seems to be that of enlightenment. It's a path on which to learn, *know* (intuitively accept as truth), and remember the truths of our existence as both humans and spirit beings. Enlightenment is gained, not from reading books or listening to wise teachers, but only from going within to one's inner soul-Self. Only the Self can enlighten, providing the truths of Reality. So, the journey is an inner one into consciousness itself.

Many years ago, I began a quest for enlightenment, an unfolding process through which I sought "truth." I eventually read everything that hinted it could teach me something. In reading others' views about human life, though, I found their answers to *why* either thoroughly unconvincing or missing altogether. Yet, as chaotic as they seem, on closer examination, the universe and our life clearly have order. The anthropic (for human habitation) nature of Earth's physical makeup and location in space is a prime example of that order. Scientists report that it takes some one-hundred conditions to make human life on Earth possible, and if any one was off by only .01° we would not exist. Those conditions have to do with our planet's distance from its sun, its orbit, our moon, and its orbit, Earth's protective ozone layer, the chemical makeup of inner earth, and much more. Where there is order, there is reason for it; there is cause and there is purpose. There must be an answer to "why."

Early in my search, I met people who were further along in their own quests and who were willing to share their wisdom with me. They taught me the single most important step in pursuit of my enlightenment: *communication with my all-knowing inner voice* (a process I call "communion"). Whether one thinks of this voice as that of spirit guides, God, Jesus, one's own soul-Self (as I do), or one's imagination, is of little importance. Consciously receiving insight from it, though, is without a doubt in my mind, the most important and thrilling thing anyone can do in this life. The mere fact of having such communication answers some of my questions, helping me see that we aren't alone in this life, that there is an unmanifest Reality—not another place but higher vibrational dimensions in consciousness—beyond this physical life on Earth.

> The soul's communication of truth is the highest event in nature... and the communication is an influx of the Divine Mind into our mind.... Every moment when the individual feels invaded by it is memorable.
>
> ~ Ralph Waldo Emerson

Through such communication, I gained answers to all of my questions, both lofty and mundane. So it was I gathered my spiritual truths. Those truths have answered my why, what, who, and how questions while helping me formulate an overall philosophy that is wholly positive and which enables me to understand, cope with, and enjoy, every moment and aspect of this life.

I'm not saying my answers are the only true ones, just that they are true for me. I have no more proof of my hypotheses than science and religion have of theirs. But I do have a complete picture of what originally occurred and what has transpired to bring us to where we are now. I know, Western fundamentalists of science and religion each offers a picture, but neither is very complete; they both leave so much unexplained, so many questions unanswered, especially those *why* questions. Neither sees us as living before becoming humans, and only religion speculates on our ultimate destiny.

While we may be somewhat interested in that big why question, it's our everyday life with which we are mainly concerned. I contend that if we knew and understood the answer to why we are in this life we would have far fewer concerns about our everyday life and would be far happier—and isn't that what we all want? In our everyday life, we seek money, possessions, and love in search of happiness and self-esteem. We measure success by the quantities of material things we can amass. When these don't satisfy us–and they never will–we seek to gather ever more, often becoming greedy and power-hungry. We lose our sense of humanity, our caring for others, and are afraid to share our wealth for fear of losing it and diminishing our hard-won status. We pretend we're happy, satisfied and occasionally succeed in convincing ourselves. When we aren't able to achieve success in these ways, our self-esteem deteriorates and we become frustrated, angry, and sometimes belligerent. Men and women both assault their spouses, abuse their children and addict themselves to all manner of substances and activities. Some take to a life of corruption or crime to gain the money, power, status, and self-esteem they long for, or merely to take out their frustrations and anger on others.

We've functioned in this pattern throughout most of our human existence without achieving the happiness we seek. And fewer of us, perhaps than ever before, have genuine self-esteem. This old way doesn't work; it can't. It can lead only to our destruction. It has destroyed whole civilizations in our past, and will do so over and over again until we learn the lesson this pattern and its results provide. We've spent our lives seeking what we don't have, and have misdirected our search. But, the good news is that we are beginning to realize our error.

It's nearing time for humanity to experience a *Shift* in consciousness. It's time to realize the folly of seeking material satisfaction and to reach out in a new direction. We were designed to ultimately seek what until very recently has not been recognized by most of us. It's time now to properly identify that which is missing from our conscious awareness, so we can set ourselves on the most fulfilling path. I believe that what we're missing is truth, the knowledge and understanding of our existence, our spirituality, our Oneness, and our divinity. We are being prodded from within to seek that understanding, to *remember* what we once knew well.

I feel that my picture of human life and the philosophy it promotes have been entrusted to me to share with others. I offer you another way of viewing life on Earth, to give you more choices on which to base your responses to your world. I feel I have some truths to offer those of you who want them, which might help you toward that Shift in consciousness.

Acquiring truth is not necessarily a mystical experience. It can be common and a normal occurrence, for others as it is for me. It's time for people to realize that no one of us is any more special than another. We don't need heroes, we need truth. Truth is available through our inner voice to each of us equally, not just to a chosen few. I call this truth-gathering "en*light*enment," because the process brings light into a world of darkness.

Those of us who consciously commune with our inner voice—which I prefer to call my "Self"—do so in a variety of ways, each using what works best for us. In some cases word-for-word dialogue is the means. Some people "channel" an ancient wise entity, ascended master, or avatar, while others see pictures in their mind's eye. Although I now regularly carry on dialog with my inner voice, I received my basic truths as insights, concepts, or blocks of wisdom, to which I then responded with questions for clarity and understanding. My questions were answered, mostly through more and deeper insights, which I digested. Then I asked more questions until I was satisfied I understood. To illustrate the point and help me assimilate it, my Self often arranged an experience for me and accompanied it with intuitive explanation. Because I view the source of my inspiration as that aspect of God consciousness that is my own higher-vibrating soul-Self, I choose to call the truths mine.

Western Religion has gotten itself so wrapped up in controlling the thinking and behavior of its followers, it has lost sight of the beautiful fundamental truths on which it was originally based. For the most part, each denomination thinks it alone has the only truth, and insists it is right for everyone. Religions focus on the worship of heroes, on the "shall not" social dogmas and on the negative aspects of human life. Tenets such as sin and the emphasis on righteousness, self-denial, and atonement stem from negativity and fear. Fundamentalist religion approaches life from a belief that creation, including us, is basically flawed and sinful. The "evils" condemned by religious leaders are social, human issues and have no basis in original spiritual truths. Spiritual truths are opening not forbidding, loving not fearful, accepting not judging; they are positive not negative. Besides, if an all-powerful God created this cosmos and us, how can we be flawed and sinful?

Although my philosophy is different from most Christian teachings, I quote the Christian Bible throughout this book. I use passages attributed to Jesus to illustrate that his words as expressed in the Bible can be interpreted in different ways, and can support different approaches to truth. I also use aphorisms of the wise from the Hindu *Upanishads* and quote other great thinkers to show that my philosophy is in sync with other notable philosophies and that much of it isn't new at all. Mine is simply a new way of interpreting and applying time-honored truths, what Aldous Huxley termed the "Perennial Philosophy."

"Truth" is not an opinion or intellectual knowledge; it is inner *knowing*—a personal *experience* of the heart. Each of us has or can gather, our own set of truths, if we want to. Each of us is a unique individual. Even when we agree on a subject, we approach it from a viewpoint different from anyone else's, so there is no single set of truths we can all understand, agree on, and follow, no single set that meets the needs of the many diverse cultures. Consequently, we must be content with whatever *resonates* best to us personally, to our heart. There is, however, something of value for us in most others' truths; so, we might look for that exquisite morsel. And sometimes it takes only a word to trigger our memory of something in Reality, our truth.

Why would anyone enjoy or get anything out of reading about my journey of enlightenment and the insights I have gleaned? I'm not a famous person who people want to know more about. But maybe that's the point. Maybe you can relate to me and my story. I offer it to help you view yourself and Earth life differently than fundamentalists of either Western religions or science have taught us. I believe they are both incomplete, even wrong, in their teaching, mostly because they don't know why we are here, other than to share in, embody, and spread God's love.

My philosophy, based firmly on an answer to why we are here, is so satisfying to me that I want to share it with others so they have an opportunity to experience the love, joy, truth, and happiness it gives me. I see life on Earth in a way that has completely removed fear from my experience and makes me so very glad to be here, especially at this time of great change.

When I began researching and writing my other book, *WAKE UP! Our old beliefs don't work anymore!* (Portal Center Press, 2013), what I had in mind was something quite different from what finally came out. It was to be informative and without much of a message. I wanted to describe the many various beliefs (ancient and modern, spiritual, religious, and scientific) about our origin, experience, and destiny as humans on Earth. I was calling that book idea "Contrasts in Perspective." But the more I read and wrote, the more I realized both how very similar some of the numerous perspectives were and how very different some were. I had known very little about the classical scientific beliefs (of physics and biology) and nothing about the beliefs of our ancient ancestors. I realized, too, that our beliefs influence our worldviews and our behavior with regard to other cultures and ethnicities, other species, and our environment. I saw that our beliefs fall into essentially two categories: materialist and spiritual, with the beliefs of classical science and fundamentalists of the Abrahamic religions essentially in the materialist category and all others—ancient and modern, Eastern and Western, as well as aboriginal traditions world wide—in the spiritual category.

It might help at this point if I were to provide my definitions of spirit and spirituality. All things "supernatural" are spirit, and supernatural, to me, merely means "ultra natural," more natural than anything material. Actually, all things, whether manifest or unmanifest are spirit, always have been and always will be. I equate spirit with energy, light, consciousness, and love. These are what we (everything) truly are. We are not our bodies, not our human egos, not our human intellect. We, spirit beings, temporarily don bodies, egos, and intellect to enact physical human life. Spirit is not a substance, it is an essence, we can think of as an idea. All spirit is the ONE of everything, what I also call the Kosmos: all that is, in all dimensions and universes, whether unmanifest or manifest, seen or unseen. Spirit can also be viewed as life, for everything has life, is alive, even the rocks, elements, and atmosphere of Earth. All cells, atoms, quanta are alive with intelligence.

Spirituality is one's knowledge, understanding, and memory of spirit Reality. It is one's inner Reality, inner beingness, inner consciousness. While religion is an outer or external expression of one's spiritual beliefs, usually shared in *community*, spirituality is an inner or internal expression of one's *individual* spiritual reality. To realize spirituality, we "go within" to our inner spirit beingness.

It was obvious to me that our world conditions today are due to exaggerated materialism. Our materialist beliefs have put us on and continue to nurture a destructive, harmful, and disastrous track, which could lead to our culture's ultimate fall. Something needs to be done. I thought that if we could somehow have a spiritual renaissance, in which the heart-based beliefs of spirituality—its interconnectedness, interdependence, and holism—rose to the forefront, we could turn our culture around and resolve our world problems. If we could get humanity's awareness raised to a higher level of consciousness, we would further an unstoppable Shift in our world consciousness. So, while keeping much of the intended information, I changed the direction of *WAKE UP!*, giving it a very definite message, one of hope in our future with love and compassion for all. My essential theme became: Change beliefs, change the world.

AWAKENING offers a spiritual perspective that I believe represents the beliefs of our very ancient ancestors, Eastern traditions, native traditions everywhere, and spiritual/metaphysical mystics and philosophers of today. It provides details of its expressed belief system that enable the reader to thoroughly examine the spiritual perspective and apply it to their life.

I have sectioned this presentation of my story and philosophy into five parts. The first part covers my personal journey of enlightenment. The second part contains the foundational insights I was given about God, consciousness, love, and perfection, then about our origin, beginnings, experience of human life, and our destiny. Then I consider these insights, how they work and what they mean to us in human life on Earth. I discuss the big WHY at length, and look at the "dark" side of human life—the evils and heinous things people do to others—viewing them as spiritual positives, even blessings, rather than the negatives we judge them to be. Parts three and four apply those insights, my "truths," and resulting overall positive philosophy to your personal experiences of this life, and are introspective in nature, encouraging you to go within. Part three specifically examines loves, adversities, health, and well-being, then healing and finally death. Part four looks at how you create your own life experience, featuring judgment, loving yourself, your relationships, creating your reality, happiness, serenity, and enlightenment, to make the most of your human experience. Each chapter in both parts provides exercises you can use to apply the insights. Part five is about our destiny: where we're going, how we'll get there and what our future holds. It examines a Shift in awareness to ever higher levels of consciousness, the cyclical/spiral nature of our human evolution, and our ultimate awakening back to fully conscious spirit beings.

You may find me pretty opinionated, especially in much of my coverage of our experience of daily human life. But I am only trying to show how my philosophy applies to life and how, by applying it as I do, you too can get more enjoyment out of life. Much of it may seem like I'm saying that my truth is how things are and how they work. But what I'm saying is only how life is and works for me; I'm merely giving you another view of life to think about, accept, or reject.

It's been nearly 20 years since I finished writing the original *AWAKENING, a journey of enlightenment* and it was published. While I had by then learned enough to formulate my philosophy and my view of "creation," I have since expanded my truths. I haven't needed to alter my basic beliefs, merely further develop and refine them. So, this second edition is updated with new insights and understandings, all of which I hope will help you refine your own personal beliefs, if only to help you decide what isn't your truth.

PART ONE - A PERSONAL JOURNEY OF ENLIGHTENMENT

God and I are one.
~ Hindu Law of Identification

1

THE EARLY YEARS: EXPERIENCES THAT SET THE STAGE FOR MY SPIRITUAL UNDERSTANDING

Leaning across his big mahogany desk, the doctor looked straight at me and said, "You have cancer." My mother and father both gasped and my mother's hand squeezed mine. My stomach lurched. I was not yet fourteen.

It was almost as if that thoughtless doctor was responsible for whatever was wrong with me. He had frightened my parents, making my mother cry. I can't say I truly understood what cancer was—not all that much was known about the disease in the mid 20th century, and I was young and rarely read, and we didn't have television, much less computers and the internet.

That night I talked my situation over with God, as I always did when confronted with a problem. I asked that nothing bad happen to me. Then, a deep calmness washed away my fears and brought acceptance of whatever was to be my fate.

Seven years earlier my pediatrician had discovered a growth on my thyroid and prescribed daily doses of iodine, hoping to shrink the mass. I had been an active, vivacious child, loving every minute of life, especially my tap dancing lessons. Oh, how I wanted to dance. Suddenly, I found myself listless and easily tired. My tap lessons were abruptly ended to conserve my energy; I had to take naps and down tablespoons of tonic in addition to the doses of the vile-tasting iodine. In the seven intervening years, the mass, instead of shrinking, grew to the size of a tennis ball sitting in my throat as if I'd swallowed it. I felt freakish.

After I was diagnosed with cancer, we didn't go back to that doctor, but instead went to a surgeon in downtown Los Angeles. Always before in any doctor's office, I was a bundle of quivering nerves, but as I walked into the new doctor's office I felt totally calm, and wasn't in the least afraid. In fact, I felt almost good, comfortable. Because of the rarity of my youth with such a condition, doctors came from around the country to observe my surgeon remove the mass—which turned out to be a surprisingly unfamiliar benign growth. With it, I made the *Journal of American Medicine*. Looking back on all that now, I think that if that first doctor hadn't been so callous, that experience would not have been so significant to me. So I thank him for his directness and help in my journey.

My early childhood memories are few, and mostly trauma-centered. Because it was so abnormal for me and I was so acutely aware of it at the time, that calm acceptance as I entered the surgeon's office left me with the memory of a wonderful experience that I would never forget.

GOD, MY FRIEND

I believe I was born with a knowledge of the Supreme Spirit I call "God." Although it's likely I heard about it from my mother, I don't remember ever being told about its existence, I just *knew* it. I was conversant with it and had an unswerving faith in its love and power. I felt we were connected in some special way, maybe as friends. I didn't know who or what my friend was; I didn't even care or question that. It existed and it felt loving; that's all that mattered to me. I read that experience of calm as confirmation of our special relationship and a demonstration to me of love. I would later yearn to recapture that easy calm.

NOT RELIGIOUS BUT WANTING SOMETHING

Although my faith remained strong, I never became religious in the institutional sense. I felt I received more wisdom and comfort directly from my special friend than I would get in church. Wisdom has come to me mostly as *knowings*. All my life I have *known*, intuitively sensed, truth on all manner of subjects. For instance, without studying psychology, often I believe I *know* why people behave as they do and feel compassion toward them and their circumstances.

I was raised a free-thinking Christian, not indoctrinated into any particular denomination. My parents were not avid churchgoers, but dabbled in spiritual metaphysics (which I knew little about at the time). My free thinking probably came from them, although I have no memory of any discussions. My brother and I went to Christian Science Sunday School, because it was the easiest to reach by walking two blocks then taking a bus directly there. (Children could do that sort of thing in those days.) I'm sure Mary Baker Eddy's teaching contributed to my unorthodox views.

During high school, I began wondering about religion. Searching, I went with friends to Baptist, Lutheran, Methodist, Roman Catholic and Christian Science services. I joined a youth group's choir. While I liked some things—especially the hymns—about each church, there were always more things I didn't like. Their sermons rarely had much meat to them, and seemed steeped in fear and negativity or were concerned with why we should give money to the church. I also didn't appreciate being told I was a sinner. I didn't want to feel guilty, and saw no good reason to; I hadn't done anything bad.

Christians seemed to worship Jesus instead of God (I didn't know then that they considered Jesus one person of a three-person God in their Trinitarian belief system.); it was usually Jesus or Mary, to whom they prayed. Since I felt I knew God personally, I wanted no intermediary. To me, Jesus was a wonderful teacher and way-shower, whose specialness was being blown out of proportion. I thought his teachings were wonderful, although I rarely interpreted them as the churches did. I became concerned that perhaps I wasn't Christian, and if not, what was I? I thought I had to be something, but it never occurred to me to explore Judaism or Islam, or even Eastern traditions.

One Good Friday while working in downtown Los Angeles—after high school and some college—a co-worker and I walked around the corner to a church service. We left in the middle of the sermon, disturbed by its negativity. As we strolled back to work, we talked about our beliefs. To our mutual delight, our ideas about God, Jesus and the Bible were similar. Even more exciting for me, my friend had a name for her beliefs: Religious Science. She told me about her church: a Christian denomination with a spiritual metaphysical slant. I was thrilled. I was still a Christian!

Excited, I rushed home that evening to tell my mother, and was amazed to learn that she was currently studying the *Science of Mind*—the philosophy of Ernest Holmes, founder of the Church of Religious Science (now called Center for Spiritual Living). For many years after that my parents and I occasionally went to church together. Although I had no interest in joining a church, it felt good to know there was one with which I could relate whenever I had a need.

THE SPIRITUAL

Throughout my first forty years of life, my brush with the metaphysical or spiritual was slight, and vicarious at that. When I was a teenager, my mother—an intelligent, level-headed woman—related some rather bizarre experiences from her childhood and early twenties. One had to do with a house in which she and her parents lived temporarily while their new home was being built. It became commonplace for the family to be disturbed in the evening as they sat in their parlor reading, sewing and listening to the radio. By disturbed, I mean it sounded as though a basket of gaslight jets—electrical lighting had recently been installed—sitting in the cellar, was being upended and spilled down the stairs, when in fact it remained intact. This was usually preceded by a rattling of the cellar doorknob, and always occurred about the same time each evening. My grandparents would sit poised to pounce, and at the first sign of activity, someone would fling open the door; but nothing was ever found to account for the noises.

Another event frightened my grandparents for my mother's safety, causing them to move from that house. One night, sleeping on a daybed in the parlor, she was awakened by the feeling of breath on her face, as if someone were bending close over her. She opened her eyes to look into the face of a man, gone the next instant, a ghostly apparition. Had she been a child given to fantasies, that easily could have been taken for the workings of an overactive imagination, perhaps stirred by the eerie noises. To her it was another very real ghostly experience.

Mother also told of coming home from school one day and greeting her father at their front door as he was seeing two men out. (Her father was a psychiatrist, with a home office.) When the men had gone, the doctor turned to my mother and said, "Well, he won't be back!" "Why?" Mother asked. "Well, for one thing he won't be able to find his way back here," he answered. "Can't the other man bring him?" asked my mother. "What other man?" her father asked in astonishment. One man had visited the doctor that day, and my grandfather thought he might possibly be possessed, i.e.: taken over by another disembodied spirit being, whom my mother apparently saw. Hearing such stories at a young age, I easily accepted the existence of spirit life beyond the physical. I knew there was more to life than we could validate with our human senses, but gave it little further thought until much later.

OTHER INFLUENCES

After college in the mid 1950s, I worked for ten years in administrative management in the space industry at TRW's Guided Missile Research Division (which later became Space Technology Laboratories) in Los Angeles. Among my friends there was a man to whom I was immediately attracted. He taught hypnosis to a small group of us, giving us post-hypnotic suggestions to later verify its effectiveness. He also taught us mental telepathy and self-hypnosis. We learned to relax one small part of our body at a time, a process that has been widely used in self-help programs. This was at a time when hypnosis was used for parlor or stage tricks, and the only things said about it inspired fear. To me it was fascinating, not at all scary and quite wonderful, a tool for deep relaxation that I would use later to great advantage.

My friend left STL for greener pastures and we lost touch. A couple of years later, after a traumatic relationship breakup, I yearned to see my friend. He called the very next day, and told me that he had recently divorced, so we were free to enjoy each other, as we had always wanted. If you believe in coincidence, then for you my wishing and his calling may have been just that. I, however, don't believe that anything is coincidental, and I know mental telepathy works. I think our affinity created a bond felt over time and miles, a bond which facilitated telepathy; that and the fact we were both believers in spirituality, put us in resonance with each other's energy. I also think my Self wanted me to know about this inner sense we call telepathy, and perhaps wanted to bring us together for other reasons as well.

Through my mother's influence, I have always tried to live by the Golden Rule: "Do unto others as you would have others do unto you." She also persuaded me to believe in the "Pollyanna" principle: that behind every cloud is a silver lining; all things work out for the best. My mother also convinced me I could do anything, if I believed I could. On my own, I borrowed a line from Shakespeare: "To thine own self be true." These beliefs, along with my strong faith in God, have virtually piggybacked me through life. I gratefully thank my mother for her insights. To my great benefit also, I was born an eternal optimist.

Sometime late in the 1950s, one other person had a great influence on, not only my approach to life, but ultimately on the philosophy that now guides and drives my life. That person was Ayn Rand, and besides the movie from her book *The Fountainhead*, her book *Atlas Shrugged*. I picked up *Atlas Shrugged* and began reading it, and although I was not yet a reader as such, I couldn't put the book down. I loved it. I went on to avidly read everything she wrote, learning something important with each book. Until then, I had no direction, no focus, or meaning to my life and few original thoughts. I was not my own person, not much more than a clone of my mother. I was so impressed with Ms. Rand's philosophy of self that I wanted to learn to recognize, honor, and revere my own self. I wanted to know myself. This, I can see now, put me firmly on the most important path of my life and led straight to where I am now, spiritually. Rand helped to prepare me for easy acceptance of the importance of self and of strong self-esteem.

Her philosophy was actually atheistic and political, designed to fight Communism as seen by her in her native Russia. But to me it was considerably more profound. I initially accepted her political views and, heavily influenced by them, remained conservative in my own approach to politics for a long time. It wasn't until I began to recognize the greater significance in her ideals that I came to see them as basic truths. They ultimately were reinforced by my own intuitive analysis of self.

While working in STL, a small group of co-workers and I met a couple of times to talk metaphysical philosophy. We posed questions, such as: What is reality? Is life on Earth possibly only illusion? Are the chairs, tables, things of life really there or do we create them with our minds? We had only questions, no answers. I left it at that, then.

CAUGHT UP IN MATERIALISM

Having earned an MBA at UCLA for women executives, I bounced back and forth in my career between STL and UCLA, I finally quit STL in 1966 to work ten more years at UCLA. I was consumed by intellectual and material pursuits instead of spiritual ones. I became Associate Director of Planning, responsible for coordinating campus-wide academic planning, and later for campus administrative data processing and information services. I focused my mind narrowly on my analytical and managerial responsibilities. I was an early yuppy, on the trail of lofty position and financial success. Some of my friends and I were racing to see who could advance the fastest, and I was leading. I was already earning more money than most women in business in those days, and, as a woman in an executive position, was in a minority.

I drove a new powder blue and white Buick Riviera with sunroof. I owned a rambling home on the Palos Verdes Peninsula overlooking the Los Angeles basin. From a long wall of glass I could enjoy the coastline and on clear days the San Gabriel Mountains, while all of Los Angeles out to Whittier lay at my feet. The Christmas-tree-like sparkling lights of the sprawling city at night made a glorious panorama. My game room had not only a wet bar and dancing area, but also a pinball machine and a regulation-size pool table with smooth, hand-polished walnut sides and legs and apricot/beige felt—green was too common for me. I had a high-powered stereo system surrounded by hundreds of LP record albums and cassette tapes. In one of the bedrooms, I had set up an easel, stacked pre-stretched canvasses next to it and laid out tubes of oil paint on a specially designed paint stand my father built for me. My brushes were artistically arrayed, bristles up looking like flowers in a vase. A colorful, paint-smeared smock dramatically draped over the easel.

My life was full. It was full of things, but it was shallow. I knew none of my neighbors. I never had time to paint, and I'm not sure now that I had intended those props for anything other than effect—they let me feel artistic. My twenty-two mile drive to and from UCLA took from an hour and a quarter to two hours each way, bumper to bumper, stop and go, wait and inch along on the San Diego freeway and surface streets. I sometimes spoke into a tape recorder as I drove to help me recall ideas or things to do. Day after day I participated in or led one meeting after another, and traveled to other university campuses almost weekly to more meetings.

SPREADING MY WINGS

I didn't mind spending my time that way; I didn't know any better. I had lived in Los Angeles all my life, so it and what it had or didn't have to offer was all I had ever known. To get away on weekends, I bought a motor home, as did many of my friends. Between fifteen and twenty of us met regularly at a mountain lake—Casitas, Cachuma or, most often, Lake

Hemet on Mt. San Jacinto above Palm Springs. We parked our rigs end-to-end, forming a circle around a campfire pit to block the wind and provide privacy. We fished for trout and catfish, while sitting in colorful plastic folding chairs and catching up on each other's life. After dinner, we built a roaring bonfire and sang for hours to the strums of a lilting guitar.

I found there were places without supermarkets and shopping malls, neon lights and billboards, cement sidewalks, freeways and crime. I learned the feeling of relaxation and how clean air could smell. I grew to appreciate mountains, lakes, streams, and trees. There really was more to life than what the big city had to offer!

This was the mid-1970s, when I began feeling that something was missing in my life. I felt a longing, but didn't know for what. Terrible burning sensations were attacking my stomach, diagnosed as precursor to ulcers. The longing persisted and grew more insistent. I experienced almost a loneliness, an emptiness unfamiliar to me, along with a certain anticipation bordering on excitement. Without knowing the cause of these feelings, I yearned to think aloud with someone. I realize now looking back, I had never shared inner, private thoughts with anyone. And, I hadn't for many years had a philosophical discussion. I didn't know where or how to begin. I wanted almost desperately to recapture that gentle calm I had experienced just prior to thyroid surgery. I tried to talk with a friend, but chose the wrong person with whom to begin. She was raised Roman Catholic and steeped in dogma that would not let her question. She didn't want to talk about it, whatever "it" was.

THE REAL BEGINNING

Then I met a person with whom I felt free to explore my inner thoughts, someone who was ready to do some exploring herself. To begin the process, she brought me Richard Bach's *Jonathan Livingston Seagull*, then *Illusions*, and started me reading. We both read other books, recommended to her by friends: Fynn's *Mr. God, This Is Anna* and Dick Sutphen's *You Were Born Again to Be Together*. I had never been much of a reader, so it took forever to finish a book, and I would lose its continuity. The books my new friend brought were small and easy reading, but of great depth.

I began using the relaxation (self-hypnosis) techniques I had nearly forgotten. My stomach aches grew worse, though. I found myself conducting business meetings from a couch, lying on my back sipping milk. (I don't know why lying on my back helped, but it did.)

Finally, I took a medical leave from UCLA, sold my house, put my "things" in storage, and traded my Riviera for a Jeep Wagoneer and my motor home for a thirty-two foot travel trailer. I thought it would be fun to rock hound and make cabochons from my findings, so I stocked the trailer with lapidary machinery and some jewelry casting equipment I had recently acquired. I also took fishing gear, oil paints, a tape deck and lots of music cassettes.

As I was leaving the university and Los Angeles, my absolutely superb secretary gave me a going away present, a wonderful little book: *Siddhartha*, by Herman Hesse. Although a novel, that book was based on the awakening of Siddhartha Gautama to Buddha. In thinking about that book now, I realize that it was probably the catalyst that pointed me toward the spiritual. It may have been the beginning of my enlightenment journey.

All of the books I'd been reading found and breached a hidden void in me that now ached to be filled. Excursions to bookstores produced works by Ruth Montgomery, Jane Roberts (channeling Seth) and Vernon Howard. One book in particular, that had truly, literally fallen off a bookshelf at me, led me to especially valuable insights: William Samuel's *A Guide To Awareness and Tranquility*. From it I learned that judgment of people, things and events causes stress, and that tranquility can be enjoyed only in the absence of judgment, through nonresistance or acceptance of what is as it is. I began a personal campaign to be less judgmental.

WE TOOK TO THE ROAD

It turned out that my new friend, Mauri, like me, had been an art major in college, and had also taken night courses in jewelry making and in lapidary, learning to cut stone and shape it into cabochons. So Mauri, along with two German-Shepherd-mix dogs, joined me. We headed east through Arizona, spending as long as we wanted in each spot. Sedona, Prescott, the White Mountains, were some of our favorite spots. I read books and insatiably sought others. I felt wonderful. Sometimes I would just sit with a contented smile on my face and excitement in my heart. I had no stomach aches.

I delighted in watching my wonderful young shepherd/collie mix, Stormy, herd cows, chase rabbits and ground squirrels and bound through streams. Mauri and I bathed in the Gila River and were rinsed off by Stormy, who, prancing at us and skidding to a stop, drenched us with sprays of water. With a grin on her face and glint in her eye, she would tear away to regroup for another lunge.

In New Mexico, Taos captured our hearts. We camped by a gurgling stream in the mountains outside the city. A winter ski resort, in the summer when we were there it drew little attention, so we had the campground to ourselves much of the time. Taos, with its eighty art galleries and wonderful restaurants, appealed to both the artist and gourmand in me. We got some soldering tips from a local silver smith, then moved on to Colorado, then Wyoming.

In Wyoming I took and filled my first commission for custom jewelry: a pair of wedding rings. Spending a month in the mountains at 10,000 feet, we enjoyed hiking and rock hounding. We found colorful petrified wood and lacy red and green moss agate, some of which we sliced and shaped into cabochons. We camped in what turned out to be a cow pasture bordering a lovely river. Where Stormy got her herding instincts I don't know but she was very good at it. She wanted the cows to keep their distance from our trailer, so set up an imaginary line past which they were not allowed. Whenever cows strayed across the line, Stormy quickly and effectively herded them back, leaving them alone to graze peacefully when they stayed in their place. She was a joy to watch. We headed further north to the gorgeous Flathead Lake area of western Montana and Glacier National Park and after that to southeast Washington and finally Oregon.

I had friends who owned and operated Humbug Mountain Lodge on the southern Oregon coast, nestled on the lee side and at the foot of Humbug Mountain on Highway 101. In addition to groves of endangered myrtle trees, the resort had a well-stocked trout pond and a full-running creek that meandered behind cottages and lodgettes.

SETTLING IN OREGON

After enjoying my friends and their beautiful setting for awhile, I decided not to return to Los Angeles and the stress of my UCLA career. I had changed during the six months we had traveled the western states. I had read several thought-provoking books and was nearly overflowing with partially formulated ideas. I felt if I returned to my old life, I would never resolve those issues and satisfy that old longing, finally identified as a serenity that I believed would somehow come with spiritual enlightenment, whatever that was.

My friends suggested we set up a custom jewelry business there at Humbug Mountain Lodge. We could remodel the old garage building they were using as a mini-mart, if we would also continue that service. After I drew up plans, Mauri and I, Nancy (one of the Lodge owners) and Mark (Nancy's brother, Lodge cook and a qualified contractor) did the remodeling.

Before opening our jewelry shop, Mauri and I spent two weeks in Ennis, Montana, taking private lessons in jewelry making from a couple we had met in our travels. In March, 1978 we officially opened for business as Demori Designs, fine original jewelry designers. It felt great to be creative and use my artistic talents again.

Humbug Mountain, the highest point on the Oregon Coast, was near the north end of a sixty mile stretch of the most beautiful coastal scenery I've ever seen. Rugged, off-shore rock formations resembled haystacks, arches, spires, and in one case, an elephant's head. Spruce, fir, hemlock, and juniper, grew lavishly to cliff's edge above the great Pacific Ocean, interspersed with myrtle, cedar and alder trees. Delicious wild blackberries were abundant. Sheep grazed peacefully on pasture hillsides and valley floors etched by rivers and creeks. Pure white egrets and great blue herons waded in marshy river basins, while nutrias and otters swam, fishing for their food. Frequent vista points offered magnificent views. From high above crashing breakers, one could watch spindrifts curling along waves like their etheric bodies and occasionally see gray whales roll and blow. Other turnouts were low to give easy access to white sandy beaches strewn with driftwood and wave-smoothed agates, jasper, and petrified myrtlewood. This area was not only beautiful but peaceful and somehow spiritual.

A few yards from our jewelry shop was a wonderful spot, perfect for taking breaks from work. An old moss-covered log spanned the gurgling creek and was ideal for sitting and relaxing in meditation and deep thinking. Although the sun's rays could warmly reach it, my special spot was nestled in trees and brush, hidden from intruders.

A wonderful new life was underway. I was to make great strides here on my journey of enlightenment.

2

THE DAWNING OF ENLIGHTENMENT

My enlightenment progressed, but slowly during the first few months at Humbug. I read what was available, frustrated by the nonexistent supply of metaphysical books in rural Oregon. My questions persisted and multiplied. Then, suddenly, people began entering my life who had seriously studied spiritual metaphysics and were ready and willing to share with me.

LEARNING NEW THINGS

One of our new friends, Bev, gave me a "reading" to determine the number of my spirit guides and some of the things with which they were helping me. It was her guides, she said, who told her about mine. She pointed out that each of us has spirit guides to help us through everyday life, and that there is always a core group of five to seven, with others joining in for as long as needed to help on specific issues. A new guide, she explained, might help a person get through a difficult experience, such as overcoming an addiction or facing the death or illness of a loved one, a troubled marriage, a maiming illness or accident.

Bev taught me to cleanse my aura. She had me stand still with eyelids closed, then run my slightly cupped hands around my head and shoulders and a little away from my body, as if I were brushing something off and away from me. While doing this, I was to repeat this phrase as many times as I felt necessary: "In the name of God, I cleanse my body and I cleanse my soul." In place of "God" I could use anything with which I felt comfortable or which was meaningful to me. I could use this practice to prepare for meditation or communion with my guides or to cleanse any unwanted energy from my aura. It helped calm and center me.

To help me communicate with my guides, Bev suggested I stand with my eyes closed and ask questions that would require yes or no answers. My guides would rock my body to indicate their answer. Bev also taught Mauri and me relaxation techniques helpful in meditation. For some reason, though, no matter how diligently we each tried, meditation did not come easily then, nor has it since for either Mauri or me.

Despite my near failure at meditation, I was excited. I now had tools to help me pursue answers to the questions burning inside me. The concept of my guides was one of them: Who or what were they? How did they relate to the God I had always known and trusted? Were they another go-between? Were they angels? Were they discarnate human beings?

Another of our new friends, Terri led three of us novices in weekly metaphysically-oriented classes. The one lesson I remember, and which plagued my mind at the time conveyed the message that: "We are all one *with* God." It was a nice phrase, but what did "one *with*" mean?

Terri also introduced me to a wonderful little, anonymously written book, *Impersonal Life* and to Baird Spaulding's fabulous five-volume set on *The Life and Teaching of the Masters of the Far East.* They were published by DeVorss and Co., a major publisher/distributor of metaphysical and spiritual books, still strong today. Taking advantage of my ability to buy at wholesale prices, I began stocking metaphysical books in our jewelry and gift shop, selecting many I wanted to read. I could now amply supply my ravenous spiritual hunger.

I spent as much time as possible atop my favorite log, feet dangling just above the gurgling creek. Sometimes Mauri and I put a "gone fishing" sign on our door, and did just that, mostly during salmon and steelhead seasons. I didn't really want to catch fish, but "going fishing" gave me a great excuse to sit quietly by the water, soak up sun, and talk with my guides.

As I've said, I wasn't good at the common version of meditation as deep quiet. I either wakened my nerves and got jumpy, mentally designed a piece of jewelry or dozed off. I found I was able to relax and focus my mind most easily when near water. Being surrounded by water—the Pacific Ocean, creeks, streams, and rivers galore, along with the resort's trout pond—and able to take time to stroll or sit quietly, I quickly learned to commune with my guides.

COMMUNION WITH MY GUIDE

In my vocabulary, communion means conscious communication between myself and my inner voice. But because I didn't know enough to formulate spiritual questions, Terri suggested I begin by asking for words, not just any words but meaty ones I could find in the dictionary and ponder for special meaning in the context of some part of my quest. I then moved to phrases and ultimately began a wonderful communion with that voice within. This communion is the most important lesson I was to learn and I am so grateful to Bev and Terri for teaching it to me. (For a chart of steps to Intuitive Communication, see Applying the Insights at the end of Chapter 19.) Two things still occupied a major share of my thoughts: who or what were my guides with whom was I communicating, and what was meant by, "We are one *with* God"?

CHANNELING

Another new friend, Dea, brought us Jerry, a trance medium who was willing to give a group reading. We gathered in the Lodge to hear him. A large blond man in his early twenties, Jerry sat comfortably in an easy chair, his eyes closed. Shortly, his head and chest began moving as if he were belching. A deep, rich, heavily accented voice spoke. The accent, I learned, was ancient Abyssinian (Ethiopian). After a few phrases in a foreign language, spoken almost as a blessing, English became recognizable. I think he was saying (from tape recording):

> I wish to say Jubal is the Lord of my soul and is within me. Bless his holy name. It is indeed my great pleasure to be with you on this time, giving you the guidance and directance from beyond the veil. My name is Jubal. I'll be taking you through this time.

I remember nothing specific about that session, only that I was impressed. I had enjoyed the experience, coming away from it feeling I had met an extremely loving and positive being. Dea said Jerry was tested by Duke University's Parapsychology Department and accredited as an authentic medium. But, as might be expected, I wondered who or what was Jubal? I wondered if he was one of Jerry's guides, an alter ego or perhaps himself in a different role from a past life. It's not that I didn't believe in spirits, I did. But I could no more envision an ancient, discarnate being talking through Jerry than I could accept the fact that we each have a number of spirit entities guiding us. These were difficult subjects for me. I knew there was something important here, but didn't yet know what.

GOD

Despite these perplexities and ever-present and growing questions, those days were exciting for me, with each day holding new and wonderful revelations from my guides. The most wonderful insight of all occurred one day as Bev and I strolled along the creek, chatting. In addition to my question of what it is to be one *with* God, I was asking who or what our guides are, not really expecting her to answer. Had I all my life been talking with a spirit guide rather than God? Suddenly I knew with all certainty the answer to those questions.

Of course I had been talking with God, and I still was talking with God. It was perfectly clear to me that my guides, Bev's guides, everyone's guides are God. More importantly, we all are God: Bev is God, I am God! I looked around at the deep green myrtle trees, Humbug Mountain towering above us, the blue sky, the clear water rushing at our feet, the colorful mallards and trout swimming by, and I recognized God. "God is not a personal being, but is the all of everything," I nearly shouted. The phrase "We are all one with God" was obvious to me. I would say it a little differently, though: "We are all God and there is only ONE; everything is an aspect of the ONE."

I had never been so thrilled. It had come to me so suddenly and so clearly. It wasn't a bolt of lightning, a clap of thunder, nor a burning bush, although maybe it was all three. I had no vision, heard no voice. It was intuitive inspiration—infusion of thought into my consciousness—and left no room for doubt in my mind. That *knowing* was so positive, so definite for me. It made certain I could easily discern intuitive *knowing*—my truth—from a rational, intellectual thought. And, *knowing* our Godness, our divinity, clarified many other things.

INTUITION

After that, my intuition deluged my consciousness with so many insights, truths, that I couldn't digest them all. But then I realized I didn't have to, truth wasn't going anywhere; it would be available whenever I needed it. I often got the questions only milliseconds before their answers.

My questions were many and deep, including things like:

> If created by and of God, are we physical or spiritual beings? If God is perfect and we were created by God and of God, are we not perfect as well? Is everything, as part and expression of God, not beautiful, pur-

poseful and perfect? Can evil exist of and within God? Why is there so much "bad" in life? What happens in death? Is there life after death? Will we meet our maker and be judged? Why are we here?

And I received insightful answers to every one of them.

One day as I sat on my favorite log, meditating in my own way, I calmly watched a spider crawl slowly toward me. Rather than shy away or brush it off, I remained relaxed, watching the spider. This calmness was unlike me—all my life I had been terribly afraid of spiders. The thought struck me: *That spider is as much a part of God as I am.* I knew then I had no reason to either kill or fear the spider. I went back to my daydreams and the spider, too, went on its way. Never since have I feared spiders; how could I? I look at all creatures now from a different perspective. I knew my God within had given me this experience to help me in my journey of enlightenment.

MOVING INTO NEW TERRITORY

With the gas shortage curtailing tourist travel, and closure of lumber mills and poor fishing seasons hurting local economy, our business was slow. Humbug had been a perfect place for Mauri and me to learn our craft while allowing us quiet time, but we needed to move on.

Since we loved the Oregon coast, we decided to remain on the coast but relocate farther north where our business could draw from the population centers of Portland and Salem. We chose a resort town with year-round attraction for most of the major cities of Oregon and Washington. We made detailed lists of both our shop and home requirements and retained a realtor to accommodate our home needs. Then we returned to Humbug to let our plans materialize. This list idea, by the way, was a method Bev and Terri had shared with us for achieving or obtaining what we want. It's a matter of focusing on the specifics of what one wants, listing them, and then trusting they are already satisfied.

I began making notes about the truths I was gathering in communion with my inner guide/God. Writing helped me to focus them, helping me solidify my *knowings* (intuitive understanding) into specifics, and identify gaps or questions that remained unanswered.

A VERY SPECIAL TIME

Humbug Lodge was always closed for the month of January. That January, 1980, while the owners were away vacationing, Dea and two other friends came to babysit the Lodge and animals. Mauri and I were biding our time, waiting for escrow to close on our new home. Having nothing more pressing to do, the five of us sat in the Lodge living room, a log fire blazing hours on end, day and evening, for three weeks. Dea was my mentor. We talked. I asked questions; others offered answers, and I thought about them. Not all answers sat right, but I found them all stimulating. Late at night, in solitude, I conversed with my inner guide, refining my truths.

SOUL, WHAT IS IT?

I remember being preoccupied with the concept of soul. It seemed that, as disparate as many of their tenets are, nearly all of the world religions share a common concept of soul. It's as if to them the soul and human being are one and the same: the soul occupies the human body and experiences human life. The various traditions diverge only when it comes to before and after human life. Most Christians believe that a new soul is born with each new human life and after death may or may not live on, depending on denominational doctrine. To Eastern, Western, and ancient metaphysical philosophies, our souls are part of a Universal or World Soul, always existing, and separating from it to enter and partake of human life, ultimately returning to the World Soul.

As I read about these concepts, something inside me became uncomfortable. It didn't take me long to realize these descriptions did not fit my emerging definition of soul. I realized that what other people referred to as "soul" was what I called my "human self," and what I called "soul" was what some others might refer to as "spirit," if at all.

I felt, too, that there was more to this issue than mere definition, so I sought my own truths on the subject. Here are some of the questions I considered:

> Are my soul and human awareness totally one and the same? Is no part of me pure spirit and more knowing, more powerful than what I am conscious of—my human personality? Am I really only an ego that will die with my body? Did I exist as my soul before I was born? If so, and assuming I will go on living after my physical death, will I reincarnate? Are spirit guides actually souls that have somehow risen above Earthly

human life? Isn't it possible that our human selves are only illusion or dream-state sort of beings, not the whole, Real us?

Again I received answers to my questions.

One day, taking a solitary break from the group discussions, I sat on my favorite log and pondered about souls. Once again my intuition was filled with *knowing*. I had my truth. I knew with all certainty that our souls are never separate from the Oneness, never lost. Our souls are pure intelligence, spirit, energy, light, and remain ever thus. I refer to my soul as "Self," or "God." My little "human self" I see as an extension of my soul-Self, the small part or aspect of my whole being that enters human life to experience. I now knew, too, that my inner all-knowing friend and guide, my God, is my own individual soul, my Self, infusing thoughts into my human mind through intuition.

Settled on this issue, I could move on to other concepts and questions, like:

To what extent am I a material being and what has that aspect of me to do with my identity as a spirit being? How and why did I get into this physical life? Do I reincarnate? If so, why? If I'm a spirit being, how will I get back to my spirit home, and where or what is it? If we are aspects, embodiments, of God, the Oneness, how could we have sinned, and why? How could we be separate, and why? Why was the universe created?: the big WHY question.

My Self also answered all those so important why questions.

REGRESSION TO A PAST LIFE

To help me understand reincarnation, Dea regressed me. She had me cleanse my aura, lie on the couch and relax. She asked me to expand my awareness as if I were a balloon; I was to float up to the ceiling, then through the roof so I could look down and observe the Lodge from a hundred feet overhead. Then I should expand to float a mile above Earth. There I was to take a leap, stepping into a former life. I was to look at my feet and tell what shoes I wore.

I looked down at soft leather moccasins, apparently those of a Native American brave. I then looked around at my wife and children, family and friends coming and going between tepees on a sandy, desert-like mesa. After leading me to identify two of my then family as two members of my current family, Dea suggested I go forward in time to an important moment in my life as a brave. I saw myself on horseback, with other braves riding through a ravine to confront a group of horsemen in navy blue uniforms. It was clearly a battle situation.

Suddenly I began to tremble, writhe, and cry. Dea asked if I'd been shot. Was I dying? I said that wasn't it. I felt a devastating loss. Sobbing, I said my wife and children had been separated from me and I felt I would never see them again. I was so upset that Dea brought me back to the present. She later said that probably either my family had been killed or I had been and I didn't want to leave my family behind without my protection.

I was sorry Dea had stopped the proceedings. Although I had shown deep anguish, in my current life I was not affected. I view that experience as interesting, not at all bad. I had enjoyed being regressed, particularly the balloon and floating parts. I was thrilled to know I could actually feel my consciousness expand. I really seemed to float up and out over Humbug, and was able to see the buildings and grounds from above them. I actually looked down on rooftops! I recall being amazed and delighted with each part of the experience.

I was not altogether convinced by the regression experience, however, that reincarnation was fact. Except for the anguish part, I have never been sure I had truly revisited a life I had once lived. Had I been influenced by Dea's words to visualize what I relayed back? Also, because I had read about regression experiences, was I relating based on programs of what I thought I *should* experience? If that was true, what had caused me to become so upset? I was ever the questioner.

Spiritual Love

Throughout those wonderful three weeks in the Lodge, I experienced feelings I would have given almost anything to have on a regular basis, and now often do. The energy surrounding and in us was that of pure spiritual love. I was filled with joy, with my bliss. I was relaxed, pleasantly at ease, serene. The discomfort in response to some of the answers to my questions was part of my learning process. My mind was working, to be sure, but in total harmony with my Self and every part of me. I had achieved that heavenly calm I had longed to recapture from my youth. Without the use of any kind of substance, I felt a euphoria beyond my imagination.

Those feelings of bliss originated within me! I don't know how anyone else felt about those days, and it doesn't matter. Having known those feelings over a fairly prolonged period of time, and realizing their source is within me, I know I can experience them any time. It's a matter of alignment, balance, and harmony, of Oneness, as my Self has explained to me. I often feel that love and serenity while writing, which is for me a form of meditation.

I BEGAN WRITING

Since we had closed the shop at Humbug and could not yet move north, I spent time writing. Originally my writing was merely in note form on eight-by-five cards. Now I began writing my truths as letters to a friend—another way of composing my thoughts. I confined each letter to one major subject, as I had the cards, subjects such as God, reincarnation, karma, adversity. As I wrote, my truths began to fall into place. After I had written about ten such letters, I wished I could really share my truths with other people, not just my friends and family, but make them available to anyone who might be interested. I decided to flesh out each subject into a chapter and organize them into a book. My first attempts were crude and simple, but by the end of March, I had written a one hundred and ninety page, twenty-eight chapter book. I was committed.

I felt I had some truths that were different from what we'd been taught by either religion or science, ones that were more positive and plausible than any others I'd read. They were helping me understand and get more enjoyment from life, improving my relationships, and getting me closer to my goal of awakening. I hoped that someday my truths would be of use to others as well. Although I had come far, I was to realize that I still had a long way to go; what I had in bits and pieces was not yet formed into the cohesive whole it would become.

3

GATHERING, DEVELOPING AND REFINING MY TRUTHS

Mauri and I moved into our home on the north central Oregon coast early in 1980. Shortly afterward we got our shop. It was ideal—in the most desirable location, more spacious than we had stipulated in our wish list, and we could remodel all we wanted. It even had a large double stainless sink with drain boards, so we wouldn't have to install them, as we had at Humbug. We built walls around the sinks, adding counter space and shelving for storage and for holding the more unsightly tools of our trade. We took a two-year lease for less monthly rent than we had planned to pay. Sometime later we came across our wish list, having put it away for safekeeping during our move. We were amazed and delighted to find that every one of our listed items had been met or bettered. We had done as our friends had suggested, and the process had been validated to perfection for us.

After a month of remodeling, using the skills Mark had taught us at Humbug, we opened for business. Our slowest winter days were usually far better than our busiest summer days had been at Humbug. Another segment of our life and my pursuit of enlightenment had begun.

GATHERING WITH LIKE-MINDED FRIENDS

Cathi, whom we had met as a friend of Jerry/Jubal on one of his trips to Humbug, stopped in the shop to invite us to join a metaphysical discussion group there in our town. With one of the members, Dixie, leading us, we meditated and chose topics for discussion from books we were reading. She also shared correspondence from other similar groups. Dixie also was intuitively receiving messages from what were referred to as the *Great White Brotherhood* or the *Space Brothers*. The messages came to her through automatic writing at her typewriter, often in the middle of the night. Not knowing what she was typing and unconcerned about spelling, punctuation, or phrasing, her fingers flew across the keys until they abruptly stopped. She then shared the words of love and wisdom with the group at the next meeting.

SPACE BROTHERS AND THEIR MESSAGE

Although I'm not certain they ever said who they were, I generally thought of the *Space Brothers* as multi-dimensional spirit beings, somehow channeling through Dixie from a great spaceship somewhere in Earth's spiritual environs. Since I didn't think of them as physical beings, I never understood what their connection was to a spaceship. I likened them to Jubal, although I couldn't explain him either. They professed to be members of what they called the *Hierarchy*, and at least implied they somehow ruled Earth. The hierarchy idea only heightened my confusion.

What I remember most of the *Space Brothers'* messages, related to our being prepared for upcoming earth changes. They promised to help us through that difficult time by lifting us off the Earth at the appropriate moment and returning us later after the changes. We were to prepare for that liftoff by becoming as pure and spiritual as we could; that is: quit doing anything that might hinder our ability to receive their communications telling us where and when to expect liftoff. This purifying included not smoking, drinking alcohol and coffee, or eating red meat. Eating lightly, we would lighten our vibrations, putting us in a better position to receive their messages.

As usual, although I could understand automatic writing and accept telepathic communication with spirit beings, these particular messages didn't sit right with me. First, I could not conceive of a hierarchy of beings in the spirit world or their rule over Earth—why would either be necessary? Second, they made the predicted earth changes seem bad, and that wasn't my truth. Their purification demands didn't feel right to me either, unnecessary. But, since I had wanted to quit smoking, their message provided added incentive.

Amazingly, many of the channeled messages conveyed in newsletters from other metaphysical groups around the world had similar content. People everywhere were talking about cataclysmic earth changes, the Hierarchy of the *Great White Brotherhood* and liftoff.

JUBAL'S EXPLANATION

I decided to check it out with Jubal during one of Jerry's monthly treks to our town. (We didn't know about these visits when we located there—ah, synchronicity.) After his usual greeting and preliminaries, I jumped right in, asking about the validity of upcoming earth changes and liftoff and what preparation, if any, was necessary. He answered (as taped):

> Always remember that when you are dealing with the spirit world, the spirit world comes through a medium and has to work through a medium's consciousness. There is no higher attainment than attunement with yourself. There, in the vibration of preparing for liftoff, do not prepare yourself to leave this Earth. Only prepare yourself to be at one with it. I do not say, go out and buy silver because this world is coming into a very hard time. You don't need to get caught up in it. 'Prepare yourself so you can become spiritual with us so you can go to the higher planes with us'; that is not the word of the spirit. That is the word of the medium. For in the vibration of the spirit, the spirit recognizes that Oneness is all that is necessary. It does not matter whether you eat meat, smoke cigarettes or are an alcoholic, as long as you know your Oneness with the Father. That is where the flow is.
>
> The Father never said to you, 'Okay, I'm going to put you down here and here is a list of what you can do and here is a list of what you cannot do, and get by as well as you can.' The vibration is that 'I am the center of your life, make me the center of you life. For when you have me as the center of your life all other things will fade away. All things will be made brand new.' Do not prepare for all of those secret things, such as liftoff and reincarnating, but have your mind fixed on the Father [Self].
>
> Have your mind fixed on the love of the Father within you, for your love will grow very, very much. That is our purpose here to have our mind totally attuned twenty-four hours a day to God the Father. Hard to do? While at work, repeat, 'I am one with my Father, I recognize my oneness.' Program yourself during the day; you will find your life will flow into beauty, more moneys will flow in, freedom flows in. Because once we are with the Father, He gave us the whole Earth and says, 'You can do with it as you want. If you do bad you're going to get something bad happen to you and if you do good, then I will bless you with much good.'
>
> Lift-off is releasing the old and taking on the new. There is nothing to be afraid of. It is going to be a very exciting time to be here.

Despite my reluctance to accept Jubal as claimed, nearly everything he said felt good to me, and jibed with my intuitive sense about the changes. I especially liked his interpretation of "liftoff." Maybe we had misunderstood the Space Brothers' messages. Unsure, I let it ride.

A Spiritual Center

Our group opened a book store and metaphysical center, the "Open Door," across the street from Mauri's and my jewelry shop. When it became evident the group as such could not manage the store, Dixie took over the full responsibility of it. The group disbanded, some members moving away, others losing interest. A little later, Jim, a quiet and shy man in his mid-thirties who had a tea and coffee shop up the street, became a partner with Dixie in the Center and moved in his wares. Then Dixie phased out, leaving it to Jim alone. Jim and I became good friends. Whenever I needed a break from jewelry designing, I walked across the street and joined him for coffee and sharing of thoughts and ideas.

Jim began holding group meetings that offered a way to share love, growth, and common interests. After leading group meditation, he talked awhile on one subject, then often fielded questions. He talked of love, enlightenment, and "how to be in the world and not of it," judgment, negativity, our programming and other limitations. Jim's teaching centered on what he called the "golden triangle," of which the sides represented unlimitedness, unconditional love, and Oneness.

Jim's meditation and talks reminded me of Jerry's Jubal, except that Jim didn't go into a trance like Jerry did. In both cases their voice changed and the words and phrasing weren't quite their normal way of talking. Their messages, though, were similar and positive. At first Jim thought he, like Jerry and many others, was channeling messages from the spirit world. But, since he was always fully consciously awake, he knew there was a difference. In time he came to the conclusion that he accessed the Oneness directly. By his own choice or by others' questions, he focused on a specific body of wisdom contained in the Oneness, perhaps the "Akashic record."

He eventually was in that space of the Oneness most of the time and changed his name to Ishvara, which he said is Sanskrit for "God in man." He always encouraged us to raise our vibrational rate by staying centered and expanding our awareness. He was leading and showing us the way. He is a wonderfully spiritual, loving man, my friend. We finally lost touch after he moved away.

QUESTIONING "KARMA"

I remember being nearly obsessed throughout the early 1980s with the concept of karma. At first I wasn't even sure what it was, but it struck me as essentially negative: Whenever I heard it mentioned it seemed to be in relation to something bad or fearful. By then, I saw everything as perfect, based in love, and beautiful, so I couldn't imagine what karma could be or how it could have so much influence in our lives, as believers seemed to feel.

I read everything I could find on the subject of karma, and also about reincarnation because rarely was one mentioned without the other. This research helped me solidify my truths on not only the subject of karma, but the whole picture that was forming in my mind about us humans and our life on Earth. I finally settled in my own mind what karma meant to me and what I thought of the generally accepted metaphysical concept. I was quite happy to disagree completely with what seemed to be the world view. Because karma is an important issue through which I learned so much, I'll discuss it thoroughly in a later chapter, along with reincarnation.

Once my truths had been clarified regarding both reincarnation and karma, I was again ready to move on to other essential elements of the grand and glorious puzzle I was dedicated to solving. My steps on the path of enlightenment were becoming larger as I progressed.

WRITING FROM WITHIN

My enlightenment continued but more subtly than before, and involved more a gathering and developing process. The fragmented truths I'd amassed needed refinement, cohesion, and focus, which rewriting helped. I tried to get one of my original attempts at writing a book published and, although devastated by rejection and frustrated at the time, am very grateful I was unsuccessful. I had left subjects out of it because the insights I had received on them seemed so radical. I finally realized I hadn't been true to myself or readers of my work. Those truths were just as important to the totality of the philosophy I wanted to convey as any others of my truths, maybe more so. In 1984, while laid up with a shattered foot bone, I began to revise the book, putting in those truths. Writing in earnest, I enjoyed every word of it. It became an obsession—as it turned out a life-long one. I was driven to write, spending every spare moment doing so. Often, I began on one subject and shortly changed to another entirely, writing pages almost before I knew it. The new subjects were usually ones I hadn't yet finished formulating into truths, so I learned with every phrase.

Although the process could be considered automatic writing, I like to think of it as my Self expressing, doing its natural thing as my human self. By writing freely, without judgment or regard for composition and wording, I keep my intellect, my little self, from getting overly involved. Instead, I allow my intellect to flow in partnership with my intuition, writing words to express the sense of a concept. This writing process has become for me a form of meditation, enabling my consciousness to open and be receptive to thoughts from my soul. And it brings me serenity. Besides, from where does the wisdom come in automatic writing if not from within?

In communion with what I now *know* to be my soul, the larger, higher-vibrating part of me I call my Self, I had moved from words to phrases and eventually whole concepts, thoughts or questions. I found that as I fleetingly thought of a question, not really asking word for word, my mind flooded with insight. I realized that the presence of a question in my mind signifies my readiness for the answer. This was another joy-filled time for me. I will always love to ask questions and have answers implanted as if in a complete package, like a brick of truth being put in place to fill a hole in a great wall of wisdom. What thrilling experiences these are!

MY BROTHER'S INFLUENCE

One day while in Los Angeles visiting my family, I got into an "animated discussion" with my one-year-older brother, Chuck, about our origin and evolution. He was a devotee of Darwin's theory of evolution, and without knowing why, I had some doubts. Although I had not formulated a clear view of our origins, I also could not accept the concepts of "spontaneous happenstance" and "survival-of-the-fittest" to which my brother was devoted. I had never given these subjects much thought, but just knew that whatever occurred did so with purpose, order, and divine cause.

Chuck was adamant that all life had somehow begun in the sea and had evolved to its present state through natural selection. He claimed that his position reflected proven evident facts, not merely unsupportable theories. What disturbed him most was that I couldn't argue against his position, but still didn't accept it. I just didn't know. I intuitively sensed there was much more involved in both our origin and evolution than those theories could offer. My totally unsupported position was terribly frustrating to him, so he took on the job of "educating" me to the "facts."

Over the next few years, Chuck sent me books on Darwinism, archaeology, and paleontology, all of which I enjoyed immensely. I learned a great deal, but not what he had intended. The more I read, the more obvious it became to me that nothing was certain about either our origin or our evolution. All of the theories seemed at best flimsily supported. I felt that scientists had a tendency to create hypotheses and then seek out evidence to support them more often than letting evidence dictate theories, and often ignoring evidence against them.

To make matters worse as far as my brother was concerned, I intuitively accepted the existence of Atlantis as an advanced civilization that existed thousands, and perhaps millions, of years ago. I saw Atlanteans as the ancestors of Sumerians, Egyptians, Hindi, Maya, Olmecs/Incas, American mound builders and the builders of henges like Stonehenge in Britain. To me they were more advanced scientifically and spiritually than we, and were the forerunners of most ancient civilizations we know about today. Because of the limitations imposed on their thinking by Darwin's idea of evolution, scientists assumed global travel, like air and space travel, had been nonexistent. My thinking had no such limitations, so I was free to imagine anything. I figured that global and even space travel was ordinary, so naturally cross-cultural similarities would exist. This theory solved for me many of the mysteries pertaining to ancient cultures.

My brother had instigated an insatiable drive in me to know about our origin and evolution. I gathered anything I could find that might shed some light on these issues. I read Hawking, Adler, Huxley, Darwin, Plato. I also read H.P. Blavatsky, Edgar Cayce, and a number of books on Atlantis. I read about ancient civilizations and about the unexplained mysteries of the world. I read about UFOs and extraterrestrials. I studied science and metaphysics. Overall, I believe I had one great advantage over scientists in that I was not confined to academically justified positions. I was free to explore any theory. I had no limitation, self-imposed or otherwise, on my thinking.

FORMING MY OWN CREATION STORY

I began to develop theories of my own concerning our origin, beginnings, and evolution. In formulating my own theories on these deep and almost magical subjects, I ultimately realized two things: First, since there is purpose behind everything, *why* the universe came into being and we became physical human beings needed to be answered before a complete picture could be seen; second, all the books in the world weren't going to provide me with the answers I needed. They could never answer my *why* questions. And without those answers, they could also not answer my "how" questions. I had done the reading, now it was time to do—literally—some soul-searching. Now it was time to let my soul, my Self, my God, help me put it all together.

I wanted very much to know why and how human life began and what human life was all about. As usual, I asked questions:

> Could our wondrous human intellect truly be merely a result of four billion years of chance evolution? If everything is part of God, why would we humans alone have such intellect? If we are God and there is only the ONE, why are we so obviously separate? How can we humans do the heinous things we do? Do such actions serve unknown good purposes?

As always, I received wonderful answers to my questions, and before long these new answers amassed with those I had already gathered to give me my set of truths, including a new hypothesis about our existence. Such a set of aha's they were! I wrote.

I finally wrote a letter to my brother spelling out my new theories as conveyed by my Self. This letter eventually formed the basic outline for my version of "creation" that puts all my truths together and into perspective. I look back now on that fateful day when Chuck and I argued, and am thrilled by what I see. Apparently I was getting ready for a giant step on my path of enlightenment. There is no doubt in my mind that my soul arranged for that discussion to take place and for my "education" about it to thus proceed. My brother was part the process of my enlightenment, and I am eternally grateful for his help. I marvel at the workings of God and the ways in which we are taught. Every person in our life contributes to our growth—our awareness expansion—just as we, usually without conscious knowledge, help them in theirs.

An enjoyable and truly exciting part of this process is being aware of and able to discern the synchronicity and God's teachings as they occur. It's wonderful to realize how swiftly and easily one can gain needed help in getting firmly on a personal spiritual path. The nearest town to Humbug had a population of only about 250 people, and the town we moved to had less than five thousand residents. My experience tells me that "when the student is ready to learn, the teacher[s] will come."

If I could get all of what I needed to pursue my quest for enlightenment in very rural Oregon, I believe that anyone who wants enlightenment and awakening strongly enough will get it, no matter where they are. Teachers and insights came to me. I didn't have to go looking for them, and I wouldn't have known how or where to look anyway. All a person needs is to want help and to be open to whatever comes along.

GATHERING IT ALL TOGETHER AND REFINING MY TRUTHS

Although less dramatic than the enlightenment stage at Humbug, the years after our move north were also significant for my growth. I gathered together, not only my truths and people pursuing a similar path, but my own self. My Self taught me, sometimes with Ishvara's help, about my many selves and the sum of them that I am. I learned to revere and honor all that is me, not only my larger Self, but also my little self (ego), my intellect as well as my intuition, my human body as well as my etheric spirit body, my human consciousness and my subconscious, the child in me as well as the adult, both wise in their own way. I came to know my strengths and weaknesses, not as assets and faults, but as equally essential parts of the experiencing me. I also learned to honor myself with regard to my priorities, choosing mainly to follow my heart.

I have come to realize that every person and event in my life has led me and contributed to each successive moment of my life. I've written about only the most obvious contributors. I know, though, that everything and everyone in my life, no matter how seemingly insignificant, has helped me to follow the path of enlightenment on which I travel. And, too, numerous past events and people led me to express myself in writing so I might write of my truths to help others in their search. All those events and people brought me to the place I am now: firmly on an exciting segment of my journey, having long ago traded in my jewelry design business for writing.

During the several years immediately following my "retirement," I often felt I was stagnating, perhaps even backsliding a little. I wasn't adding any new major truths to my repertoire. Most of my spare time was spent in learning more about the English language and in improving the presentation of truths in book and article form. That period was more intellectually technical and detailed than spiritual and enlightening.

I now realize, though, that my truths were being refined, not only in writing, but in my mind. Looking back, I see that as I received insights I had interpreted them into words, for my own clarification. I now know that in putting words to them, I sometimes missed something in the translation. Often the answer was so complete, so encompassing that my intellect, putting it into words, couldn't possibly do it justice. I then forgot the rest. Later, a word from someone, something I was reading, or an answer to another of my questions jogged my memory of those lost thoughts, often triggering ahas. So, although the basic truths were given to me in a short period of time in the late 1970s and were added to in the 1980s, the last decade of the 20th century recalled to mind, refined and clarified many of the details. I also have been shown practical applications of concepts which were before only fine ideas. Of greatest importance to me is the fact that all of my truths came together into a cohesive whole. They formed an overall philosophy of life that is not only totally positive, but liberating and exciting

Now, the 21st Century has so far led me in yet another direction, one that includes learning about ancient cultures and their wisdom, and the realization that we nearly lost our spiritual roots and are reclaiming them in a spiritual renaissance. But the ancient spirituality and wisdom, along with my assessment of both fundamentalist religion and classical science (that research fostered by my brother) were for another book— *WAKE UP! Our old beliefs don't work anymore!*, (Portal Center Press, June 2013).

MY TRUTHS, MY INTUITION, MY SOUL

Truths come to me through my intuition, which I trust completely. My intuition is my connection to my Self and through which I will one day achieve a *conscious* unity, a reunion, with that inner me, and be consciously whole. Through intuition my enlightenment continues. The more

I use and rely on intuition, the closer I come to the Oneness and awakening I seek.

My soul has always been me; the only difference is that now I know it. I'm not always consciously at one with my soul. Not yet. My journey there is what I'm enjoying now, and is probably more important anyway than the end result. My years of search and discovery have been wonderful, my joy enormous. My awareness has expanded immeasurably. My understanding of life (and death) gives me comfort and peace of mind for which I had before only dreamed.

A few years ago I realized that my drive to write was one of the many ways in which my Self directs me toward our jointly intended plans and goals, including our conscious unity. For some time I wasn't sure that my writing wasn't merely to help me assimilate my truths, not for publication at all. If that was the case, fine; it certainly was successfully doing that. But, finally, I knew there would be more to it. Not only was I to learn through my writing, but others might too.

My intuition told me to persevere, finish the work and get it published. That book was published as *AWAKENING, a Journey of Enlightenment* in January 1996 (copyrighted 1995), but with its publisher's bankruptcy, it never reached distribution. Since I firmly believe there's a good reason for everything, I'm sure that book's failure was in my best interest or in the best interest of its content and message to readers. And so, this new version, one that is updated, expanded, and better written

The foregoing has been my personal story of enlightenment. The rest of this book relates the insights, I have gleaned from my Self throughout my journey. I feel our soul-Selves use all sorts of tools to guide us and to inform us of our truths. The words of others are often such tools. I hope this book will be of help to you, if you want that. I am very grateful for every bit of enlightenment I am given. I lovingly share all of it.

PART TWO - THE ILLUSION OF HUMAN LIFE

All the world's a stage, and all the men and women merely players: They have their exits and their entrances; and one man in his time plays many parts.

~ William Shakespeare

4

THERE IS ONLY ONE: GOD

By going within and communing with my higher-vibrating, always in spirit, soul-Self, I received—or remembered—insights which I call my "truths." While I received most of them in only a few months time, others have been scattered over the thirty-five years since then, as my journey of enlightenment has continued. This part of *AWAKENING* is all about the fundamental insights given me by my Self. These are my basic truths.

Throughout my journey of enlightenment, certain insights virtually fought for my recognition and acceptance. Among them is a particular one I have come to view as the foundation upon which all other truths rest. It is that everything is ONE, and that ONE is God, if you will. Ernest Holmes, founder of the Church of Religious Science as part of the New Thought Movement, put it: "God is all, there is nothing else..." Amen!

GOD: THE ALL

In Chapter 2, I told about my wonderfully exciting revelation about God, when it was made clear to me that God is *All-That-Is*. So now, I believe that everything in our physical universe is a manifestation of God. We are God incarnate. Our mothers, fathers, friends, and neighbors, even our enemies are God incarnate. Trees, plants, fishes, animals, and rocks, too, are all God. God is not merely the source of everything but *is* everything. Our feelings, thoughts, words, and actions express God. God is the air we breathe, the energy that maintains movement of every atom in the universe and the love in and behind everything that goes on, the cause, the life, the truth, and the direction. God is the Oneness of everything seen and unseen, manifest and unmanifest, spiritual and material, what I call the "Kosmos"—borrowed from Theosophist H.P. Blavatsky and integral philosopher Ken Wilber—the All-of-Everything, physical and spiritual, in all dimensions, so much more than the physical cosmos or universe.

The word "God" is sometimes confusing, often wrongfully used and exploited. It can elicit reverence but also fear and hatred. Some people avoid using the word because it connotes to them a personified idol or religious symbol often associated with hypocrisy. They may even relate it to evil, for throughout history we find the use of the word God to justify horrendous actions. In America today, God's name is often spoken in justification of the hate and bigotry of prejudice and discrimination. To many women (and some men) the word represents patriarchal dominance and much that is wrong in the world today. To some people who have been hurt and are disillusioned, God is either nonexistent or a being who can't be trusted, someone who makes promises but doesn't fulfill them, someone who takes away loved-ones and who kicks us when we're down, instead of helping us up. To orthodox scientists—those who believe in this material existence as the only reality—God is nonexistent, a religious fantasy.

PERSONIFICATION OF GOD

The Hebrew Scriptures, which also make up the Old Testament of the Christian Bible and what in Islam is called the Torah of Moses say "God is one." They also say that in addition to being all knowing and all powerful, God is omnipresent: present everywhere, and that God created us humans in his image and likeness. Only in the interpretation and subsequent use of those teachings do distortions and misunderstandings occur. Those misunderstandings have caused fundamentalists of the Abrahamic religions (Judaism, Christianity, and Islam) to visualize God as a supreme male being, separate and apart from his creation.

Not realizing that God's likeness is spiritual, they have assumed a physical likeness, and created the metaphor of God in *our* likeness: a person, only more knowing, powerful, and pervasive. All ancient cultures personified their gods to help their uneducated populace identify with them and enjoy the stories written about them. Hidden within those stories, though, were the wonderful spiritual truths of the elite *Mysteries* of each culture. While Jews had Kabbalah (a mystical practice that has been rejected by Orthodox Judaism). which I think of as a Mystery teaching, neither Christianity nor Islam had a well-defined Mystery tradition. Both have always had mystics with highly spiritual teachings. Certainly Sufism could be likened to a Mystery tradition of Islam, as could several monastic groups of Christianity. Gnosticism, while never organized and largely considered heresy by the powerful Christian bishops, might also be seen as a

Christian Mystery. The Mystery traditions taught the true meaning of scriptural texts, which were probably written much later to reflect those traditions rather than to put down new truths. Fundamentalists of Judaism, Christianity and Islam primarily address to this day what they consider an uneducated populace.

We've all heard people refer to God as "The *man* upstairs," and we are prone to visualize *Him* as a white-haired, bearded old man, sitting on *His* throne high in the clouds, passing judgment on us. Pope Paul VI said that a woman can't be a priest "because our Lord was a man"! In *Cayce, Karma, and Reincarnation*, I. C. Sharma relates a tale told him by Edgar Cayce's son, Hugh Lynn, of a young boy who had learned at Sunday school that Jesus Christ rose to and is sitting on the right hand of God. In week-day school he read in the primer, 'God has painted the beautiful world. He has painted the leaves and the flowers with His own hands.' At home, reading this passage to his mother, the little boy said, 'Mother, God certainly is a wonderful painter. Isn't it wonderful that He did all this with only His left hand?' The embarrassed mother asked, 'How did you come to that conclusion?' and the little boy answered, 'Don't you know, Mama, that God can't use His right hand, because Jesus Christ is always sitting on it'?

While sitting *at* the right hand of God generally signifies a valued assistant and second in command, this literal religious personification has done a great deal to limit our idea of God. It not only encourages the male dominance of a continuing patriarchy, but furthers the separation and dualistic approach to life many of us would like to change. It supports the dichotomies of dualism: spiritual/physical, God/human, good/evil, we/they, male/female, black/white.

Many "New Age" thinkers use a less limiting, genderless word in place of God. Some use The Powers That Be, Creative Force, Intelligence, Energy, Source, (Universal) Spirit, Mind, Oneness, The Light, or simply Love. Judaic teaching still today uses what in ancient Hebrew was the name God told Abraham: "YHWH." They have left it in its unpronounceable four consonants so it couldn't be spoken and thereby limit the unlimitable. (Ancient Hebrew was written in consonants only, with vowels added when reading aloud or speaking.) To give Jews a name to pronounce, their priests used "Adonai," meaning "Lord." Adding vowels to YHWH, German scholars formed Yahweh, later rendered Jehovah. The fact that YHWH and the Babylonian word for God, AH-YAH, both translate to "I Am" is meaningful to me. That is, since I believe that we all, everything, are God, we could each say "I Am," and be and mean "God." The 12th-century poet Rumi wondered "When will I ever see that Am that I Am?"

Some of Huston Smith's words, in *The Religions of Man*, helped me to see from another perspective and better understand the separatist view *Bhakti*, for example, the Hindi term for the spiritual path of love, can refer to anyone who is devoted to the personal God:

> As love when healthy is an out-turning emotion, the bhakti will reject suggestion that the God he loves is himself, even his Self... [H]is aim will not be to perceive his identity with God but to adore him with every element of his being.... As a Hindu devotional classic puts the point, 'I want to taste sugar; I don't want to be sugar.'

Biblical Christians believe the sugar they want to taste is actually three male *persons* somehow being the one God: the Supreme God, the Son of God, and the Holy Spirit. The now familiar God/Goddess term also implies the involvement of gender, furthering the image of a personal Being.

The God to which I refer is not a personal being, no matter how Supreme, and is way beyond gender. My God is Oneness—the All-That-Is, always has been and ever will be. We could say that in a sense we material manifestations are the personal aspects of God. I often also use the term "God" to mean my (or another's) soul, for I see our souls as our personal always-aware, always-in-spirit aspects of God's/our Oneness. My inner, soul-Self is my individual, intimate connection to the Oneness. It is the only "God" as such I know, my "special friend." I am the human embodiment of that God, its physical expression. My Self is my life's breath, the I-Am of me, my guardian angel, my spirit guide. My Self is my intuition, providing insights amounting to wisdom and truth, while also directing me through my play of everyday life.

Although much of the Bible depicts God as a being and separate from His creations, some passages attributed to Jesus seem instead to support my view of God:

God is in you (1 Corinthians. 14:25).

In him we live, and move, and have our being (Acts 17:28).

While superficially these may seem contradictory, I see them as complementary. Together, they describe the totality of God as the ONE, within and without. To me, God's "omnipresence" says it all. The Qur'an says "And do thou, O Muhammad, remember thy Lord within thyself."

THE ABSOLUTENESS OF GOD

Although I often find words inadequate and even misleading to describe things spiritual, I see *absolute* as the single word that describes my idea of the nature of God for my intellect. Some of the words Webster uses to define absolute are: "...free from imperfection; complete; perfect; pure; not limited in any way; unrestrained; ultimate; intrinsic; not comparative or relative; positive; unconditional; not dependent upon external conditions for existence or for its specific nature." The absoluteness of God means there can be only ONE. If any part of us is God, then the entirety that we are is God, and everyone of us and every thing in existence is God, expressed in a variety of forms, dimensions, and levels of complexity. Either God is the all of everything or is completely separate and apart from everything. And if God is omnipresent then there can be no separation. If, as Emma Curtis Hopkins, the great teacher of spiritual teachers of the New Thought Movement—including Ernest Holmes and the Filmores' (Unity)—put it: "All that I call my good is my God, Omnipresent, Omnipotent, Omniscient."

Those "Omnis" of God mean to me that if God is everywhere present, nothing can be separate. Not only separate but, for God to be everywhere, that means inside every part of everything, not merely *in* everything but *as* everything. If God is powerful, God must be all-powerful, never partially so, never limited in power. If God is perfect, positive, and good, then every expression of God is also perfect, positive, and good. If God is love, everything is love, always and ever. If God is good at all, God must always be the ultimate in good. But, this means also that if evil exists, it, too, must be of God. So, this tells me that evil exists only in our human perceptions and misunderstandings, not as a true idea. If evil is seen to exist, it is by misinterpretation or is part of the illusion of human life, serving loving purposes, so isn't truly evil. The same goes for hate as the opposite of love, or for any negative condition or emotion as an opposite of a positive. Actually, there really, other than for us in human life, is no positive or negative, there is only perfection. Everything just is, always in perfection.

GOD AND US

If God "created" us, we must be of God. If God is omnipresent, what else was there from which to create us? And, if we truly exist, we must be expressions of God's omnipresence, and also God's omniscience and omnipotence. If God-consciousness thought the universe into being—as I believe—we cannot be anything but God; we are each—every being, every particle of the universe—by virtue of our existence an expression of God, not just a "likeness." Therefore, everything, having its inception in and of God, is God.

HIGHER INTELLIGENCE BEHIND IT ALL

To nonbelievers I ask:

> Why is there order in the universe? How is it maintained? Why, when honestly examined, does it all seem somehow to make sense? How does a pumpkin seed know to grow into a vine producing more pumpkins and not peas or beans? You might answer "DNA." But how and from what was DNA created? What causes it to work? How did the human body evolve and develop to the magnificent and complex enterprise it is? How does each cell in our body know its role in the preservation of our life? How did we acquire consciousness, and what is it? How did life begin, and why?

I don't see how these questions can be answered without suggesting cause and direction, without implying the existence of higher intelligence in the design of things. Even Charles Darwin saw "life,...having been originally breathed by the Creator." He also had to admit:

> Another source of conviction in the existence of God, connected with the reason, and not with the feelings, impresses me as having much more weight... I feel compelled to look for a First Cause... and I deserve to be called a Theist.

Nearly everyone who has thoroughly studied the cosmos and/or the wonderful workings of nature at some point comes to realize that a higher intelligence must be at work behind it all.

ONENESS

Not only is the existence of higher intelligence so obvious to me as to be without question, so is God's all-encompassing Oneness. This Oneness, I believe, is the number one concept for us to understand, even though it may be counter to our perceptions. It means we all are part of the ONE and the ONE is us. Everything we see as we look around, as well as everything we don't see, is the ONE. Nothing is separate and apart. As O. T. Bonnett put it in *Why Healing Happens*:

> The first concept to embrace is that humankind is an inseparable part of the universe... an integral part ... just as each single cell within our bodies is an inseparable part of us. Second, ... the universe is a living, sentient being... 'an infinitely vast field of intelligent consciousness.' ...This would imply that the universe and God are one and the same. God did not create the universe. God is the universe. The universe is God.

Rather than "universe," implying the physical, I prefer to call God the "Kosmos"

You are God. You are an expression of the ONE, an individualized point of view of the ONE. You enable the ONE to expand its awareness by experiencing contrast through you as the unique viewpoint of itself that you are. Each of us manifest expressions is one of the ONE's unique viewpoints. Each of the possibilities or Intelligible Forms is a unique expression of the ONE: God. It's not that together we make up God, the ONE, but that we are the ONE. We each are a way for the ONE to know, love, and enjoy itself. We are not created by the ONE, for we have always existed in the consciousness of the ONE, its thoughts, its possibilities, its viewpoints.

CONSCIOUSNESS

Another insight that has become foundational to my belief system, one that has made its way into my philosophy through both my heart and my intellect, is that *God is consciousness*. This "truth" finally made it possible for me to understand our Oneness. I had earlier accepted as fact that we all, everything, are ONE, because my Self told me so, but my intellect hadn't been able to make it our own truth until we learned about consciousness. Allowing that consciousness is far more than a function of the human brain is central to understanding it, ourselves, and life more generally. Through such understanding we can *know* that we all, everything, are ONE, and we can realize that we are not truly material beings living this Earth life.

To me, consciousness is irreducible and fundamental to the Kosmos in all its dimensions. It is pure intelligence, love, light, energy, and creativity, and it permeates, entangles, and interconnects everything as the ONE. It is the Hindu "ground of being," the Gnostic "fullness" containing quantum physics' "possibilities," Plato's "Intelligible Forms," the information of the "akashic record." It is the "Mind of God"; it is God. Consciousness is the "creator," quantum physics' "observer," who thought the material into existence, the "First Cause."

Quantum Hologram

As the father of quantum physics Max Planck found, "there is no matter as such." Einstein later explained that "what we call matter is energy whose vibration has been so lowered as to be perceptible to the senses. There is no matter." And, quantum physicist David Bohm, a protégée of Einstein, discovered that everything, animate or seemingly inanimate, is conscious at the subatomic level. Bohm also realized that everything is ONE and that the ONE is a "quantum hologram."[1] He found that each aspect of the ONE—including each of us—is like a holographic shard and, while unique, is also the ONE, not just in "image and likeness," but truly is the ONE. This holographic concept means that everything the ONE is, each of us aspects is also, and anything that affects one of us also affects all shards in like fashion to some extent. We shards are quantum physics' possibilities, the multitude within and as the singularity of the ONE.

The Material Is Consciousness Made Manifest

The material is not apart from consciousness, it is consciousness made manifest. We are within and of consciousness, and it is within and of us. Consciousness is what everything is. There is nothing but consciousness—manifest or unmanifest—so consciousness is the ONE and we all are it. We all, being aspects of the ONE, are the ONE. We are not parts of the ONE but are expressions of the ONE, each a perspective from which the ONE views and comes to know and love itself.

The expressions, the possibilities of the ONE consciousness are individualized spirit beings. Some of those possibilities, choosing to experience physicality, projected themselves, or parts of themselves, into the materiality we call the universe and Earth. Each aspect of the universe is an emanation or face of a possibility made to appear physical by slowing its

---

[1] A hologram is an etheric illusion, a projection, which when shattered into pieces can be seen in its entirety in each piece, each "shard" in full spiritual expression.

rate of vibration. Each is consciousness expressing in materiality. The possibilities are like blueprints, Plato's Intelligible Forms, from which the material forms are projected into physicality.

INTELLECT

Although many people believe that the energy which surrounds and interpenetrates everything is consciousness, most also believe that only humans have consciousness. But I have to ask: "If consciousness interpenetrates everything, how can anything lack it?" I think they believe that because most other species don't seem to be particularly "aware of themselves and their surroundings"—Webster's definition of consciousness—at least to the extent that we humans are. They also equate consciousness with intellect and think we humans alone acquired it at a relatively recent point in our evolution (only about 100,000 years ago), a time they call our "mind's big bang." But it isn't consciousness we acquired then, it's intellect, when we became self-aware—and that was a lot longer ago than 100,000 years. Intellect, with its perceiving, reasoning, learning, judging, and reacting with emotions is a tool we humans use in enacting our daily life. We didn't acquire consciousness at all, none of us did, for we all *are* consciousness, ever and always.

While all other beings retain pure intelligence, we humans are the only beings who hid their natural intelligence with intellect. We did so to help us experience interactions and dualistic states and, applying its judgment, make choices and react with emotions. Intellect is the questioner who helps us understand our human life; it is also our conscience. It's a small aspect of our consciousness.

OTHER LIFE AND CONSCIOUSNESS

Most people believe that we humans are the only Earth beings who are self-aware and conscious of our surroundings, so the only ones with consciousness, what makes us different from other animals. Many people believe also that other creatures aren't as intelligent as humans because they don't have consciousness. Because we've been taught, whether by science's evolution theories or religion's creation story, that we humans are the pinnacle of Earth life, many materialists feel that other species are beneath us and are ours to dominate, even abuse. Many seem to think that other species are incapable of feeling, so abusing them isn't really hurting them. But they are as much consciousness as we are; they just don't use intellect, so aren't involved in the processes of self-awareness—or self-centeredness and indulgence—judgment, emotional reactions, and the kinds of perceptions and reasoning we humans use in experiencing this life. I believe that other Earth life never took on intellect, never hid their pure intelligence, or their natural spirit beingness. Everything in existence, though, has and is consciousness, in *equal* measure. Nothing can have more or less consciousness than anything else; it's what we all are!

Other Earth life may even be less material than humans, higher vibrating. It's said that cats and dogs live seven years for every one of ours, maybe because they vibrate seven times faster. Not having limited their natural selves, other animals function from awareness and pure intelligence. They have sharper senses than ours, and many are able to see colors and hear tones beyond our perception. They communicate telepathically, and may know exactly what's going on in this theater we call Earth. They are enacting their parts in our joint venture to help us in our experiences and awareness expansion while enjoying other aspects of Earth life. Bees, with their beautiful intricate hives, who contribute to all life by spreading reproductive, renewing pollen, and making tasty, nutritious honey, may be fully aware of their part in Earth life. Horses, sheep, and cows, grazing in grassy meadows, may be enjoying glorious spirit music we humans can't hear, may be basking in the deep love they feel for each other and for their human friends.

We need to take to heart the fact that inside we all, each and every being, are spirit and consciousness, all equal in our being. We all *share the same One consciousness*, the ONE of which we are each an aspect. We are that consciousness. We, of course, don't see that while living a relative, conditional reality of ordinary experience. But in Reality *there is nothing else*.

PERFECTION AND LOVE

Two other insights are also foundational to my philosophy: (1) everything is inherently perfect; (2) love is in and the basis of everything, every one, and every event that occurs. Earth revolves around the sun and the moon around Earth. Deciduous trees awaken with new green leaves in the spring, flourish in the summer, shed their leaves in autumn and slumber through winter. Dogs wag their tails and kittens purr to express their love and pleasure. Rivers flow to the seas and oceans ever circulate, evaporate, condense, and become rain, snow, and ice to return to rivers. Babies are born and volcanoes erupt. We meet and interact, all in perfect order. There is no such thing as an accident, no accidental injuries, deaths, or conceptions. Nothing occurs by chance, no actions or discoveries by happenstance. There is no such thing as luck, good or bad. Nothing is done that "should" not be. It all is perfect.

PERFECTION

You may question my use of the word "perfect," so I'll explain. In Webster's words, perfect means: "(1) having all the elements or qualities requisite to its nature or kind; complete. (2) without defect; flawless." I mean the same thing, but from a spiritual perspective. From my view, we are never flawed, never incomplete. We are God and spiritually express only love, only our divinity, so we can't be less than perfect. In any moment, who and what we are and what we do is correct for us at that time. We are all that we can be and are perfect in that being. We humans equate "perfect" with "ideal," and don't seem very perfect to our human perception. Ideal is determined by judgment and means something different for each judging human. No judgment is involved in perfection; it's not comparative, it just is.

Be ye, therefore, perfect even as your Father, who is in heaven, is perfect.

~ Matthew 5:48

I see this line from Jesus, not as a command to become perfect, but as a statement of fact. I think the biblical Jesus meant that all people, all things, *are* perfect. Being aspects of the ONE, we can't be less perfect than God. Manifestation doesn't change that fact. I see everything that anyone does—despite our human judgment of it—as serving a (spiritually) loving purpose, so is perfect. It fulfills our individual and often collective needs.

One day at Humbug an incident helped solidify my understanding of all this and helped my intellect to accept it. I mentioned earlier that, in addition to our jewelry shop, we ran a mini-mart. Part of that responsibility included selling gasoline to Lodge tenants and passing tourists. On this occasion, both of our gas tanks needed filling, so we'd ordered a truckload. The gas supplier stuck a hose nozzle into first one tank and then the other. While Mauri chatted with the gas supplier, I tended to business in our shop about six feet away from the fume-spewing truck. Since the shop door stood open, I could hear parts of conversation, but paid no attention to anything other than what I was working on. I absent-mindedly put a cigarette to my lips and raised my lighter. A horrendous bang outside stopped my thumb in mid-flick. I became aware that our non-vented shop was filled with gas fumes. Shaken, but curious about the noise, I ran out to see what had occurred. As the truck sat there pumping, one of its tires had blown; for no apparent reason, it just blew. Perfectly timed, it did its job, preventing my blowing up us and much of Humbug with one flick.

Awed by the perfection of this event, I realized that we are never alone. I have never since doubted the existence of higher intelligence, purpose, and perfection in and behind everything that exists and occurs. You may think I'm driving with only a joystick, or at best stretching a point to form the conclusion I did, but think about it. Can you prove it was purely coincidence? Is there such as coincidence, really? The Christian Bible—as does every religious text in its own way—tells us: "Remember, I am with you always" (Matthew 28:20). Are we ever truly alone? If God in omnipresent, can we ever be alone? As we proceed in this book, I'll explain this perfection concept in depth. It is the soul of my philosophy. Now to the heart.

LOVE

My Self has impressed upon me that there is loving cause behind everything that exists and occurs. Everything, no matter how insignificant seeming, has its place in the scheme of things. Everything is in harmony, in a cooperative, coordinated pattern of life. Humans alone, because we believe we're separate, sometimes behave disharmoniously. And yet, on a spiritual level, there's love behind that too. Kosmic law dictates that love is the only force and rule in the Kosmos. It enables us who live in physicality to do or be anything we want, yet, it also keeps us from doing or being what is not based in love. Although this law is narrow, we don't feel the constraints imposed by it because love is our very being. It would be impossible for us to be anything but the ONE's loving expression. So, nothing occurs that is not based in love. No matter the appearance, everything serves a loving purpose, and is perfect.

I know, you look around and think, "Love can't possibly be behind all this!" Read on; I'll explain what I mean, and if you can't buy it, you'll at least learn why I say it. And, you just might find some grain of truth, some morsel of use in your life.

Everything, being part of the Kosmos, has the ONE's perfection and the ONE's love, and cannot exist or take place by happenstance; it must exist by design, God's, our design. It's clear to me that every form in Earth life exists because on some level its inner being wanted to experience materiality and does so to serve specific love-filled purposes. It cannot be otherwise; there is nothing else; love is part of the absoluteness of God. Love is synonymous with consciousness, energy, light, spirit. All are the ONE, and we are it.

SEPARATION

A major aspect of our human life experience is one of separation. That is, the background we chose, our costuming, and our scenario details all help us see everything in our life as separate and apart from us and each other. Because our Reality is one of unity, we wanted the contrast of separation and multiplicity to help us see the individualized possibilities in order to know and love both them and the ONE. We wanted such definition to enable us to focus on details and see each aspect of the ONE as unique, beautiful, and wonderful. We wanted our initial human focus to be on separation and materiality as real so we would be able eventually to put it all back together into the spiritual ONE. We wanted the wonderful experience of awakening and remembering Reality, our spirituality and, our Oneness.

To us humans, by design our individual body with its consciousness seems unique and separate from everything else, each of which we also see as a unique entity. But put yourself in the place of a cell in your body. As that cell, because you don't know the truth and can't see or imagine the larger picture in which you exist, you would likely think you are separate and apart from all the other cells you see around you. But are you? You are individualized within the One that is your body. Return to your human awareness. Are you still separate from everything you see?

You may say, "But, some of us do terrible things, how can they be part of God?" Some of the cells in your body, with the same DNA, are malignant. Those malignant cells could join forces and do what you think of as harm to other cells and to the One they are, called "You." We all have some malignant cells in our body, but that doesn't mean we're all going to get cancer. When it serves some purpose individually or in the scheme of things, some of us get cancer. Some of those malignant cells hurt, even kill their larger self. But each cell is governed by its oneness and fulfills the needs of that oneness. Those cancer cells don't strike out on their own; they follow instructions from the mind of their larger self. Being cancer cells doesn't make them "bad." They act what we judge as "bad" when directed to, for purposes they probably don't know and don't have to know. That is their role in the scheme of things. They, too, are God, perfection, and love.

Eastern traditions don't like to speculate on the nature of God, saying we can't know. And some people are agnostic due to an inability to define God in finite words. While fundamentalist Jews and Muslims see God as a male being and biblical Christians see God as a trinity of male persons, to me God is not a Being and certainly not an individualized person. God is the Gnostic fullness and all possibilities of Plato and quantum physics. God is love. God is wholly spirit, pure energy, out of which all matter comes into being. And, because all aspects of the ONE are expressions of the ONE, we are all equal; no one is special, no one is better, higher, wiser, or older than anyone else. We are eternal beings.

When we try to describe God, we use the limited terms available to us in our human language, clearly associated with materiality. But, it's not that we can't adequately describe God; it's that *everything defines and describes God*. Everything is God: the ONE.

5

OUR ORIGIN, EVOLUTION, AND DESTINY AS HUMANS: MY IDEA OF CREATION

Since I couldn't imagine that our glorious universe came into existence by happenstance, without cause or direction, I felt certain there had to be cause and purpose to it. And, since our beautiful Earth clearly seems to have been "designed" specifically for us humans,[2] I felt there also had to be cause and purpose to Earth's existence, and especially human existence. Furthermore, I felt that until we knew why the universe and Earth were created and why we live in Earth life, we could never know what it's about and its meaning. We could never truly know ourselves. Many people say that we are spirit beings who enter human life of our own free will to experience and thereby expand our awareness, to know and love ourselves. But, why do we want to know and love ourselves, and why can't we do so as spirit beings without human life? Why physical experience? By learning answers to these why questions, we can understand the nature of our experience and why it often seems negative. Only then can we begin to understand our life on Earth. In garnering answers to those whys, I also got so much more.

Every idea I expressed in the previous chapter about God, the ONE, consciousness, perfection, and love were basic insights given me by my higher-vibrating soul-Self, and have become the foundation of my belief system and resulting philosophy of life. What follows are additional basic insights given in answer to my specific questions about our origin, our life experiences, and our destiny. As you read these insights keep in mind that they, like the stories we call myths, are learning/teaching tools and not necessarily factual history of "creation" and our human life here on Earth.

---

[2] This idea is called the Anthropic Principle, *anthros* referring to humanity.

It's not my intention to explain details of how things came about. My focus in presenting these insights is on answering the why questions, to help us better understand our life. These insights are reflected in my philosophy of life which works well for me. I don't ask you to accept any of it, but I hope it will give you things to consider for your own belief system.

WHY THIS ILLUSION

Although it all seems so very real, everything physical is only illusion. As spirit beings, we together thought the material into existence to serve our awareness purposes. We "created" not a material universe but a holographic image of what we wanted to experience. Why?

Before the "creation" or "big bang" of our universe, there was only ONE, an unbound sea of consciousness. Within that ONE, though, was an infinite number of eternal possibilities: the multitude within the singularity, as taught by Plato, ancient Kabbalah, and today's quantum physics. We spirit beings were those possibilities, Plato's Intelligible Forms or potentials. But because we were ONE consciousness, we were unable to know our individuality and uniqueness. So we also couldn't appreciate either our individuality or our Oneness. Everything was spiritual so we couldn't know what "spiritual" was, its nature. Contrast alone enables definition, and we had no contrast. We had nothing that wasn't spiritual, nothing that didn't express love, nothing separate to define individuality, nothing dark to illustrate light, nothing inert to help us know of our vibrating energy. Because we were omniscient pure intelligence, though, we knew we were missing something. We knew there was more to us than what we could feel and see about us.

Some of us were playing a game of illusion, creatively imagining things then slowing their vibrations to give a sort of form to them. A few of us slowed our own vibrations very slightly so we could enjoy our creations more on their level. When we returned to our full vibrational level, we were amazed as we looked around. We marveled at the vividness of color, the beauty of harmony, the absolute vibrancy of lilting sounds, and the enormous depth of love we feel in our natural state. We hadn't realized how glorious it all was. We'd never noticed, because we had no reason or way to do so; we never before had diminished Reality or us in any way. We'd never before had contrast to define anything, no way to see Reality differently than we had always known it. That slight slowing had provided a little contrast, enabling us to focus on and see some differences. We found our new awareness thrilling.

CREATING THE UNIVERSE

From this very minimal experience, we thought how fun and enlightening it would be to create other existences in which we could experience a variety of form and contrasting limitations, through which we could learn more about the wonders of ourselves and Reality. We wanted to know and appreciate ourselves as both the many and the ONE. Using emanations of our consciousness, we imagined a universe through which we could experience all manner of contrasts. Our universe was within and of our consciousness, each aspect interconnected to the whole, inseparable and interdependent. It contained many globes we could further develop to be theaters in which we would enact plays of differing experiential lives. Each aspect of our universe was an emanation from a possibility of the ONE, an expression of our consciousness, each an intelligent, loving part of us, not separate but individualized. We thought or projected our universe into etheric existence, then we gradually slowed its vibrations to create the appearance of material form. Everything still vibrated, in fact oscillated between their natural rapid pace and the new slower one, in and out of materiality, in and out of spirituality. Everything was and is alive, aware, intelligent, and loving.

EARTH

On one of the globes in our universe, which we now call Earth, Gaia, or often Mother Earth, we developed a theater especially for humans. We gave it varying and beautiful scenery as background and an extensive array of flora and fauna as co-inhabitants to participate in our plays while enjoying their own experience. Because we wanted to experience contrasts to help us define ourselves, we at first very slightly reduced our own vibrations to interact with our creations on a level closer to their materiality. We played in etheric form in semi-physicality for what would be in human terms a very long time. Not needing it, we didn't have language; our communication was far deeper, open and honest through thought and feelings. Since there was no disease or decay, we also in that early stage had no death and no birth and we were naturally androgynous, that is without gender and with a balanced mixture of masculine and feminine energy. Also, we interacted with all life on Earth and Earth itself, in complete cooperation, harmony, and love. We were developing our theater, our plays, and our creativity. We spirit beings, the souls of the Kosmos, were the First Cause, the quantum physics' observer, the infinite possibilities, the Creator. We are the ONE that in the physical is an expression of the ONE consciousness viewing itself in materiality.

REDUCING VIBRATIONS

As we experimented with different levels of vibration and their resulting denseness, we became aware that the greater the contrast created by slowed vibrations and the longer we were in that slower state, the more beautiful everything appeared when we returned to our Reality level of consciousness. We found that by applying to Reality the focus we were learning to use in our illusory world, we could see and appreciate so much more. As we experienced, we learned how to create an ever greater variety of conditions. Our joy in creation grew, especially as we learned more and more about ourselves from a perspective of something very different. We were becoming ever more aware and better able to know and love ourselves as well as our spirit existence.

EXTENDING OUR CONSCIOUSNESS

We finally realized that to truly experience the contrasts we wanted, we would have to considerably decrease our vibrations, and cut ourselves off from Reality, something we didn't want to do. We decided instead to express or extend a small part of ourselves into reduced-rate consciousness as human actors, so the larger part of us could remain in spirit while being fully connected to our extensions. In this way, our higher-vibrating soul-Selves could direct our slow-vibrating actor-selves through our experiences and our evolution while indirectly gaining from everything in our experience. We would expand the awareness of our whole being through the contrasts of our human lives.

To us human actors those larger, always higher vibrating, unmanifest spirit parts of us are our souls, what I call soul-Selves. It is that part of each of us who directs our plays, arranging for us to meet, bringing to us the contrasts necessary to our awareness expansion. I believe that our Selves are our guides, often thought of as several different beings, and sometimes also considered an avatar or ascended master. We each view this connection, this intuition, this source of wisdom, in a way that we personally can accept and best deal with. Regardless of how we each see and interpret our inner voice, it is, I believe, our Self.

We don't have emotions in Reality, so our experiences in this particular theater are designed to offer us opportunities to react with contrasting emotions. Our relationships are the most effective in this regard. How we emote, what emotions we feel, and the extent to which we feel them is entirely up to us individually, our choice.

The defining contrasts were not seen by us as lesser than Reality in any way, but rather as ways of getting a better look at and an understanding of Reality. Slower vibrations enabled us to see everything in component parts rather than in wholeness, as we had always known it. The result of slowing was as an expansion of our Reality and a truly exciting and joy-filled experience. Being able to see enumerable aspects of the ONE was just as exciting to us originally as it is now when we as individual humans occasionally glimpse the Oneness that is also our Reality.

PLANNING AND ENACTING OUR PLAYS IN SOUL GROUPS

From what my Self tells me, I see that we enact many overlapping plays together in groups, reincarnating over and over together into Earth life under differing conditions and different relationships. (I explain about our use of reincarnation in Chapter 6 - How It Works.) Before we first entered Earth life, we each joined with others to form a relatively small soul group, so we could together experience a specific set of conditions which would give us emotions most beneficial to our individual and collective awareness expansion.

To help in our play planning and enactment, we, in those soul groups, plan the course of our play experience together. Each group has planned and enacted many plays together and will continue to do so as long as we want this physical human kind of experience. While throughout our play life we each interact with numerous other actors, the members of our soul group take the roles in our life which are the most significant to our experience and awareness expansion. They may be our mothers, fathers, siblings, teachers, friends, co-workers, or our enemies. Our significant lovers, mates, partners are certainly in our soul group.

MASCULINE AND FEMININE ENERGY

At some point in our evolutionary experimentation, we realized that death of our physical bodies would provide a great array of plot opportunities for our plays, as would birthing, developing, and aging processes. We also saw that we would gain greatly from limiting our individual human energy to predominantly that of either masculine or feminine and see to it that our bodies, emotions, and intellectual patterns reflect our choice of gender. All this gave us considerably more to experience and emote about, especially the love, mating, birthing, and parenting aspects of our relationships. We also concluded that our play scenario would benefit from background conditions in which the planet's energy, and with it humanity's collective unconsciousness, was unbalanced to be heavier with masculine energy. This imbalance would create an atmosphere in which competition, conflict, power, aggression, and greed could flourish and dominate. This gave us a truly extensive mix of contrasts to experience.

When we extend ourselves into human actors, we have to put that part of us into a sort of sleep or dream condition so it can forget the truths of our existence and realistically enact our individual role. A few years after birth, most of us program ourselves to forget Reality, our Oneness, and the fact that we are spirit beings. We further cause ourselves to believe that the play is not only real but that the material we see is the *only* reality. That's what we teach ourselves and our children. We exchange our great spiritual powers for five limited physical senses: seeing, hearing, smelling, tasting, and touching. I say "limited" because we have these senses in Reality but in different non-physical ways and considerably more intense. We also temporarily exchange our pure intelligence for what we call "intellect." In learning to use intellect we gradually program our human minds to think rationally, judge what we see, hear, and experience, make choices from the great array of dualistic (positive and negative) conditions as they present themselves, and emote accordingly. Long ago, we established a law of cause and effect so we could experience the effects of our thinking, behavior, and attitudes through intellect. Intellect is our ego, our persona, and the part of our consciousness that wants what it thinks of as success, power, control, and does or intends that we do what will satisfy those needs. We did all this so we could effectively experience the contrasts of physical human life from a material level of awareness. Although this life is limited in many respects from what we have in Reality, it gives us experience in physicality. And in that experience, we feel, see, hear, touch, and taste many wonders we can't get in Reality. I'll talk more about this in Chapter 7 - What Does All This Mean?

INTUITION

Because we cut ourselves off so completely from Reality, we also enabled a strong link between the small actor part of us and our larger, unmanifest, always in spirit part of us. This link is what we call "intuition." It allows our individual soul-Selves to keep in constant communication with their actor-selves, directing us in enactment of our play. With gentle nudges, including feelings, desires, ideas, and thoughts of wisdom, invention, and insight, our souls direct us actors through the plays of life, one interaction and experience after another. In this way, we continually advance and unfold, seemingly naturally, greatly expanding our joint awareness. Not only are we directed throughout our plays by way of intuition, but we can also get help in remembering who and what we are and all things about Reality from our personal source of all knowledge and wisdom: our Self. Most of what we get through intuition is subtle and not consciously or knowingly received, but we can make it a conscious connection, if we want that. We can intentionally go within to commune with our Self, our inner voice. I'll even teach you how to do so and give you a practice that helped me establish a wonderful conscious communion, giving me constant access to my higher-vibrating soul-Self. See Chapter 19, Going Within To *Know* and Love Our Selves.

SLOWING VIBRATIONS TO CREATE PHYSICALITY

As we slowed our universe's vibrations to appear more solid, "creating" physicality, causing what scientists have called the "big bang," we left consciousness replicas of it at each descending level. These replicas are what amount to parallel universes which we would use later in further experience. These parallel universes are also alive and aware, each higher one more fully aware of all those at lower levels, while slightly aware of higher ones. And the consciousness of each affects the level of awareness of beings living at that level. These are not material places, they are levels of consciousness.

Some of the experiences we want are physical; many, too, are not physical but are spiritual. By using different vibrational rates, we create different levels, or dimensions, in which to interact and experience. Some of us slowed our vibrations only slightly, some more so but not to a material level. Much is going on in many dimensions, but those of us in physicality can get only occasional glimpses of those other levels until we begin to awaken.

In slowing vibrations, we also created space and linear time and established duality, in which everything would have an opposite, such as good and bad and weak and strong. Duality would enable suffering and help in defining everything. Without both opposites, we couldn't define, know, and appreciate the one we had. They are not truly opposites but are contrasting complements making definition possible.

HUMAN EVOLUTION IS CYCLICAL

Before we actors entered Earthly human life, we decided it would be especially effective to use many lives in reincarnation to go through a process of circular evolution. We are beginning now to enjoy the fruits of that process. When we first entered Earth life we were fully aware, intelligent, love-filled and creative. This may have been when we were what are now called Lemurians. But because we had no way of focusing on our individuality or uniqueness, we didn't really know ourselves. We weren't truly self-aware. We needed the contrasts of a very different, physical life to help us see and appreciate both ourselves as possibilities and our self as ONE. In the process, many of us then went through a devolution (evolving downward) process, slowing our vibrations to materiality and veiling our great minds and memory of ourself/selves and Reality. This devolution and veiling put us under the dream spell I've mentioned, which is really a form of amnesia, a forgetfulness, forgetting our Real life and spirituality. Some of us remained high vibrational, choosing not to fully devolve, to look after and help the devolved "children." Those who remained higher vibrational helped the children learn to fend for themselves and develop language. They built megalithic cities, with temples to keep some of the children in touch with their spirituality and, to some minimal extent, the knowledge of their Oneness. They also left wisdom in symbolic form for future use and created what are called the "Mystery" spiritual teachings, eventually adopted by nearly every ancient culture. They were often held in awe by the less sophisticated children, and were the original heroes and deities on which myths were based. They were the early Atlanteans who finally themselves also went through the devolving process.

When we had fully devolved, we took on intellect to replace our pure intelligence and the five physical senses to replace our great natural "extrasensory" abilities. We got really into our experience of human life on Earth. We learned how to use our intellect and to judge everything using the dualistic criteria to make choices. We became self-aware, and learned to interact with each other. As our intellect developed, we learned how to use it to cause emotions as reactions to each other and our environment. With each new incarnation, our intellect grew stronger and we advanced into ever more sophisticated modern humans. We have continued evolving, becoming largely intellectually based and highly inventive technologically. Believing this material existence is the only reality, we have tried to become independent, self-sufficient, and intent on surviving through power, control, and material possessions.

Most of us in that first group who devolved, though, are now evolving in another direction. We are waking up from our self-imposed amnesia and are realizing that we aren't truly material beings at all and that this human life is an illusion. We are raising our awareness to ever higher levels of consciousness, coming full circle Our awakening will bring us to a new higher level than the one from which we entered human life, so it's really spiral. Our wonderfully awareness-expanding experiences have so perfectly done their job. We see, know, and feel so much more than ever before. We are now fully self- and selves-aware, and can appreciate all that we are and have. Through numerous reincarnations, we have defined by contrasts our multiplicity and the uniqueness of our individuality. Now, though, for many of us it's time to learn more about our Oneness, what I believe is every human's destiny: That is to *return* to full conscious awareness of our spirituality, our Oneness, our love and perfection, and our divinity.

Atlanteans' Devolution and Ultimate Evolution

Not long after the first group of us devolved actors began our upward evolution, the other group (those who had remained in higher consciousness) began their planned devolution. Those later Atlanteans became less and less spiritual and more materially oriented. They got very wrapped up in technology, trying to replicate spiritual powers and bodily workings into material "things" and became competitive and combative. They may have caused the split in land mass that separated the Americas from Africa and Europe, creating the Atlantic Ocean and breaking up their once huge and great civilization. While geologists would say that split probably occurred over 60 million years ago, time was completely different then from what it is now, much slower, so can't be counted in the same terms we do today. Even today's time is constantly changing, speeding up, as we raise our vibrations and evolve back toward our spirituality. Gaia (Earth as a single complete living system), too, is evolving.

The first group of humans is experiencing a Shift in our awareness to higher levels of consciousness. We are becoming more aware of our spirituality and our Oneness and are more loving, sharing, and compassionate. The second group is once again thoroughly wrapped up in technology, competition, power, war, and greed. They are in a sense reliving their experience as Atlanteans, only on an upward path rather than the downward one of their earlier devolution. They, like the rest of us are on the upward arc of our circular evolutionary path, just slightly behind the first group. This distinction is not meant to imply lesser in any way.

Once the first group has made its Shift and raised the collective unconsciousness of humanity to a higher level, the second group, too, will begin shifting. Their shift will be more quickly accomplished, having been made easier by the first group's shift and the lightening of humanity's collective unconsciousness. What I call "collective unconsciousness" is the energy of humanity collectively, of which we are unaware, but which greatly affects us and our world generally. It collects the intellectual programs and beliefs we have imposed on ourselves as well as all the negativity we believe to be real. See Chapter 6, How It Works, for more on our collective unconsciousness.

COMING FULL CIRCLE ON THE SPIRAL

Soon we all will have come full circle, and Utopia—or heaven, or a golden age, if you prefer—will be a fact of life on Earth. We will, once again, fully cooperate with each other and all Earth beings in the knowledge of our Oneness. We will understand them and they us. We will have peace on Earth, everyone (humans and all other life) living in harmony, enjoying the beauty, love, and tranquility of spiritual life in this beautiful physical environment

Wondrous are the scenarios available to us through interaction, love, physical and emotional attraction, mating, birth, illness, and well being. We also have adversity, deformity, challenge, abuse, injury, tragedy, imagined successes and failures, and death. Then we have application of intellectual reasoning and judgment on the opposites of duality. Of course, we didn't know to plan all this originally, but learned as we actors developed and experienced. Our creativity, like our awareness, has evolved.

The feelings and emotions we use in human life are parts of a continuum, with high vibration love at one end and low vibration fear at the other end. In between are all the other feelings and emotions vibrating at different frequencies. There's no difference in value between the higher feelings and the lower emotions; they just serve different purposes in human life and at different times. All serve loving purposes, helping us human selves and our soul-Selves to better know ourselves, our whole being. In using emotions not natural in Reality, we actors have wonderful new experiences that contrast to Reality, enabling us to realize and appreciate all we truly are and have in our spirit dimensions. Emotions are reactions to outside stimuli—interactions with people and events in our lives. What I call "feelings" are the spiritual love, harmony, serenity, joy, and bliss native and natural to us as spirit beings. Our soul-Selves sprinkle these into our lives to help balance and reduce the suffering of the contrasting negatives in our experience. We also get feelings—of pleasure and happiness, sadness, worry and concern—every day as we go about our life, which I'll call "worldly" feelings, to distinguish them from the feelings we get from our Selves, and I'll call those "spiritual feelings." Worldly feelings, like emotions, are responses to outside stimuli, but are more subtle, not as reactive as regular emotions.

Evolving Back to Spiritual Understanding at Higher Levels of Consciousness

Once we have experienced at the lower levels nearly all we have planned, we human extensions, with the help of our Selves, begin to expand our conscious awareness to work our way back up through ever-higher levels of consciousness. As we rise higher, we open to more and deeper spiritual feelings and reduce our use of emotions. For example, the more love we feel, the less fear and other negativity we experience. As we evolve consciously back toward Reality, our physical vibration rate increases and our body lightens; our awareness rises ever higher, getting closer in vibration to that of our souls. As we gradually re-attune our outer human consciousness with our inner, larger, higher-vibrational Selves, we raise our overall vibrations. We begin to awaken, gradually diminishing the veil created by lower vibration energy amassed into our collective unconsciousness. The more we *know* of our true Selves the more awake we are. We begin to recognize our interconnectedness and our Oneness and begin to exercise our divinity. Our consciousness shifts from strictly worldly (material) to more and more spiritual. Our energy becomes ever more balanced, with the feminine energy returning to balance the masculine. We realize that we never really lost the other half of our male/female energy, and see that our inner self is androgynous; that is, both female and male in balanced combination. We are then able to express more love and caring in our relationships and in our approach to people and events in our daily life, our worldview. In time, we each will fully awaken.

THE SHIFT AND CONSCIOUS REUNION OF self WITH SELF

As we human extension actors rise in consciousness, with each level our soul-Selves are better able to express through us. The more we attune ourselves in communion, the more directly our whole being can express. The Shift will make it possible for our larger Selves to enjoy Earth life ever more directly and without the dualistic contrasts. Once each human extension awakens to its Oneness with its soul, the unmanifest part of our whole being will finally be able to directly experience in physicality. We have eagerly awaited our reunion ever since we began the physical plays and extended ourselves to become actors to perform in them. We are beginning to enjoy our own true loving nature, our divinity, in experiences of human life.

HARD CONCEPTS

I know these are hard concepts, very different from what we've been taught. Keep in mind that we actors in these plays are not separate from our high-vibrating souls; we are each an extension of our soul's consciousness. We are an expression, a point of view, of our Self, just as our Self is a viewpoint of the ONE. What an actor experiences, so does its soul, and indirectly so does the ONE. Participation in a play is always voluntary and done for everyone's benefit. While experiencing suffering in human life seems like something a sane, loving being wouldn't choose to do, we gain so much awareness from it that it's worth every pain. Also, Earth life is illusion and suffering is only physical and temporary. Remember that time, too, is an illusion, created by slowed vibrations; a lifetime on Earth is the equivalent of a much briefer time in Reality.

Reality is not a remote spot in the universe, but is all around us, in interlinking and interpenetrating energy/consciousness. Reality, is not a separate place from Earth, but is a different dimension in consciousness. Our souls enjoy the same material universe that we physical extensions do, only to them it is more vibrant and beautiful, since they don't have the haze of our current veiled physical condition and collective unconsciousness to obscure its glory. But, since they're not material, they don't physically experience materiality.

Enacting plays of human life is not much different from starring in a human movie or stage play. In the latter there are breaks between scenes or acts when actors return to their real life. In our plays, actors often return home to Reality at the end of a day's act while their role (ego, intellect) sleeps. Actors are never far from Real life. Speaking of a movie brings to mind the Harry Potter movies. It seems to me worth noting that J. K. Rowling, in writing the *Harry Potter* books from which the movies were produced, was well aware of the illusion of Earth's materiality. One example is Harry's ability to go through walls. We all could, too, if we hadn't programmed our intellects to believe that it's impossible because matter is solid.

WHAT WE'VE LEARNED

We've learned so much since we set all this material creation in motion, and greatly enjoy our power of creation. We see much more of Reality now, and are able to focus on details we hadn't before realized existed. We will continue to use Earth for semi-physical and spiritual experiences any time we want; for much goes on in several dimensions above (higher vibrating) what we humans are familiar with. We also have much more to experience on other globes, in other, different theaters. Also, in Reality our spiritual feelings are far deeper than what we get as humans, and our music and colors are glorious. More precious than any other advantage we have in Reality over humans is the love we feel for all life. We manifest materially to know and love ourselves/Self. Before, we had no way of knowing what love was, but now after eons of experience with love in limitation, we realize what it is to *be* love. In human words, it's incredible. And now we know that.

The remainder of this book elaborates on and explains the insights I offer here only briefly. For a more detailed description of my "creation" ideas in story form, see *WAKE UP! Our old beliefs don't work anymore!* In that book, that story is told by my higher-vibrating, soul-Self. *AWAKENING* elaborates on that story and applies it and my resulting philosophy to our everyday life.

6

HOW IT WORKS

According to my soul-Self, although we perceive it as "real" in human terms, our beautiful Earth is not Real in absolute spiritual terms. It is illusion of our own design, a living theater where we enact the plays of physical human life for everyone's great benefit. We humans are merely actors, performing our roles. But, on a spiritual level, being shards of the ONE hologram, we are also our Real Selves and the ONE. We are our Selves' expressions manifest in physicality.

THE WHY OF IT ALL

In answer to the big question of WHY the universe, Earth, and its life were created in the beginning, my Self says it was to define and know ourselves and to appreciate (love) what we were and had as spirit beings. Self explains that we spirit-light beings chose to create the universe to house theaters in which we could enact plays to help us know and love ourselves—both the ONE and its multitude of unique possibilities—through contrasting material experience.

Because I had found no explanation in the Bible for why "creation" occurred, I thought that all three of the Western religions of Judaism, Christianity, and Islam had no answer for the why. But a friend of mine says, "it's not that Christian religion doesn't have an answer to why all this exists; they do have one [although it's not in the Bible] that has served them well for nearly two millennia. It's just that now we don't like their answer, aren't satisfied by it."

"The Life of Man—To Know and Love God" is the heading which opens the Catholic Church's Prologue to their *Catechism of the Catholic Church*—commissioned by Pope John Paul in 1986 and released to the public in 1992. It is "a compendium of all catholic doctrine regarding both faith and morals...." That opening phrase is the Roman Church's answer to why we exist, and in a sense is the same as mine, but quite different in interpretation and intent. The Prologue elaborates:

> God, infinitely perfect and blessed in himself, in a plan of sheer goodness freely created man to make him share in his own blessed life. For this reason, at every time and in every place, God draws close to man. He calls man to seek him, to know him, to love him with all his strength....
>
> To accomplish this, when the fullness of time had come, God sent his Son as Redeemer and Savior. In his Son and through him, he invites men to become, in the Holy Spirit, his adopted children and thus heirs of his blessed life.

Chapter One of the Catechism further explains:

> The desire for God is written in the human heart, because man is created by God and for God; and God never ceases to draw man to himself. Only in God will he find the truth and happiness he never stops searching for.

The God the Roman Church teaches we must know and love is a personal God in the form of three male persons. That God is outside and apart from us, and much of the time the, love, truth, and happiness we were born to pursue is in practice more devotion and worship than knowledge and understanding. The Church does say that we can know God by his works—mostly in nature.

The Roman Church's answer doesn't for me fully explain why God created the universe in the first place, or Earth and its life. Was God lonely? Did God seek companionship in the form of humans? And, if He created us, why did he have to adopt us as His children?

Long before Christianity, the Mysteries of our early civilizations taught as their prime directive the knowledge and love of God but, like me, they said to go within to find God and to know and love that God in ourselves. And, neither the ancient Mysteries' teachings nor I give this as a reason for our being here but rather a practice to pursue for enlightenment and awakening.

As we saw in Chapter 4, God can be viewed in several different ways. Clearly the Roman Catholic Church wants us to see him as a male being separate from us; ancient *spiritual* traditions saw God as within us all; and I—both human self and soul-Self—see God in and as everything. We—spirit beings—wanted to know and love God. But that God was ourselves, not some outside being. Realizing that we needed contrast to define ourselves individually and our Oneness, we built this Earth theater in which to experience a great array of contrasts.

THE PLAY

When we took on intellect, in order to more realistically experience materiality, we temporarily veiled our pure spirit intelligence, wisdom, and knowledge. As I've said we gave ourselves amnesia, in a sense put ourselves under a sleeping spell. As we experience human life and become ever more aware of our true spirit nature, we gradually awaken. This process is part of our individual evolution, toward which our soul-Self guides us through intuition.

As a soul group, during the time spent on other planes between incarnations, we discuss our evolution. We evaluate past-life experiences and individual progress toward our ultimate goal of awakening. We formulate plays, agreeing to play new roles in upcoming sojourns on Earth.

THE SCRIPT

In a sense, we use a "script" for each play, but it isn't a word-for-word dialog, nor does it specify the details of each scene. It is more an outline defining the essence, purpose, intent, and aims of major events and interactions of the particular segment of human life it covers. It sets the overall goals for the lives involved and the general ways we intend to fulfill those goals in terms of the who's, what's, why's, when's, where's, and how's of the individual scenarios in each play. And it is flexible, allowing a variety of ways to provide what each entity wants to experience. It enumerates each major happening or event, each relationship, and each major interaction the group will use to accomplish its aims and purposes, both as a group and individually.

Those aims and purposes, the experiences we want at our soul level, are in the form of emotions, not the physical experiences themselves. Physical experiences stimulate the emotions which are our true experiences; it is only through our feelings and emotions that anything affects us. In most cases we can achieve the emotions we want in many different ways, through various physical events and interactions. So our script merely suggests what some of the means might be. Rather than providing specific conversations, for example, it points us toward people and encounters that offer the environment through which we might potentially evoke the emotions we want. It's up to us humans to respond to those people and the environment as we choose. If we don't react with the emotions we want at our soul level from one set of experiences, we get other opportunities to create those emotions.

No one tells an actor it has to enter an Earth play or what must be accomplished. A soul doesn't send its actor into Earth life; it's not like that. Every life is strictly voluntary and intended to provide opportunities for awareness expansion, with specifics chosen by participating actors. Just as actors and audiences participate voluntarily and enjoy human stage plays and movies, so too do we enjoy human life plays. We are enjoying it all, together. And it all is based in Love.

Planning Our Plays

Our soul group decides where, when, and how love interests will develop and what obstacles we characters will encounter for the greatest plot interest. We also predetermine what if any tragedy will occur, who will be involved, and how generally we will react to it. We preplan the circumstances and timing of death for maximum effect. Every character who is a significant contributor to our plot does and becomes what serves best the purposes and aims of the play as far as their role is concerned.

We jointly select our family and friends, each choosing the combination of gender, physical attributes, mental powers, capabilities, and talents to provide the perfect conditions for the experiences we wish to create in our life. These are our costuming and makeup. We plan our loves, our successes and failures, our adversities, afflictions, and challenges, our joys and sorrows, and we plan our death. We vary these with each of our numerous roles (through reincarnation) to give us maximum exposure to conditions offered in Earth life to serve specific planned purposes. All human actors play their parts to perfection, at the time aware only of their personal roles, usually forgetting Reality almost entirely.

Planning Emotions Through Interactive Relationships

Human life is all about relationships, interactions, and emotions, with most awareness-expanding emotions coming to us through personal interactions. Emotions provide the contrasts we want to experience and our relationships and interactions create circumstances through which our intellect can emote. So, before we begin an Earth life, we plan our individual and joint play scenarios, deciding on the emotions we each want an opportunity to experience. We, together, figure out the interactions and/or events which will provide those opportunities. We cast our play. We decide on the country and its living conditions where the play will mainly take place. We each choose the race, ethnicity, gender, physical, mental, and emotional characteristics, talents, and strong interests, and the economic, educational, religious, and social environment that we want to use in our new life experience. We, along with those who play our loved ones or care-givers, consider adversities, for example: whether a physical or mental challenge will provide what we want, and whether it would be best from birth or later in life. And we often involve tragedy in our scenario.

Each member of our soul group is an important participant in the play of each other member. Some are loved ones, some are family members who express little or no love, some are instruments of harm or great challenge, some act as mirrors, helping us see ourselves as others see us or as we need to see ourselves. These mirrors often help us individually work on a specific issue—something we may want to change in ourself. Everyone is vital in the role we are playing.

Many human actors in a given group are at a similar evolutionary stage and, despite contrary appearances, at a like point on their spiritual path. This similarity provides an affinity of interests and values which helps draw group members together during a life's scenario and often gives them a commonality to share in relationships. Differences serve plot needs through contrast. Because of this group travel, as we meet new people, we frequently have an immediate rapport with some of them. We feel as though we've known each other forever (and, of course, we have), when we've seemingly only just met. This helps us create necessary interactive relationships and is the origin of "love at first sight."

Usually, we take a different role in each others' lives from one incarnation to another. Except lovers. We seem to journey through our many lives with the same lover or couple of lovers over and over again. We often think of ourselves in connection to one of those as "soul mates." Not all enacted relationships are pleasant, though. The point in participating in these plays is not to enjoy love and beauty as constants but to experience emotional contrasts to what we truly are and have as spirit beings. It's to help us see the true love and beauty of ourselves and our Reality. That's not to say that all human life has to be tragic, frustrating, or challenging, but certainly some of it must be. We give ourselves only enough pain and heartache to stimulate the emotions we chose to experience and never more than we can handle.

LOVING FRIENDS

Studies through regression into past lives show that nearly every entity with whom we closely associate in this life has played a major role in many previous incarnations. They are not always loved ones; when necessary, they are adversaries or those from whom we experience injustice, bodily harm, or other suffering, possibly as mortal enemies. When Jesus said for us to love our enemies, he knew that each enemy is truly a loving friend, playing the part of an enemy or instrument of harm or injustice only because they and we lovingly agreed to play those roles for mutual benefit. Five hundred years before Jesus, the great classical Greek philosopher Socrates, too, said for us to love our enemies. Everyone in our life is truly spiritually a loving friend, there for our mutual advantage. Every one of us is needed in the role we are playing for the benefit of everyone with whom we come into contact. Without our knowing it consciously, our words, actions, and attitudes are what others need to experience. Nothing we do can be wrong, bad, or even ill timed. Each of us is important, with purpose and value just as we are to each member of our soul group and possibly to the whole of life on Earth.

OUR SOULS DIRECT US IN OUR PLAY

Our play is produced and directed by and from the spirit plane. Our souls are the co-directors of our plays, using intuition, to prod us human actors into enacting the scripts we've chosen. Our souls cause us to meet and create events for us to experience. They feed us feelings, desires, hunches, nudges, insights, ideas, and occasionally things to say as we enact our play, all in conformance with our planned scenario. What we think, do, and say, though, in response to the people and events we come across, are the crux of our experiences and are our choices to make. Most of the time we aren't consciously aware of being directed. Oh, we know we suddenly get ideas, feelings, or hunches, but seldom do we stop to think about them, rarely asking from where they've come. In fact, we don't always follow those proddings, but sometimes reject or ignore them. Yet when we go against them, more often than not we regret it. We're apt to later think: "Oh, if only I'd followed that hunch," or "... my first thought." Our own choices, when opposing our highest good (planned direction), usually produce uncomfortable outcomes. Then we respond to the discomfort, sometimes getting back on track and sometimes getting further mired in the muck we've chosen. The closer we are to oneness with our Self, the more directly our Self can act in our life and the more comfortable we can be with our Self making more of our choices.

Throughout a play we can fulfill the intent and create the feeling of a scene in various ways, giving us flexibility in our interactions, enabling us to experience the variety of emotions through which our awareness grows. It also enables our human selves to feel we are exercising a little free will and freedom of choice, necessary parts of our human experience. No matter the specifics we use to enact our scripts, we always fulfill the essential purposes and goals we set for each life.

Occasionally the experience we want comes not through direct interaction and behavior but is something in us triggered by someone, and has otherwise nothing to do with them. Our Selves set up the scene so that one of us can trigger something in the other, and that may be the only purpose of the scene. The trigger may be merely a word that reminds us of something, or it could be a feeling that does the reminding or causes us to think about something.

COLLECTIVE UNCONSCIOUSNESS

As I've indicated, humanity has what I call a "collective unconsciousness," which holds negativity, limited programs, and dualistic criteria over our heads like a cloud. It is not in itself negative—nothing is—but is there to help us experience the negatives as we choose to draw from it. Its primary purpose is to gather and hold the ideas and beliefs we collectively have sold ourselves to be true as we've experienced life and make them available to us for continued experience. It includes: the idea that we humans are all sinful and need to be saved from ourselves or from Satan; the idea that God is outside and apart from *his* creations; the idea that this material existence is the only reality, there is nothing spiritual or supernatural. It also includes all the terrible acts people have perpetrated and our reactions to them. It is like a mesh net in which heavy thoughts of fear, limitation, and other negativity can't escape and are held for our use. Lighter thoughts of love and harmony can't get caught in it and pass on through to be enjoyed by all the Kosmos. Our collective unconsciousness can be weakened by loving thoughts, and will eventually be dissipated when we raise our consciousness to higher levels.

REINCARNATION

To co-create every possible expression and experience, we human actors return to Earth in physical form of our own free will over and over again for the benefits we derive from our experiences. It is our great pleasure to enact these plays. It is our joy to experience human life and all of the conditions associated with it. It isn't that we *need* some experience, there is nothing we need. It isn't that we have to overcome, perfect, or correct something. We return only because we get pleasure out of doing so, like we humans do when we go to see a movie or play, or because of the satisfaction we get out of enacting our role in a play or movie. While in them, we find our roles entertaining, and benefit greatly from them. When we return home, we find Reality that much more glorious as a result of the contrasts in our Earthly sojourn. We know and better understand ourselves individually and our Oneness. We're able to focus our awareness as never before and see and appreciate details we had no idea existed.

Many spiritual metaphysicians see reincarnation as a means of "perfecting our souls." Through human life experience, they say, our souls are tempted, tested, and tried; they learn lessons, grow, clean their karmic slate, and thereby ultimately become perfect. Soul perfection, whether through karmic cleansing or through trials and tribulations, result in the soul's release from Earth's ties to enjoy eternal bliss, say many New Age thinkers and spiritual metaphysicians.

In my understanding, though, our evolution through reincarnation has absolutely nothing to do with cleansing, purifying, or perfecting; involving neither physical perfecting of the species nor soul perfecting. Neither souls nor we human consciousness extensions need to be perfected; both are in a constant state of perfection (from a spiritual perspective). The human species is just what we want it to be in any given moment. It is perfect as it is. Besides, how could perfect gods extend their consciousness as imperfect actors? Second, we're not here to transcend this life, we're here to make the most of it and evolve; and we're here to help our fellow actors do likewise.

Since there's no mention of reincarnation in the Bible, most Christians exclude it from their beliefs. Many emphatically deny it, saying it's contrary to the concept of resurrection and Jesus' special divinity. Actually, both Judaism and Christianity deliberately removed belief in reincarnation from their creeds, and Islam followed their lead. References to reincarnation originally in the Bible were removed early in the first few centuries CE (common era, formerly called AD)—although some phrases can still be seen as implying reincarnation. Prior to this exclusion, all ancient cultures taught reincarnation as part of their *spiritual* traditions. Kabbalah still does. Hinduism and other Eastern traditions, unaffected by Christianity's influence and attempts at eradication of other beliefs, have maintained most of their ancient teachings, including reincarnation. Of course, orthodox Darwinian science denies reincarnation entirely since, by its theories, we don't have souls, and this material life is all that exists; there is no spirit world, and consciousness is a physical attribute of the human brain.

While considering the possibility of reincarnation, think about the experience of a friend of mine. One day while my friend was comforting her granddaughter after a minor mishap, the three-year-old child looked up at her and said, "Grammy, remember when you were my baby and I rocked you in my arms?" Was that child's question evidence of a previous life they'd had together? Was that evidence of reincarnation? We often wonder where children get some of the ideas they voice, and are prone to say they are products of active imaginations. But are they? Remember, youths have recently come into the physical world from spirit Reality and have not yet programmed their intellect. They have not yet pulled the veil of collective unconsciousness over their individual spirit awareness as we did. And their spirit being is not really a child.

KARMA AND ITS LAW

It seems that the vast majority of people drawn to the spiritual have been convinced of the "never-failing justice" of the "law of karma." For awhile early in my search for enlightenment, I was obsessed with understanding the concept of karma. Wanting to know what is meant by "karma" and how it's applied, I read numerous books on the subject. I finally decided that most believers think of karma as "action," and most of the time they associate it with a "law" that separates karmic actions into good and bad categories. That law of karma then states that we in a sense reap in each new life what we have sown in previous lives. That is, past-life actions affect subsequent lives on Earth, with mean or harmful past actions (bad karma) bringing about challenging rebirths and kind, compassionate actions (good karma) providing pleasant future experiences.

Some say there is family or ethnic karma through which one suffers the consequences of their family's or ethnic group's actions of prior times.

Believers feel this is unerring justice because it never fails to be applied and affects us only to the extent of our own prior actions. Some people believe we often return in the same or reverse relationships with major characters in our plays to re-experience some karma left unsettled in a previous life together. Others say our karma isn't with other individuals at all but is with God.

DISAGREEING WITH THE LAW OF KARMA AS PUNISHMENT AND RETRIBUTION

This understanding of the law of karma runs completely counter to everything I believe about human life. First, categorizing behavior into good and bad is completely subjective and judgmental—what's good to some people may be very wrong to others and vice versa. And, good and bad are human concepts only; they don't exist in Reality. Besides, who decides into which category a behavior goes or how and when it's to be experienced on the receiving end? Second, our Selves and selves—together as one in Reality before our play begins—plan each incarnation within the overall design for our individual awareness expansion and humanity's evolution. We plan each affliction for the growth it offers. It isn't retribution for past bad behavior. We use deformities, disabilities, and other challenges to enable us and those near us to experience conditions and emotions not otherwise attainable. Whether deformed from birth or physically impaired later in life through illness or injury, we chose such conditions for our experience. And, our so-called evil deeds are preplanned actions designed to be of experiential benefit to the "victims" and their loved ones, and also to us as "villains." These actions create some of the most mutually valuable awareness-expanding circumstances of our lives, and cannot be returning energy from past negative karma. They aren't anyone's to judge and categorize.

There is never a need for retribution or justice. In fact, justice would be ill served by what amounts to punishment in some future life. Who would want to ever play the part of villain if they ultimately had to be on the receiving end of something similar? Also, every mass consciousness evil (like the Holocaust, the 9/11 terrorist attack, genocide wherever perpetrated) is staged and orchestrated to help humanity in general raise its awareness to higher levels of consciousness. Each is committed in love (on a higher soul level), jointly by the perpetrator and the victims.

Sometimes, for more rounded growth, we elect to act out both sides of a situation in two different plays to experience emotions associated with both sets of conditions, and learn, such as, compassion. Or, we may want to re-experience like conditions of a prior lifetime to afford us the opportunity of acting and reacting differently. The knowledge of a lesson handled one way in the earlier life might unconsciously influence our behavior in the subsequent life. But, it's always our choice, never something we *must* experience for any kind of justice or compensation.

For example, in one life we might play the part of a glamorous movie star, whose fame, fortune, and temperament make her despicably haughty, difficult to direct, mean to underlings (which in her eyes is everyone), and demanding in all personal relationships—in short, an unhappy person. In a subsequent life, we might attain similar fame and fortune, but demonstrate humility, generosity, and kindness, achieving great personal happiness, having lived through a life of misery in the prior experience.

In each new life, we have available for our use all of the effects of our many experiences as well as our talents and capabilities of prior incarnations, but use them only to the extent they are helpful in our new experience. Many have influence on our current life and behavior. Such influence is usually subtle or even latent, because we've chosen to hide our past life experiences from our conscious mind. The nature of and extent to which experiences in earlier lives affect us in subsequent lives depend entirely on whether they fit into the play's scenario. Nothing is either good or bad, but is perfect; no judgment is involved. We select from the tools available to us, and prior experiences, relationship interactions, and talents are some of those tools. If the memory of an earlier experience will help us to react toward someone in a way of benefit in a new life, we use it.

Any injury that occurs during the course of a play affords the "victim" and those near and dear to them a growth experience or possibly needed change in the direction of their life, depending solely on their own individual plans. There are no victims. Positive and negative are dualistic concepts we created for our physical experience in Earth life. They don't exist in Reality. When we actors return to Earth life, we enact a different role and are not the same person in whom we last expressed and emoted.

Sometimes we plan past-life experiences into a current life scenario to serve a useful purpose in our new relationships and experiences. Such then, might show up in past-life regressions to help resolve a current-life issue. But, the current-life situation or condition is not dictated by the past life or even influenced by it unless it lovingly (on a higher level) helps the participants in the current play. We often extend previous-life talents and interests into a subsequent life because they make learning easier in the new life and bring to the new scenario similar yet different conditions, situations, and relationships—more like a continuation of a previous set of circumstances than a wholly new scenario. The savant in this life remembers (usually unconsciously) his or her training and accomplishments of the previous life and draws on them wonderfully.

To me, what believers in the common concept of karma call the law of karma is judgmental and unfair. It's a human-contrived social tool and, like the Abrahamic notion of Hell, has nothing whatsoever to do with spirituality. And, it isn't a fact of life. I see it as coercion, made up to explain suffering and apparent evil and to influence an improvement in human behavior—and not very effective at that. And, I don't think coercion is necessary anyway, nor do I consider that law of karma one of justice. If we truly are enacting plays, and this Earthly human life isn't real and is lovingly pre-planned and enacted for awareness expansion, there is no need for returning karma, good or bad.

I doubt that the Eastern traditions who began the idea of karma see the law of karma as retribution, they perhaps see it as compensation, if defined as balance. I think that, while rooted in ancient Hinduism, the retribution concept was a Western interpretation when Eastern thinking was brought to the West. Helena P. Blavatsky, founder of Theosophy in the late 19th-century, Edgar Cayce in the early 20th-century, and others in between popularized karma and its law in the West. Then New Age believers in the 1960s picked it up and ran with it, perhaps taking it to an extreme.

My Version of Karma and Its Law

As I see it, karma, like all of our human experience, has more to do with attitude in any given moment than anything else. Our attitudes toward the people and events in our world reflect back at us and implement the "law of cause and effect." So, if I have a law of karma it is that we affect only ourselves by everything we think and every way we act, now—within the confines of our scenario—not in some later life. Affecting everyone equally, the law truly is impartial and non-judgmental. We see its effects as good or bad only because of our human judgments of them and our subsequent reactions. Our experiences are made by our attitudes and reactions.

So, why is there so much disease, challenge, hardship, heartbreak, and suffering of so many kinds in this life if there is no returning karma? We don't have any such conditions in our Real spirit life, and we seek contrast in Earthly human life to help us know and understand ourselves as spirit beings and also our spirit Reality (home). We invented this illusory life to experience contrast; so, of what value would it be to us were we to experience only, or even mostly, pleasant, peaceful, healthy, prosperous, happy, love-filled lives? We have all that in Reality.

Once we've experienced most of the contrasts and raise our awareness to higher levels of consciousness, we get more of the "good life" to actually experience in physicality. But without the contrasting conditions we wouldn't recognize and appreciate the more pleasant, satisfying conditions as they come to us. The higher we raise our consciousness the more loving and wise our beliefs become, resulting in more compassionate worldviews and behavior. As we expand our awareness into new, higher dimensions, we find we need fewer contrasting states to help us *know* ourselves. When we are more loving in our thoughts and behavior, we are less likely to let negativity affect us.

I did my research on karma in the early 1980s. And now, I can't help thinking that to more spiritually enlightened people that interpretation has changed as they have risen to higher levels of consciousness. Couldn't karma be thought of as a combination of "relationship" and "thought" rather than action. It could merely mean the connections between each of us and everyone and everything else in our life. Then it just is, without judgment, justice, or compensation of any kind. Karma may be our thoughts and the emotions they evoke, creating a pattern within our consciousness. This pattern changes as we change our beliefs about ourselves, all other beings in this life, and life itself. This pattern isn't categorized, it merely is, in accordance with our beliefs, attitudes, and emotions. As we raise our awareness to higher levels of consciousness, self-centered, negative patterns give way to heart-based, positive patterns, and our life changes accordingly.

For example: The movie star in the earlier example in her first life created a pattern of negativity that she never considered changing. Had she realized her life could change by changing that pattern, she could have created a new life for herself and everyone around her, perhaps more like that of her second life.

Our life is a reflection of the patterns of thought and emotions in our consciousness. We all have habitual patterns of thought. Look at your thought habits to see if you might want to change any. Take responsibility for the conditions of your life, without blame, and look inward to yourself rather than outward for the cause of both the pleasant and the not so pleasant conditions. The people and events in our outer life are not the source of our conditions (emotional or health), only our inner selves are responsible for them all. The people and events in our life are attracted by and respond to our thoughts and emotions, whether negative or positive. Like attracts like. Earth life is about relationships, attitudes, emotions, and change, and the people in our life give us opportunities for such experience. Karma depends on our own personal beliefs and attitudes and the emotions they evoke. That seems to be what human life is about: our personal beliefs, attitudes, and resulting emotions and behavior. Change those, and you change your life.

AWAKENING TO ONENESS

Since we humans are extensions of our soul-Selves, we don't awaken directly to the overall Oneness. We awaken, instead, to our whole Self. Although we've never been actually separated from our higher vibrating soul-Self—or from the ONE—we think we are individual, alone. We each want to eventually reunite with our Self. We want to consciously *know* the unity, wholeness, which together we are, always and forever, and seek to be in alignment with that, our Oneness. My soul is not somewhere up in the ethers, but is right here with the visible me, every moment of every day. It is in me, in my consciousness. The reunion of self with Self is a matter of the self consciously awakening to its oneness with its soul-Self, to the memory of its true, whole beingness, and once and for all attuning itself with its Self.

QUESTIONING MY TRUTHS

You may have problems as you consider the ideas I offer as my truths, perhaps because you have endured some of your afflictions or adversities for a long time. It's hard to equate many years of suffering with the misery of an actor in a two-hour play or even a six-hour TV mini-series. Yet, I'm sure in Real time (in Reality) one of our lifetimes takes only days or at most weeks to enact, some only moments. Because of our slowed vibrations our years seem long, as intended.

We are in some way responsible for every bit of our own experience. We are in error when we either blame or give credit to other people or circumstances, or even to "the powers that be." We are responsible for our life's original design—the scenario and script we chose to enact in this performance of Earth life. We also are responsible for our choices and responses while enacting our role. Only through our reactions do people and events affect us. And, only through our reactions and responses do we accomplish our self-set goals for Earth experience. There is no reason for blame of any kind. All is perfect. What we see in our world is a mirror reflecting what's in our role's heart: our thoughts, attitudes, fears, beliefs.

People have said to me, "Hog wash! I'd never have chosen this experience for myself." They are looking at only the negatives in their experience and are hurting. For some, time will heal their wounds and offer them a different perspective. If later they are happy and healthy, they may recognize their earlier experiences as stepping stones to their ultimate fulfillment. Others may go through their whole life in misery, blaming others for that misery. Most of us occasionally play the victim by laying blame outside of ourselves, and many of us only rarely accept credit for our own joy and happiness. Even our acceptance or denial of responsibility and the extent to which we wallow in self-pity may be important parts of ours and others' experience.

I personally think we'd be smart to accept the responsibility. Doing so in itself can be cathartic. It can help us stand tall against adversity, raise our self-esteem, and actually ease whatever pain we feel. When we take responsibility, we are in control of our life and, believe me, that is empowering and feels good. When we choose not to accept responsibility for our life, we let life control us, and it is debilitating and demoralizing. And, too, if we aren't responsible, who is? Is God responsible? Who is God? If God is responsible and you are God, aren't you responsible? Or, is everything accidental, occurring by happenstance?

Accepting responsibility in no way means to feel guilt or shame. It merely is recognition that everything is perfect as it is and is being enacted for your highest good. In most cases it will lead to more fulfilling circumstances. No one is to blame, least of all the loving friend(s) who supplied or aided in the experience. Your emotions resulted from your reactions, and weren't they fun! Now you can move on toward that something more fulfilling.

7

WHAT DOES ALL THIS MEAN?

This chapter covers some of what you may think of as the "dark" side of life, not to dwell on negativity but to explain and show that it isn't truly negative. There may be some parts of what I've written that you will vehemently deny, some things I say which you just can't accept as true. That's okay, these are my truths and not necessarily yours. Don't, though, be deterred by this discussion. Reading on, you might come to understand—not necessarily agree with—why I believe as I do. You might find that at least some of it makes perfect sense, either to your intellect or your heart or both.

COMPLETING OUR EVOLUTION

We humans have come a long way in our evolution, and although it may not seem so, many of us are not far from having come full circle. We realize our spirituality and Oneness, have made the Shift, and before long will consciously awaken to unity with our souls. The veil over our conscious human minds will be lifted forever. Not all of us will awaken at once, for many of us have not yet set our sights on awakening, are not ready to, and so will take a little longer. Such people are in the second wave, having begun their devolution later than those of us in the first wave. The second wave people aren't far behind, though, and will begin shifting shortly, perhaps through enlightenment. They will begin to go within to know and love God as themselves and as their neighbors.

GOD'S WILL

God is everywhere, knows all things, is all things, and does all things. Since we are God, every thought we think is God thinking, every word we utter is God speaking, everything we do is God in action. While we humans have freedom of choice, in a sense we don't exercise our own will and because of that are constrained in our choices.

Our God, who art our winged Self, it is thy will in us that willeth.
~ Kahlil Gibran

Like us, our will is an extension, a physical manifestation, of our Self. So nothing can happen that isn't planned for in our play scenarios; there are no accidents

No Accidents

Recall my earlier story in which a tire blowout prevented disaster; that was neither an accident nor coincidence. My Self punctured that tire to startle me and keep me from flicking my cigarette lighter. Similar things occur in people's life on a regular basis, in varying degrees of severity. Some people miss airplane flights that subsequently crash, killing all on board, while others move away as something heavy falls where they had been standing. At such times we're apt to say, "It must not have been their/our time." Many people, who would normally have been in one of the World Trade towers on September 11, 2001, were not; something occurred in their personal lives which kept them away. In other cases, of course, people are directed toward those fatal or maiming events. No one is a haphazard victim. All such events in our lives are pre-planned, staged, and directed by the souls of participating actors to fulfill specific purposes.

That day at Humbug was not our time to leave this life, but that experience and my awareness of it were, to me, clearly purposeful. I believe my director Self had me pick up the cigarette and lighter in the first place (I did so automatically, unconsciously), and directed the whole scene to illustrate to me its role in my affairs and the impossibility of accidents. Then, through intuition, it showed me what it had done and why. It gave me a wonderful aha. I was enormously grateful, not only for the life-saving blowout, but actually more so for my awareness of its meaning. It felt wonderful to know with certainty that I am never alone and that nothing can happen that isn't intended. This event occurred at a time when it was right for me to learn those specific lessons. When the time is right, we all will be shown: the veil will be lifted. It is, after all, the will of God, our Self. God's will is our will; our will is God's will in physical manifestation.

Lifting the Veil

In this way, both events and other people help us lift a corner of the veil. We can read hundreds of books, hear a multitude of speakers, have many intimate discussions, all without experiencing truth. Then something happens or someone utters a word or phrase that strikes the right chord and we experience understanding. Like my tire blowout, those events and words don't occur by chance, but are said and take place for our benefit, as is true of every event in our experience—whether seemingly good or bad. What we "hear" from others may not always be what they say but is what we need in that moment, so that's what our Self gives us.

We learn something from everything we think, see, hear, feel, and do. We store it up, awaiting a moment when we can finally assimilate it. When it fits, we say, "Ah hah, so that's it; I see." In fact that's what happens—a corner of the veil is lifted, providing a glimpse of light. No one lifts that veil but our Self off stage, having prepared us for such moments. The words uttered may not be important at all, while the feelings or emotional reactions are the learning factors. Our Self sees to it that we view and understand events in ways that best serve our needs.

THE GOOD OF EVIL

Philosophers and psychologists both debate the question, are we humans basically good or intrinsically evil? I say one is no more true than the other. Assume for the moment that my concepts of God and perfection are true and that we all are God manifest in human form, can any part of us be evil, or even sinful on a soul level? In our veiled state, so long as we are directed or guided from within by higher consciousness, can we do anything truly bad or wrong, anything that is not perfect? If we are only actors in plays, we are neither good nor bad but perfect in enactment of our play.

WHAT IS EVIL?

Think about the possibility that what we consider evil is not evil at all, but a crucial aspect of our chosen scenario and as such is based in love. Since every thing and every condition surrounding it has a purpose that is perfect and love-filled, and since we humans have no will of our own apart from our soul's will, there is no such thing as evil. Evil is only an interpretation or judgment in the minds of human beings, yet like everything else, purposefully perfect.

This means that such as murders, rapes, beatings, robberies, and child abuse are in themselves not evil deeds but are planned parts of scenarios. They provide essential elements that fulfill many growth experiences.

They are only evil in the context of our human plays and in our human judgment of them. Ralph Waldo Emerson said of evil: "The first lesson of history, is, that evil is good." Yes, it's good, for without evil we would have no way of knowing good; they define each other. Without evil we would have no way of experiencing fear. And without fear we wouldn't know serenity. We would have no relativity with which to define and know ourselves, on our spirit level.

You may ask if God creates wars, steals, kills, maims, and persecutes, if God permits millions of God-manifestations to suffer from painful disease, injury, or hunger. I say yes, but not some, perhaps angry being, separate and apart from us. We are the gods who design and create our own experience for our joint benefit. Were Jack the Ripper, Jeffery Dahmer, and Ted Bundy also God? Was Adolf Hitler God when he ordered the annihilation of millions of people? From my perspective the answer to these questions is unequivocally yes. Without exception, every one of us is God and everything we do is done by God. Nothing is outside of God. Nothing is exempt from the Kosmic law of love. No one can do anything that does not have love as its soul-level purpose.

Without the seemingly terrible acts against humanity, we would not experience the sorrows, revulsion, outrage, indignation, and compassion they evoke. Our reactions to them create experience from which we learn. Millions have given of their human selves in this way that humanity in general might learn, strengthen, and rise to higher consciousness. They have added to collective unconsciousness and have contributed immensely to our individual scenarios. Many of us now see and view terrible acts against animals in a similar fashion.

We consider Hitler and his murdering henchmen mad, as we do other mass killers. Were they insane or under the control of their Selves, doing as directed from within? Were they following a planned path and script, actually serving humanity? Isn't it true that many so-called evil people think of themselves as God or as God's instrument, fulfilling God's wishes? Occasionally the defense of a killer is that they heard a voice telling them to kill and whom. It may be true. We haven't believed that sort of defense because we haven't before known of our divinity or our Oneness. Those killers may have been listening to their director Selves in performing their parts in their play, and we haven't known it was a play or that we are being directed.

The "victims," too, played their parts perfectly. They were not randomly chosen, but were directed toward their final scene. Those "victims" of the Nazi Holocaust voluntarily (on a higher soul level) agreed to play that role for the benefit of humanity. Remember, the Jews going to their death are said to have inexplicably put up no fight. Death by another's hand is under prior agreement off-stage, a contract, if you will. All such agreements have love as their source, intent, and purpose.

As we experience terrible mass consciousness events, as survivors or witnesses, we are often caused to stop in our everyday routine and rethink our life. We may decide to modify our ways of thinking and behaving toward the other people and beings in our world. We may realize our own involvement in creating the atmosphere in which such terrible events can come about or need to be enacted. We may see our own culpability in bringing about the events because of our beliefs or our behavior toward our neighbors.

COULD SOME PEOPLE BE OUTSIDE OUR CONSTRAINTS?

A friend asked, "If we learned about limitation by slowing our vibrations, isn't it possible that some of us—rather than creating consciousness extensions—actually slowed ourselves and continued slowing until we completely lost sight of our connection with the spiritual and with love and perfection? Couldn't Hitler have been just such an aberration?" That supposes we can be less perfect than our original nature, I told her, and that is impossible.

PERFECT GOD, PERFECT HUMANS

The Oneness and all its individualized souls, are neither good nor evil, beautiful nor ugly, but are all of these, and perfectly so. It takes the judgment of human intellect to discern beauty, ugliness, good, and evil, and that discernment is subjective and variable. Only open awareness knows the perfection of what is.

As Socrates concluded with Adeimantos in Plato's dialogue of *The Republic*, it would be impossible for an all-perfect God to create anything either more perfect or less than itself.

S: God and what is God's is everywhere in a perfect state.

... Then in this respect God would be least likely to take on many transformations.

... Would he change and alter himself?

... Does he change himself for the better and more beautiful, or for the worse and more ugly than himself?

A: He must change for the worse,... if he does change, for I suppose we shall not say there is lack in God of beauty or virtue.

S: And if thus perfect, do you think... that anyone, god or man, would willingly make himself worse than this in any regard?

A: Impossible...

S: Then it is impossible... that God should wish to alter himself... each of them, being the best and most beautiful possible, abides forever simply in his own form.

From a spiritual perspective not a human one, for any of us to modify ourselves and allow ourselves to degenerate would have gone completely against our nature and be outside the Kosmic law of love, both impossibilities. Our friends wouldn't have stopped us from doing anything we truly wanted to do, but never would enact plays that include us and real evil in their script. Also, if any of us actually "altered" ourselves and have lived and acted from such a state, it would make accidents possible and Kosmic order impossible. We would have had no reason to do such a thing. We would not have needed to, we wouldn't have wanted to. Being, as Socrates said: "the best and most beautiful possible," we would never have altered ourselves in this or any other way. That's why our souls created us as extensions. Our soul-Selves "abide forever simply in [our] own form," which is spiritual love, light, energy, consciousness. Soul extensions, as alter egos, on the other hand, give our whole Selves all the experience we want without altering us and without risk. We remain ever in full control.

What our souls created in the way of their consciousness extensions and human physical experience are not in any way less perfect than they, neither less nor more than they. Our souls and we extensions slowed our human vibrations and exchanged our inner senses with five physical senses, pure intelligence with intellect, and feelings with emotions, but not to create something lesser, only different. Even when we split into female and male, leaving some of our energy behind, the intent was not to make us inferior, only purposely and temporarily incomplete. Good, ugly, better, and less are value judgments which can be made only by our human intellect; they aren't part of spirit. Spirit beings are incapable of judging, so no value is associated with anything they or we humans do. All is perfect.

ALL IS PERFECT

Hearing my answer regarding Hitler, my friend asked how something so perfect as God could have conceived of something so vile as Hitler and his Holocaust. I answered that the creation of such horrors was not the visualization and manifestation of something vile or lesser in intent than the perfect Oneness; it was expression of the revelation and appreciation of that Oneness. Without human judgment, nothing is vile, heinous, evil, or ugly except as another way of viewing the perfection that is also loving, awareness-expanding, and beautiful. In devising horrible plots, we (our whole Self consciousness) thought of them as different ways of experiencing. And we knew that enactment wouldn't be Real and no one really would be hurt. They led to death of the physical only. The human actors returned home, not only without ill effect, but with greatly expanded awareness.

Today, as we review drastic contrasts to our true nature, our heartfelt and humane conscious and subconscious responses give us quantum leaps into higher levels of consciousness. The greatest shocks of extreme contrasts are often the most effective attention-getters and learning experiences. In this way such atrocities truly do serve humanity as they were intended. Are the people who write horror stories or devious, cruel, despicable characters, themselves despicable and horrible? How do they come up with their plots? Creative imagination is wonderful, not evil.

While serving the mutual needs of our soul group members through interaction in our joint plays, many of us also serve humanity more generally by what we do, produce, or say, in what we are, or in our contribution to the dissipation of collective unconsciousness. We do so by vile acts against our fellow human beings which disturb humanity, or more gently by our own enlightenment, compassion, and love.

If everyone is God or was created by God and has the spark of God at their core, can anyone be any different? If anyone or anything could be different, the universe would not exist. No order could be maintained; no perfection would exist. We know there is order; we know there is perfection; therefore we know there is no anomaly. The Kosmic law of love either exists for all and everywhere or it doesn't exist. If God exists at all, God is absolutely all powerful, all knowing, everywhere present, loving, and perfect. I don't see how it can be otherwise.

COMPASSION

We don't feel compassion as spirit beings because we have no reason to experience it; there is no condition that would require our applying it. In human life, though, compassion is a necessity, if we are to create a better, more harmonious, caring world society. We have to be able to see others' pain and suffering, feel for them, and want to enable better conditions for them, want to lessen or remove their pain and suffering. But in order to ever be compassionate, we have to have experienced something similar; we have to know by experience what others are going through. We have to hurt right along with someone hurting, perhaps knowing that, because we are ONE in consciousness, we are affected in some way by their plight. When we raise our level of consciousness, we automatically become compassionate.

THE WONDERS OF PHYSICALITY

Our evolution has been primarily spiritual in nature. Our human awareness is doing the evolving. Our bodies have only undergone change along the way to best accommodate our experiential needs. We are, as former astronaut Edgar Mitchell eloquently put it, "conscious and immortal [spirit] beings evolving a physical experience." As spirit consciousness, we are truly grateful for our physical experience. As human beings, when we understand what our life here is all about, we too are grateful. The marvel is that only through physicality can we experience what we are not, so we might know what we are. Soon, having had all the contrasting experiences we've wanted, we will begin to experience in physicality more and more of what we truly are. Physicality offers us a depth to our experience we could get in no other way.

Although in Reality we spirit beings are able to see and hear using our native inner senses, we don't get the enjoyment out of tasting and touching that we get from these senses in physicality. The physical realm offers us all the glorious tastes of whatever culinary delights we care to invent. We probably have some taste ability in Reality, but it's in the physical that we enjoy our powers of creation, not only in what and how we prepare our food but also in how we present it. Also, the flesh of the various animals, fishes, fowl, and plants—leaves, and other vegetables, berries, nuts, and fruits—is available only in physicality.

This material illusion also offers us a great deal to enjoy by touching, especially in expression of love. Hugging, kissing, hand-holding, and stroking/caressing are expressions of love we can enjoy only in physicality. Making love is something we can do only here in Earth life. We can't pet a cat or dog in Reality, can't fondle or caress a loved one, can't walk arm-in-arm with a friend or hold hands. While in Reality our expression of love is so much deeper and for all beings, our experience of it in physicality more than compensates for its lack of depth. And because in physicality we have form, we can enjoy the great variety of such form only imagined in our native Reality. Now we can see each and every material expression and marvel at the exquisite detail of each that we have formed—detail of form, fragrance, color, and texture, and maybe taste.

Until we all have regained our original state of conscious awareness, the true beauty of Reality on Earth must remain veiled to the human eye in general. Earth must continue as a causal workshop until we have all experienced everything we wish to, have grown in awareness, and can lift the veil of collective unconsciousness to consciously *know* the true beauty of Earth and life in the Kosmos as ONE. Those of us who are ready or nearing readiness – are in the process of awakening – will get glimpses of all the wonders of Reality, encouraging us to proceed and spread the word. Earth will eventually be one of many globes in the universe where we, if we choose, can enjoy our being in a physical environment, using all of our senses, both physical and spiritual.

It's hard, I know, to imagine that this world and your life isn't real. Everything you see around you appears so solid, and everything you experience seems so real. But don't some of your dreams also seem real? Life is a dream, or nightmare if you take it as such, and you can wake up from it by applying yourself to doing so. In fact, I believe, waking up is the destiny of every one of us. Sooner or later we each will realize (remember) our spirituality, our Oneness, our love, and perfection. We will awaken.

8

THINKING IT THROUGH

When we in a soul group plan our human life scenarios, we do so from a consciousness of love, planning interactions for the benefit of those involved. With love in our hearts for all our fellow participants, we each agree to play our role, whether lover, family member, friend, enemy, hero, or villain, abuser, or victim. As we perform our roles, we aren't usually aware of the love in and surrounding us, nor do we see the loving intentions behind the people and events that we think cause us distress and pain. We feel as we are supposed to in the role we play.

CHOICES

As we can see, we actors have little more free will than a story's characters. While it may seem constricting and limiting in contrast to unfettered freedom, we don't feel constrained. We provide the words and actions ourselves, and most importantly, we make our human choices and experience the emotions ourselves. We may occasionally get some help with our choices, but in the main they are ours. Our reactions and responses are spontaneous and heartfelt. We have plenty of choices available to us and can, within the confines of each scene, focus our attention on whatever we want, discerning, discriminating, and even judging, all we wish to. Our choices often dictate the sequence in which we encounter trials, tribulations, and joyous happenings. Our attitudes and responses determine how we view situations. By our own choice we see our world as beautiful, loving, and happy or ugly, evil, miserable, and fearful. In itself it is just a play.

CONSTRAINTS ON OUR CHOICES

Our choices help us create our world and our life, to experience both all that we are not and all that we are. That is the only purpose of our choices, so they are neither right nor wrong, good nor bad, but are just choices through which our self-awareness grows. Our choices are constrained by the intentions being played out in our scenario and the nature of who we are spiritually: extensions or expressions of our souls. And because we are governed by only the spiritual law of love, it's not possible for us to do anything that is not spiritually based in perfection and love. It's not that God, or Self, won't let us, it's just that our being will even consider doing what is outside its spirit nature to do, unless it's part of the play. By our spirit nature, we are Love, so whatever we do has love behind it, and only through our plays can we experience anything else.

We each have planned a certain scenario for this life and our soul is directing us in enactment of our part. Some of the choices available to us are pre-designed. In part, the background and personal characteristics (the setting, costume, and makeup) we've chosen for this particular play dictate many of our options. We plan to have certain kinds of experiences, so we specifically make those available to us, and will always do at least those things.

WRITING A NOVEL

While chatting with a friend, I described the fun and exciting process of novel writing. I had read statements from novelists that their characters wrote their stories, but had not understood that notion until I played with novel writing and wrote my first novel. I explained to my friend that once I create my characters and draw up an outline of the plot, I begin writing. I described how my characters fill in the story details themselves, with dialog, thoughts, action, and interaction as responses to each other. While I write, I am each of my characters. They are individualized extensions of my consciousness.

When necessary, I take over the story line to keep the characters on track or to introduce a twist of the plot toward some pre-chosen aim. I arrange for characters to meet and interact and for plot tensions, mysteries, heartache, disaster, injury, and illness to add interest to the story. Even those moments of happiness and pleasure I must surround with danger or put at risk of going awry, to keep the action and interest flowing. I explained to my friend that experiencing emotions with my characters as they feel them for the first time is thrilling for me. I live their lives as I write them, just as our souls do with us as we together live Earth lives.

Suddenly I realized I had just described the relationship of Self to self and the process of human life as I view it. I wonder, are we really enacting a physical life's play or are we perhaps only living the story written in our souls' imagination?

If characters in stories were alive, to them their writers would be like our concept of God—their creator, omnipresent, omniscient, and omnipotent. Although the writers (God or our souls) aren't directly involved, they experience everything the characters (we actors) do and expand their awareness of emotions through those experiences. The writer has the general plot in mind, and may have written an outline of major events, characters, and plot twists and turns. But the characters choose their own reactions, responses, perceptions, attitudes, and dialog. The characters truly do write the novel with the help of the writer, not the other way around. The writer gets characters together, then what they say and do is their choice. Writing fiction is a great experience for the author. Although the writer may know what emotion is to be experienced, when it comes the author feels it right along with the character. I once wept deeply with one of my characters. (I've never published a novel, so don't look for one.)

Personalities cannot on their own or of themselves be evil, nor can anyone act out of true malice or completely out of character. In a novel or movie are any characters or events in themselves evil, other than what are supposed to be their roles? Aren't they all (characters and events) equally perfect in fulfilling the writer's purposes and intents for the story? Doesn't each merely appear, occur, and be, when, where, and as intended? Certainly, there are characters we all like much more than others, but isn't that because we're supposed to? We've been played by the writer, the characters, and in a movie the portrayers. But as far as the tale is concerned the good and the bad are of equal value. Together, they have entertained us, and maybe taught us something.

TIME AND SPACE

Some people—Albert Einstein, for one—have said that in Reality there is no other time than now. That's not a concept that computes in my intellect. Oh, I understand and believe whole-heartedly that *now* is the only time we experience, and both past and future exist *now* only in our thoughts of them. But that's not what those people are talking about. They're saying that past, present, and future occur simultaneously, that there is no such thing as time. They insist that any lives we may have had in the past or may have in the future are all occurring right now, simultaneously with our current life. If all time (past, present, and future) is occurring at once right now, why does our experience keep going? Maybe they mean in other dimensions. If we are merely enacting plays, why would we enact more than one at a time? There's no hurry, no urgency. Why not enjoy the experience of human life in one play after another?

I view time differently, not nonexistent In Reality, but so fast as to seem non-existent to us in our Earthly slow-motion existence. From my perspective, linear time as we created and view it doesn't exist in Reality. Its current rate of speed on Earth is not real. In fact, I believe our time on Earth is constantly changing, now becoming ever faster. Today's time moves much more quickly than did our time of 50,000 years ago, 2,000 years ago, 200 years ago, fifty years ago, or even ten months ago. It also moves more slowly than it will next year. You might agree with me that each year goes by noticeably more quickly than previous years did. The year begins, and suddenly it's Spring break and nearing summer, then summer is gone and schools open, and just as quickly it's time to prepare for the holidays, then before we know it we're starting a new year. But, too, time was also much faster when we began Earth experience, before our devolution. We are now on the upward arc of our evolutionary circle, returning to high-vibrational beings, coming full circle, full spiral; that's why time is going by faster now. Also, since we plan the setting for our play and move into it as onto a stage, the past isn't really the past; it is an illusion we created to help us experience.

Einstein also said time is relative, and with that I agree. Time in Earth life is not a constant, it is actually different for each one of us humans and often from moment to moment. We individually create our own time. For example, when we're waiting for something or someone to arrive, time often seems to move slowly, to drag; but when we're having fun or working to accomplish something, time seems to evaporate, there just isn't enough of it. In Reality we don't have these sorts of situations; we don't have to wait for anything, nor do we work and become anxious. Also, in Reality events occur in what we might see as clusters rather than our human linear time.

It's not that our souls can foretell the future or look into it because everything is occurring at the same time. They are able to see the past, present, and future of our human existence, because at its slower rate of vibration, it's all laid out before them. Besides, it requires no clairvoyance to see into the future when you've written the story and can see the whole thing at a glance.

Space too was created through the slowing of vibrations. Since before that slowing all existence was the ONE consciousness; there wasn't really any space. Everything was light, energy. But we needed the illusion of space to help in defining individuality and material forms. That's why we left much of that energy high vibrational, so it would look like space, between us on Earth and "out there" between celestial bodies, everywhere defining form.

OTHER POSSIBILITIES

As we each raise our consciousness to a new level, increasing our vibrations and getting ever closer to our original high-vibrating perspective, truth of every sort will become more clear. We may ultimately find that there really is no past and no future. Maybe this is our only life.

PARALLEL LIVES

We each may have some other parallel lives going on in this same time frame. They may be here on Earth, in other dimensions, or they may be on other planets. Some people believe we have parallel lives on Earth right now. They suggest that we each have at least one other life across our globe, across our country, or our town, or even across our street. Although occurring simultaneously, our other lives may be perceived as taking place in different time frames. We may be acting out many plays at once, each with its own setting, scenery, script, and cast. If it's all illusion, why not? Perhaps our dreams are glimpses of those other plays. Past-life remembrances could be such glimpses, as could *déja vu*.

The actors who are members of our soul group may be our own parallel lives, not individualized entities at all. Our human soul mate may be another aspect of our Self. It may be another of our soul's incarnations, perhaps that other half of us—the mirror image, which when we're united, forms with us a complete whole. The permutations are endless.

ONLY ONE BEING

Perhaps there is only one being: God, and all human lives are parallel. Maybe there's no reincarnation, but each life is a different expression of the ONE, although I can't conceive of that. If we humans live a single Earth life returning into the ONE, our individuality exists only while we experience that human life; we have no individual soul. The Oneness is the single soul and higher Self of us all. The experience of one of us, logically speaking then, would be the experience of the ONE. Understandably, reincarnation would be neither necessary nor possible. Each life experience, however short or eventful, would satisfy the need of the ONE for that experience.

Why then are there repetitive experiences? Why, for instance, do so many people starve to death? Why have many human lives been snuffed out by wars or genocide? Why are so many children abused? Why would heartache, affliction, addiction, disease, and poverty be such prevalent experiences? Why would the Oneness want to experience those same things so many times?

Levels of Consciousness

The only reason I can see for repetitive experience is that on some level it's not repetitive and serves an individual purpose. If there's only one level of consciousness (the ONE), such repetition serves no apparent purpose. If two levels of consciousness—the ONE and the individualized beings that express it—always exist, then similar experiences by different souls serve different purposes. This is not to say that souls are separate from the ONE or from each other. It merely means that within the consciousness of the ONE, there are levels. We have the grand consciousness of the ONE and we have the souls that are the aspects, the viewpoints of the ONE, the multitude of the singularity. Of course, for purposes of our experiential plays, a third level is created for us actors to use while enacting our Earthly (and likely other) plays.

In my view, at least two levels of consciousness always exist. And, although each soul knows and gains from the experience of all others, each has and wants its own way of reacting and responding to those experiences. Each addresses them from a different set of previous experiences and with different aims in mind.

In speaking of these levels, I don't mean ever to imply quality or quantity. Each is different in its expression and how I describe it, but it is still God. I also don't mean to imply separation. All of the consciousness of which I speak is only ONE consciousness. There are just different levels within that ONE, the levels having more to do with their rate of vibration than with individuality or uniqueness, and we separate and delineate them for our benefit of understanding.

REALITY IS WITHIN, NOT WITHOUT

> Our unconscious existence, the inner world, is the real one and our conscious world, the outer one, is a kind of illusion, an apparent reality constructed for a specific purpose, like a dream which seems a reality as long as we are in it.
>
> ~ Carl G. Jung

Reality is in consciousness so is inside each of us, not outside. Outside is the stage and our illusion plays. Inside is the love and light of our Real Self and All-of-Everything. The soul isn't physical, it is energy, consciousness. So when we go within, it's our soul with whom we communicate and from whom we receive insight, love, light.

We humans (my third level of consciousness after the ONE and our souls) are our souls' alter egos in physicality, their consciousness extensions, their manifest expressions. Our individual expression is of our soul's inner form, their loving, intelligent, all-knowing, all-powerful being. Being always high-vibrating, our souls don't have form as we identify material form. They are energy. That's what souls are: pure intelligent energy, light, consciousness, Love, which are all the same ONE thing It is that pure intelligent consciousness, that love, that the ancient Mysteries encouraged their initiates to know by going within. That practice, I call communion between my self and my Self, which provides insights and wisdom, is what I call enlightenment

ENLIGHTENMENT AND AWAKENING

Enlightenment and awakening are two of the most thrilling and enjoyable experiences we will ever have; and we get them in physical human life only, not needing either in Reality. In Reality, we know all things and have no memory loss, so have no need for enlightenment. And it's to our Reality that we will be awakening. We all plan awakening, and many of us enlightenment, into our personal scenarios as our eventual destiny. Enlightenment seems to be the most effective path to awakening, because it helps us unite with our higher-vibrating soul-Self. And in the process, we are bit by bit made aware of truths about ourselves and our Real existence. We're helped to remember, helped to raise our awareness to ever higher levels of consciousness, helped to Shift to heart-based consciousness. As our awareness rises and expands, our perception of Reality evolves. As we attune with our higher soul-Self we begin awakening to our Oneness and a Reality entirely new to us as humans in this life. The more enlightened we become, the more of Reality we see, remember and make our own. Because in attunement we vibrate faster, with each step we are able to be aware of a different level of consciousness from the one on which collective unconsciousness had previously influenced our intellect. Soon many of us—and eventually all of us—will be vibrating at such a rate that all of Reality and its love will be clear to us. We'll know what is real and what is illusion. We'll know what Earth life has been all about. All will be clear.

When the self has experienced all it wanted to in physicality, and has opened itself to consciously remember what it wanted to know about itself and Reality—its rate of vibration increasing with every little bit—it is ready to awaken. Awakening is a case of the extension's vibrations being raised to the Self's level of consciousness, when they can then be consciously one, whole. That one can then experience their human life together with the soul experiencing human life directly rather than through an extension. When awakening occurs, the highest nature of the light being is expressed through the human being. Now that we of the first wave have had nearly all the lower level experiences we wanted, we no longer need negative conditions. So, for many of us, our goal now is to be en*light*ened and to in that way awaken to our soul Oneness, while never losing sight of our desire to help others around us awaken too.

TRUTHS

The insights given me by my Self represent one set of "truths." They serve my purposes perfectly. Your truths serve your purposes. Don't let mine or any others limit your thinking. But, please give some thought to the possibility that we truly are all spirit beings and the ONE's expressions, so that the experience of one is (on some level) the experience of all. Consider that Earth life may be, as I contend, illusory: the day-dreams of the gods that seem real to us human actors, as our dreams do while we are in them. Hindus picture the God Vishnu sleeping on a floating lotus and dreaming us! Give these ideas a chance, and see where they take you. In a recent discussion session with friends, we asked ourselves if there is such as ultimate truth. And after considerable questioning, and batting ideas around, we finally came to the conclusion that there are at least two ultimate truths: Love; ONE. We decided that everything is love and love is everything, and that love, like consciousness, makes everything ONE. But too, we need to know that we are spirit beings. We are spirit, energy, light, consciousness, and love.

Physical experience is our only way of truly knowing both our self and our Self and is a perfect vehicle for the joyful expansion of our awareness. This illusion is our useful and wonderful experience. My heart readily accepted the ideas intuitively offered me by my God, likely already knew them—and was remembering them—and needed no explanation or proof. My intellect, though, needed rationalization of each point. It knows that much of what is spiritual has no explanation within physical, human understanding, but it still seeks to make sense of a concept before it will accept it. So, my intellect has always sought answers to its ever-present questions, looking for logic and reason in everything given me by my inner voice. My intellect has been vital to me in both my learning process and my writing, and I am truly grateful as I acknowledge that fact. And now, the philosophy that has resulted from my Self's insights to me is one that both my heart and my intellect accept, and that integration feels wonderful.

PART THREE - OUR PERSONAL HUMAN EXPERIENCE

A tree has both straight and crooked branches; the symmetry of the tree, however, is perfect. Life is balanced like a tree. When you consider the struggles, difficulties, and sorrows a part of it, then you see it beautiful and perfect.

~ George M. Lamsa, *Gems of Wisdom*

9

EXPERIENCING PHYSICALITY, ESPECIALLY THE LOVE ASPECTS

In this part we'll begin to apply the basic fundamentals of my philosophy to our everyday life. We'll see insights from my Self that are more specific to daily living than the general ones we've seen.

We are here in this Earth life to expand our awareness through human experience, mostly by emotions brought out by interactive relationships and events. We don't experience emotions in Reality, so we create conditions and situations in this material existence that offer us all the emotions that, by contrast, help us know and appreciate ourselves and true Reality. To be most effective those emotions are primarily negative, because that's how we define and know the positives. So, in this part, I show how I believe we use those negatives to great advantage, illustrating the positive side of the negatives. Our physical bodies are also very different from what we as light beings wear in Reality, so they offer us wonderful experiences in human life, some in contrast to the positives and some very positive in themselves.

In *WAKE UP*, I wrote about healing our world's woes, saying "We don't need healing; we aren't sick or broken." The same is true of us humans, personally. We are merely actors enacting a play. We aren't our bodies, which are our makeup and costumes through which we enact our roles. And every ailment, affliction, physical, mental, or emotional challenge is part of our play. We use them all to great advantage.

ENJOYING HUMAN SENSES

As spirit consciousness, we see, hear, and smell not through eyes, ears, and noses, but by *knowing*. In part, it's a sensing of vibrations, with each different sight, sound, and scent vibrating differently, each generating a different energy pattern. That *knowing* is spiritually feeling the intent, the love and the beauty of each vision, tone, and aroma. Our five human senses are physical and, while available to us in our spirit life, we don't get them in the same ways. So, by playing in Earth life, we learn what it is to see, hear, and smell and also to taste and touch physically.

Touch and taste, especially, are so different in human life from our spirit life experience of them that we marvel at them in great wonder as we meet them in material life. When we incarnate, as babes we reach out to touch and taste everything we see, we are fascinated with the unfamiliar. As we mature we marvel at the wondrous feelings of our own skin and hair, our muscles, and developing bodies; we enjoy food and drink for their taste. As mentioned earlier, handshakes between acquaintances, hugs among friends and family members, caresses of parents and their children, us stroking our pets, and the intimate sharing of two people in love, all give us awareness possible only here in this physical theater. In addition, we choose much of our clothing and furniture because of how they feel to our touch and we often learn what not to do because of an unpleasant tactile experience.

Through touching we also impart and receive information on a spiritual level that we can't exchange in our nonphysical Reality, so the physical provides another way of knowing more of ourselves. We do touch and taste spiritually, but by inner feeling rather than exterior sensation. So, the physical experience adds depth to our knowledge of ourselves, what we are and what we are not. The more we experience in these ways, the greater is our awareness and spiritual growth. Touching is one of the most precious parts of our Earth experience.

In our natural state, what we feel is more intense, deeper, and is more true than it is in limited human form. Our physical existence adds dimension to our experience of senses, rounding out our spiritual experience. The fragrance of flowers, the scent of a forest, of turkey roasting, a baby's skin, a puppy's breath, as well as the sounds of the ocean's roar, a horse's whinny, and soft words of intimacy are experiences we treasure. A glorious, multicolored sunset, a brilliantly colorful rainbow, cows grazing lazily in a pasture, and a wind-ruffled wheat field are all sights we would miss if we hadn't created this material world and our physical life in it. And who hasn't been affected by a certain smile or the contrasts of color, form, and texture in a lovely landscape of purple mountains, quaking aspens, and a placid azure lake? Our physical human experience adds beauty and depth to our awareness and is a marvel we thoroughly enjoy and appreciate.

SPIRITUAL LOVE

Touching each other and realizing what it feels like to know the touch of love is perhaps our grandest experience. While all of these experiences provide us opportunities for emotions unfamiliar to us as spirit beings, our human consciousness might hope to someday be able in human form to know the true feeling, sight, sound, smell, and taste of spiritual love, the vibrations of it, the depth, vibrancy, and extent of it. When that day comes, we will realize that all love is spiritual although what we've experienced has been limited. We will *know* that everything is love, that love is around us in abundance, and that it is gloriously beautiful. We will realize that we too are love and beauty. We will realize how perfect we are and always have been. We will recognize our interconnectedness and not only remember but see our Oneness. We are making all this possible through the contrasts of our physical experiences.

OUR SCENARIOS

Meanwhile, there is no limit to the number of Earth plays we can enact, so we've afforded ourselves every possible choice of conditions for maximum experience through our physical senses and emotions. We can be sure that if we are Caucasian in this life we have been or will be in other lifetimes every other race. Those of us who are female have been male, and vice versa. Those who are now mentally or physically challenged, or disfigured have been and will again be physically whole and beautiful. We have used the great variety of scientific understanding, religious tenets, spiritual *knowings* and practices, and non-beliefs to provide us a basic belief system in each different life. Our circumstances today are whatever we chose to experience to best expand our awareness.

As with our costuming and background scenery, for greater awareness, we use a different scenario in each of our incarnations. Some of us in a given lifetime learn the most from tragedy, some from hardship, while others gain from a life of happiness and calm or humdrum boredom. Some people surround themselves with family and friends, while others want relative isolation or solitude. Intellectual or creative pursuits may outshine all other interests. The untimely death of a loved one may provide a main theme. And in some scenarios children are the important roles. Each scenario provides a different set of situations with its own array of experiences and possible emotions. We select what best serves our intent for our role in the play.

For instance, as spirit energy, we know nothing of bias or prejudice, so one of the reasons we select certain combinations of ethnic background, religion, gender, life style, and bodily conditions is to experience prejudice from various points of view. We want to feel the emotions offered by each and possibly at different times in human history. By being someone who hates others because of the color of their skin, ethnicity, gender, sexual orientation, or their status in life, we help define our true selves as non-judgmental and loving. By ridiculing people who are physically smaller than we, or are mentally challenged, or appear ugly to us, we further define our loving, caring true nature. When we experience the receiving end of any of these we learn compassion and help ourselves to know what we are not and thereby define what we are. We may also in our human life resent others' treatment of us, and learn to hate them, and adversely affect our life. But such enables us to more clearly see and appreciate our spirit life when we return to it.

THE MANY FORMS OF LOVE

Because love is a major contributing factor in the personal relationships through which we expand our awareness, we often design our scenarios around love relationships. When we speak of love, the first form that comes to mind is what we call being "in love." But we actually experience other forms more easily and often less traumatically. By other forms, I mean familial love between parents and children or between siblings, friendships, the love we share with our pets, and puppy love—that attraction between children I remember calling "twitterpated" (I think from the Disney movie, *Bambi*). The forms it takes for us individually are by design before entering our life, and we usually experience more than one form of love in our life, with each serving a purpose in its time.

Partnering Love

We don't consciously, as humans, determine with whom we fall in love. From my perspective, it is a prodding from our soul and serves some very specific purposes in enactment of our plays. Love is not a human invention, nor would I call it an emotion or a sensation. It's a deep feeling, felt beyond our physical senses. I *know* it to be spiritual. The extent to which we feel it and the nature of that feeling depend on the purposes served by each form of it in our life. In one life, our play centers around enjoyable searching, producing a love-filled marriage, perhaps with many children. Another includes a devastating tragedy of love or simply unrequited love. One scenario involves true bonding love, maybe enacted without society-acceptable marriage. Another features marriage without love and may include extramarital love and/or sexual interest(s). Sometimes our scenario has us taking one partner after another, either never fulfilled or only temporarily satisfied with each one. Our pairing may be based on physical attraction rather than love, so is only temporarily fulfilling, if at all. A partner can be of the opposite or same gender, and in some lives partnering activities are insignificant.

Our whole spirit Selves/selves are a perfect balance between male and female, possessing all nonphysical aspects of both genders. When we, as actor-extensions enter Earth life, each taking on a body and its gender, we suppress the ability of part of our nature to affect our planned course. The portion with which we enter the Earth theater is part of the costuming and makeup we've chosen for our play. Once we begin maturing and the veil of collective unconsciousness has hidden our view of Reality, we may feel incomplete, depending on our script. We may be dissatisfied with life until we find a partner whose energy helps us feel more complete. Our body, as part of our costuming, produces sexual attraction to conform to our energy needs in keeping with our chosen scenario. We have planned for such incompleteness and attraction to provide context for many of our experiences. Of course, male/female mating is also necessary for procreation, enabling others to enter our Earth theater for added interaction.

Clearly, not all of us partner for fulfillment in every lifetime. For some, the incompleteness felt without the energy of our opposite facilitates our growth. Others, not experiencing a strong lack, make few or no efforts to join with another; we are complete within ourselves for this life experience. Some of us in each group's play have needs or missions which have no use for marriage and parenting; even the pairing routine might get in the way. Many beings who enter this life primarily to assist others have no such need, unless it is part of their role. Still others are completely satisfied by the bonding of deep friendship without sexual involvement.

Choosing Homosexuality

Those who chose homosexuality as the primary love and pairing experience did so for several reasons. Many, males especially, wanted the outcast status and, in some cases, the rejection of family to give them trauma and exceptional emotions, often lifelong. Many wanted numerous partners without real love. And many have used that lifestyle to avoid the marriage and parenting roles often expected of heterosexual people. Most gays and lesbians wanted the natural affinity found between members of the same gender, an understanding often missing between opposite gender partners. Also, many homosexuals use a more balanced mixture of male and female energy than that of their straight neighbors. That balance enables them to better understand both genders, and often brings out feelings of caring and compassion. These various conditions are what gay people wanted for their scenarios.

Social and Cultural Limitations

The scenario we choose may relate in some way, whether for love interests or another part of our growth experience, to our culture's requirements and taboos, be they societal, religious, or legal. Each culture since the beginning of human history has had its own set of dos and don'ts. They've made for interesting variety in our scenarios from one incarnation to another. Some ancient cultures seem to have had an anything-goes approach to sex, with possibly little true bonding. Others, our Judaic/Christian culture for instance, define very specifically what they will and will not condone in the way of partnering and the sexual expression of it. Islam is more precise yet, as are some Asian cultures. Sometimes we conform our scenario to the rigid requirements of the culture we use as background, and in other cases we purposely defy those requirements to set up tensions in our life drama. Keep in mind that the more enjoyable novels, movies, and TV shows use tension and suspense to create and sustain our interest; our life plays are no different. Often the most anxiety-ridden scenario offers the most opportunities to emote and is our most effective awareness expanding experience.

Balance and Acceptance

In an ideal world, people would love people, some would bond, some would join in mating, some would procreate; all would freely express both their female and male energy in a balanced way. People would accept people in every aspect of life, regardless of color, age, gender, sexual orientation, ethnicity, race, religious or spiritual beliefs, stature, personal characteristics, or apparent station in life. But since this state would not provide contrasts to Reality, we would gain little from human life if such were also mainly the case here in physicality. We each will eventually experience Earth life in this way—as some do now—but not until we've completed our chosen contrasting experiences of material life and have at least begun to fully awaken to our spirituality and the Oneness.

SOUL MATES

When we enter a human life play with one gender as part of our costuming, we in a sense leave behind some of the energy that completes us. Since we've planned this void in us to provide a major aspect of our play scenarios, we also provide ourselves co-stars to help us fill that void as we enact our plays. Apparently the same souls pair up in our spirit world on a regular basis to extend themselves into human life as lovers. We humans refer to this mating phenomenon as between "soul mates." We may have many other love or mating liaisons, but all true bonding loves are experienced between soul mates, or what I think of as spiritual partners, and we enjoy a great variety of plays together. Both halves of such partnerships are not always present in their many lives. These are lives in which either love is not a prominent feature or whatever marital or sexual relationships are involved, true love is absent. This soul-mate phenomenon has been studied thoroughly through analysis of past-life regressions, strongly validating the concept. Such research also supports the idea that groups of souls repeatedly share lives together, in different roles, and using different genders and costumes.

Some of us spend a great deal of time and effort searching for the energy of our soul mate. Of course, we don't realize it's specific energy we seek. We're sure, though, we'll know that just-right person, certain that when we find the perfect mate whose energy fits ours like pieces of a jigsaw puzzle, we will feel complete. And, that is often the case.

SOMETHING MISSING: OUR TRUE SOUL MATE

Eventually, however, no matter how happy we each are with or without our chosen partner, we'll find there's only one true soul mate for us. I'm convinced that we will always feel there is something or someone missing in our life until we seek out and (re)unite with our soul in conscious Oneness. Our soul consciousness retains that energy we've missed and longed for throughout our many lives. Only it can complete us, make us whole. Our soul will continue gently prodding us to seek our soul mate until we're confused no longer about where to look. By design, we've misunderstood the longings, assuming their fulfillment to be in physical human terms. But, no satisfaction of flesh can truly fulfill that inner longing for completion. And neither the most satisfying human bond nor the most gratifying carnal pleasure can measure up to our conscious reunion of human self and soul Self.

Because our Self is our true soul mate does not mean that either human bonding or carnal mating is wrong or less divine. Love is the expression of God in our heart; when we express love, we express God in the truest sense. Love, therefore, will drive us closer to our reunion than any other experience. Only when we're ready will we seek our true soul mate. We are in these Earth plays to experience, and that's what searching and partnering wonderfully provide. Joining with our soul won't preclude our also pursuing human partnerships; in fact, it's likely to enhance our enjoyment, making us more loving, open, and understanding and less self-centered.

In its purest form, love is a feeling natural, native, and ever-present to us as spirit beings. It's the most important asset of spiritual Reality we will know and appreciate more fully after having lived human lives without it or with it in limited quality and quantity. Love cannot be manufactured, it just is. It is within us and it surrounds us. All we humans need do is recognize it, accept it and let it flow. We can enjoy spiritual love whenever our soul gives it to us, no matter how limited it may be or in whatever forms we experience it.

DESIRES

Our souls help us achieve our planned goals by providing influences or proddings. And I believe our desires—the very things we've been taught are some of the sins of human life—are in reality some of the proddings of our loving Selves within. Desire is an expression of intent, and is one way our souls direct us toward enjoyable experiences as well as heartache. Our Self directs us individually toward interactions that are apt to elicit the emotions and actions planned for in our scenario. It may now be urging us to enjoy life to its fullest.

By following our heart, we manifest the enjoyable experiences we intend for ourselves. Since the energy of our heart is the major vehicle for our soul connection, when we follow our heart, we're doing as our soul is directing us. We are going with the flow toward our highest good, in conformance with our own pre-birth plans. Only when we try to go against those plans do we cause ourselves stress and discomfort. When we deny ourselves, we struggle through life, doing things we don't really want to do, creating unhappiness ever so abundantly. For us, life is hard. If we follow our heart, we can't go wrong; life is easier and more pleasurable. We can better deal with hardships as they come along.

Since we don't need, want, or suffer from lack of anything in Real life, we make sure we are seldom free from desire or want in human life. To stifle those feelings as humans is to deny our Self. Attempts at stifling only serve to strengthen them anyway. We aren't "bad" because we have desires, wants, or longings. They aren't the "proddings of Satan" (as we may have been taught), but are of our Self. Our Self feeds them to us, one by one. If we don't allow ourselves our desires, the environment we provide others is one of denial and oppression in which love and happiness can never flourish. Yes, there are some desires which seem very bad to us, but keep in mind that everything is perfect and based spiritually in love and there are no accidents.

The ultimate desire is for awakening to conscious reunion with our soul. All desires lead relentlessly to this one. How will we ever consider ourselves worthy enough to allow this desire to blossom forth if we spend our life denying our desires? Strangely, we will become dissatisfied more quickly with the "good life" than with the trials and tribulations of lives in misery. The happier we are, the stronger is the urge for greater happiness. Isn't it true that the person who is surrounded by love often feels lonely? The more money, possessions, power we have, the more we want. The one who seems to have everything nearly always feels something is missing. Self is calling.

This phenomenon of missing energy is also a cause of the materialism and greed of our current societal conditions. People who feel that something is missing, again misunderstanding the longing, assume it is material in nature. They amass possessions to fill that void or they seek control over others, thinking that power will satisfy their need.

If we honor our desires, we may eventually realize that satisfaction of them is not enough. Our human desires can be responded to only in external ways and will never fully satisfy us. Spiritual longing will always nag us until we recognize and address it by going within. External placebos will not quench the thirst of our Self, calling for our conscious recognition and loving attention, calling us to the reunion of self with Self. Our soul won't let us remain consciously separate forever. Sooner or later its urgings will become so compelling we'll be powerless to deny them. We'll turn from separation and rise above the tribulations of our human life to be *consciously* one with our Self. For many of us, that time for fulfilling spiritual love may be at hand. Physical experience, including the seeming negatives, is wonderful for us spirit beings. It enables us to expand our awareness gloriously and to see and more completely appreciate all we truly are and have in Reality.

In this part and the next as we apply my insights to daily life experiences, we'll go through some introspective exercises. Since they are designed to help you examine your personal modes of dealing with this life experiences, they will work for you only if you are totally honest. You don't have to share your answers with anyone, so you have no reason to hide then, especially from yourself. Be honest and truthful, or don't bother with them.

APPLYING THE INSIGHTS

- Do you see what I'm talking about in enjoying the senses of taste and touch in this physical life? Think about your life and the taste and touch feelings you get throughout each day. Do you perhaps begin to see that love is spiritual? Can you begin to feel that you are love?
- Are you open to the idea that this Earth life is illusion and that we humans are all enacting plays on Earth's stage? Can you see that what we think of as negative occurrences are necessary contrasts to our true Reality to help us define our Reality and to know and appreciate ourselves? Try to recognize the benefit of some of your more negative experiences.

Has any one of them led to something better in your life, greater fulfillment?
- Do you have love in your life? Do you have several forms of love: family, friends, partner/mate, pet(s)? If you do, think about each and consider how it might be contributing to your awareness expansion? If you don't have love in your life, is there a reason(s) why you don't? Look inside yourself for the answers, but never with blame or guilt. If you are homosexual, do you feel blessed? Do you realize the benefits of choosing (at the soul level) that life style for this life?
- Whether you have found and partnered with your human soul mate or not, do you feel fulfilled, satisfied or do you feel something is missing in your life? If the latter, go within and find the true love of your life, your soul. In the next part we'll delve into "going within," and I'll give you a specific process to help you gain really good conscious communication with your inner, higher-vibrating, all-knowing soul-Self.
- Do you follow your heart or your head? If you are happy and satisfied following your head, by all means stay with it until you feel a need for change. You might try occasionally following your heart and see where it takes you.

10

ADVERSITY IN OUR EXPERIENCE

Adversity, too, is a major part of our human experience, including heartache, disappointment, failure, sickness, pain, and physical, emotional, or mental challenge. Trials and tribulations help us experience unfamiliar conditions and emotions better than anything else we could use. We are not being tested. We have preplanned adversities into our human lives so we might apply the judgment of intellect to those conditions and evoke awareness-expanding emotions.

BLESSINGS OF ADVERSITY

He is the most wretched of men who has never felt adversity. Sweet are the uses of adversity....

~ William Shakespeare

Like everything else in human life, adversity is largely a state of mind. Afflictions and hardship can be fought as adverse or accepted and taken more lightly. Our adversities and afflictions offer us choices and give us chances at both positive and negative reactions. We can suffer with them and experience such emotions as resentment, envy, and self-pity and be bitter, ill-tempered, and demanding or we can be cheerful, loving, and happy. We can rise above our afflictions and make the most of them. In either case, the experience adds to our awareness.

When I suggest we rise above our adversities, I don't mean to belittle them and don't necessarily mean eliminate them. Some will never go away. Helen Keller wrote: "Although the world is full of suffering, it is full also of the overcoming of it." "Overcoming" means getting on with life in a positive, high-spirited way, despite a prevailing adversity. It may mean not viewing an affliction or challenge as adverse, maybe even seeing it as a blessing. Actually, what some people view as adversities are not always considered such by those enduring them. Keller, for example, seems to have made the most of her particular situation, having been made both blind and deaf by a disease at the age of 19 months. Late in life she said: "I thank God for my handicaps, for through them, I have found myself, my work, and my God."

It may also be a matter of degree. It often seems that people born and/or faced with permanent physical challenges are more apt to rise above them than most of us facing minor setbacks or temporary difficulties. Maybe when we know something is permanent or when we've never known any other way, we're better able to deal with it and find ways around it or other ways to be happy. It may be as it was in our Real life before we knew a contrasting state; with no basis for knowing what we had never experienced, we don't know what we are missing.

Adversity has changed nearly everyone's life in some way. Whether or not we see and accept it as such, I propose that the change has been for our benefit. Upon reflection, we may view lost loves, failures, or disappointments, as catalysts to chains of events leading to great blessings. Many people have said that what at the times they thought were the worst experiences of their life turned out in the long run to have been stepping stones to the greatest blessings. Afflictions have forced some of us into different avenues of support or fun, causing us to develop new talents, skills, or capabilities, producing greater satisfaction and happiness. Old, unfulfilling relationships have been let go, often leading ultimately to greater love and happiness.

An Example of Adversity as a Blessing

Years ago, I read an article by a psychologist who had a thriving practice and was married and had two children. She had written a successful book. The theme of her article, and her book too, was learning to accept oneself despite a fat body. She said she had been fat all of her life, and as a child was horribly put down and abused by her father. She grew up hating herself, because of an "ugly, fat body." She claimed to have learned to accept her "imperfect body," as it was, and was busy teaching others how to do the same. I wrote to her as follows:

> While you are to be congratulated for overcoming your adversity, it sounds to me that you have accepted your body through psychology and sheer willpower. I suggest you could feel even more comfortable if you were to realize the perfection of your body, just as it is. Perfection

> is neither good nor bad, but what is, serving intended purposes, as is everything in life.
>
> Your body (and your experience with your father, as well) has served you perfectly. Your body has been just what you have needed it to be. Where would you be today if your body had not been fat? You may not have studied psychology and gotten your degree. Then you wouldn't have your psychologist's practice. You undoubtedly would not have written your book. Your body has helped you do all of these and likely much more, all for your greater good. Had you been slim, your life would be entirely different, possibly not as rich and as full. Be grateful to your body (and your father too). Recognize your body's beauty and perfection. It is now, always has been, and always will be perfect, just as it is.

That woman's father and anyone else who ever ridiculed her contributed to her growth experience.

We are enriched by every experience we have, whether it seems bad or good. Although we may not know it, every experience teaches us and adds to our growth. We, then, are teachers who add to the enrichment of everyone in whose experience we participate. Life is a joint venture.

CHILD ABUSE

As heinous as it seems, child abuse, too, is purposeful. Although it may not be apparent, there is always an effect on an abused child, one which the child takes with her or him into adulthood and often in some way through the rest of their life. That kind of experience often produces either a weakness or a strength in the character of growing children which affects the direction of their future. It may influence how they respond to members of the opposite sex or to their own children. These effects can seem positive or negative; regardless, they provide awareness-expanding experience and fulfill the intent of the planned scenario. As such, they are perfect.

Many abused children grow up to lead productive, successful, fulfilling lives, because they were made stronger in some way by the abuse in their childhood. Children are resilient for good reason; overcoming their abuses shows us how resilient they can be. Others of those children, however, grow up without respect for themselves or others. They don't care whether they live or die, and often become criminals, unaffected by promise of a lengthy prison sentence or the death penalty.

Such roles are necessary to our human plays of life. Some play the villains many of us need in order to set up events we can react to for growth experiences. They may be rapists, murderers, or drunk drivers who take loved ones from us. Some take away possessions or injure us, giving us a life-long set of experiences. Those people are in Reality loving friends participating in our pre-planned play of Earth life for our mutual benefit. How each of us responds is up to us individually. And that response, usually conforming to our chosen life scenario, is our emotional experience. It depends on what we want to do with this life, both now and planned for before our birth.

After reading the foregoing, a friend asked, What about "a child who is sexually abused from birth on and ends up mentally retarded?" My response was that in my view, mental retardation is not the terrible thing we think it is, at least not for the developmentally disabled person. It merely means they don't use intellect to the degree most others of us do. Believe it or not, that child has partially returned to her or his original spirit state of consciousness, and is less capable of judging and of being programmed by society than are the rest of us. As a result, that child will likely always be a child mentally and emotionally, will possibly be honest, trusting, and innocent, less affected by people and events in life as they come along. They offer their parents or care-givers wonderful experiences, jointly planned by them before entering this life.

We look on retardation with pity or even disgust and repulsion, because we think of people who are different from us, especially those using less intellect, as inferior to us. We think our intellect is the most wonderful asset of humanity, but it is also the bane of our existence. It is only through intellect that we judge conditions as terrible and suffer because of that judgment. It is through intellect that we react negatively to events and people in our lives, as preplanned

OUR REACTIONS

Our reactions to people and events affect us considerably more than the people and events themselves. Seldom does something outside of us impact us directly. And, even when it does, such as physical injury, our reactions are our main experience. Our thoughts and actions affect only us. If we hate, whom does it hurt, but us? Even when we love, isn't it the love in our own heart that brings us joy, rather than another's feelings for us?

Without the love in our heart, another's feelings aren't appreciated, may even be irritants.

Another friend said to me, "Are you saying we have planned our life scenarios to give us nothing but heartache and misery, and there's nothing we can do about it? I don't see anything positive about that." I responded, "No, that's not what I'm saying. Yes, we may have planned for certain afflictions, but they are not the sources of any misery we feel." Our misery comes only from our reactions to our circumstances. Some things don't work out as we humanly think we want, but that's only because those things aren't in our best interest. We don't have to be miserable if we don't want to, don't have to play the victim if we don't want to. These we do or don't do by choice each day or as we confront events or afflictions. Clearly Helen Keller didn't spend her life being miserable about her inability to see and hear. Can you imagine the isolation she must have felt before she learned to read Braille? Imagine too, though, how she might have benefitted from the introspection that isolation provided her. She didn't have the distractions of sight and sound to focus her attention on this material life, so could put her full attention to her inner life. She obviously recognized the blessings afforded her by her condition.

Why, you ask, would we want to suffer so greatly? First, I believe we give ourselves only as much pain as we can handle. For example, when physical pain becomes too severe, we pass out. When emotional pain becomes too great, we can draw our awareness inward where we don't have to deal with our circumstances. We also are able to forget traumatic experiences until such time as we are better able to deal with them. Many abused children have used emotional escapes to help them tolerate and/or forget the pain, humiliation, and degradation of abuse. Second, this life is only a play. It isn't real. But because we believe it to be real, we embrace tragedy, loss, and pain wholeheartedly. We may let them consume us. We give them whatever power they have. It is our choice how we react to the events in our lives, so the severity of suffering is up to us, here, now, consciously. Our suffering, though, is only temporary and an illusion at that. Also, what may seem to us a very long time—the eternity of a life of suffering—is only a blink of an eye in Reality. And, too, as we raise our awareness to higher consciousness, we will have fewer adversities to deal with and be better able to cope with and rise above what ones we do have.

We also want to know anguish and despair and to react to those emotions to better know ourselves and better appreciate what we really have. The end justifies the means. Also a great deal of what we experience is part of others' lives too. Some of us sacrifice our human life well-being, comfort, and peace of mind to help loved ones gain experience. But, other than our memories, emotions, and feelings, nothing we experience stays with us when we leave this life.

One of my counseling clients, Angela, has fought hard throughout the years since her father's abuse to excel at things important to her. She has honed her intellect to a sharp and effective instrument, and in many respects has developed strong character. Although she may be proud of accomplishments, those old programs have been hard for her to overcome. The abuse isn't what today causes her pain, nor is the memory of it. Her reactions to the abuse—the hate, anger, self-reproach, and low self-esteem—are today's culprits, having become ingrained with time. This situation, from start to finish, is a substantial part of Angela's lifelong drama. Because she has never healed the old hurt, only masked it, she is emotionally and physically fragile, and is prone to attract one abusive relationship after another. Her entire life has been affected both negatively and positively by her reactions to her father's abuse. Her opportunities for awareness expansion have been great and are not over. She can add acceptance, if she chooses, toward both her father and herself, and find good health and happiness in so doing. Angela can accept the fact that what her father did was fulfilling a contract jointly made before her birth, with both parties wanting such experience, each for their own awareness expansion. Both participated willingly and out of love. She has no reason to continue hating her father or loathing herself. Now that she has used these emotions to serve her scenario purposes, she may no longer need them. Maybe now she can fill herself with love, and heal. Or, she can let negativity consume her. It's up to her.

DEATH AS THE TRAGEDY

When the tragedy is death, only the loving survivors suffer. The dying person moves into a different dimension of existence without physical feeling, so no pain of any kind goes with them. We think of death as a tragedy and as the worst possible thing that can happen to us. But I say death is far from the cessation of life we may have been taught it is. When we die, our consciousness rises to the love-filled, gloriously beautiful spirit-world home in another dimension from which we originated. So, how can death be something bad for the one making that transition? More on death shortly.

CHILDREN DYING

Often these days, children leave us at what seems too early an age. In a way, though, for many of them the earlier the better. Why prolong any sacrificial suffering they may be enacting for the benefit of others any longer than absolutely necessary? While the devastating loss may seem unbearable to a parent, the pain will lessen in time. If allowed to, memories of joy, strength, wonder, and love will soften the edges of the void their child's death has left behind. The parent has the choice of remembering and reliving the fun, loving, and beautiful times or the painful, difficult, and tragic period preceding death in a lingering illness, or the shock and horror of a sudden, violent death. It's their choice of experience.

CHILDREN GETTING OUR ATTENTION

Let's look again at child abuse, so prevalent today. We adults, hearing about it, are appalled and outraged. Anything that hurts children gets our attention and heart-felt reactions. These experiences are good for us in that they give us emotions we might not have in the usual course of our lives. They also cause our hearts to expand with compassion and love for those children. They perhaps cause us to want, and maybe try, to change the world in which child abuse occurs with such regularity. They point us in a direction we want (often unconsciously) to go: inward and spiritually upward.

WHY DO IT?

Why would we want to enter Earth life for such difficult and challenging experiences? In Reality, we know our life here is only a play that will be brief in Real time, and the value received will be well worth whatever we go through. Remember, the greater the tragedy in a movie, the more highly we rate both the movie and the actors who make it so real for us. The greater the suffering and the more tears they wrench from us, the more impressed we are with the performances. In human life, the more we are able to express emotion, the greater our performance can be and the more we can get out of it. After this life we'll review our enactment of it and be impressed with our performance. We may even laugh at ourselves for taking ourselves so seriously.

Everything that happens in our life and our reactions to each event bring us closer to our conscious realization of Oneness, our goal at this point in our evolution. That goal far outweighs any suffering we do along the way. The closer we come to our Oneness, the more we understand and the less we suffer. It's time for more of us to awaken to Oneness, a major leg in our journey toward awakening. That's a journey we can truly enjoy.

EVERYTHING IS IN OUR BEST INTERESTS AND PERFECT

I *know* that if we let it everything works out for the best. It has to, because what is best for us is what satisfies our intent for this play, and because our Selves are directing every moment of it. Any unsatisfied desires we've had were because they or their timing weren't in our best interests. Something more fulfilling, may be planned for us. If we keep a positive attitude when something doesn't pan out as we want it to, we'll be open to the something better and more apt to recognize it when it comes along. Later, we may look back and wonder why we even thought we wanted that other thing (or person) in the first place. If we let our disappointment consume us, allowing it to affect how we view and approach life, we may block our receptivity to the something better when it's offered. We may turn it (or that just-right person) away by a negative attitude.

> Much of your pain is self-chosen. It is the bitter potion by which the physician within you heals your sick self. Therefore trust the physician, and drink his remedy in silence and tranquility.
>
> ~ Kahlil Gibran, *The Prophet*

I admit, our scenarios have been lopsided toward what we consider negative. They've had to be in order to fulfill our purposes for creating this theater. There's no point in our being here to experience mainly ease, pleasure, and happiness, which we have in abundance in our Real spirit life offstage. But we can learn from the negatives and maybe learn to accept their true positive nature. I'm not saying any of this overcoming is easy; it's actually easier to play the victim than to rise above adverse conditions. But when we don't accept conditions as adverse, we can be happier, more comfortable, and easier on our loved ones.

SPIRITUAL BENEFIT

Each of us has lived through many roles of varied suffering, and I believe that many of us have nearly completed that phase of our human experience. It's time to experience other feelings brought on by enjoyment. Until we're sated with full living, our human experience isn't complete. And that full living includes the joys associated with enlightenment and awakening. Enlightenment comes from within to help us realize—remember—our spirituality and our Oneness, essential elements of our awakening.

While heartache and difficulty aren't the only ways to draw our attention inward, they're often the most effective. Hardship forces us to face and consider ourselves. Through hardship and heartache, we may expose unfamiliar sides of us and gain greater insight into our behavior, to better know and understand both our human and our spirit selves. Extremes in either direction can cause us to search for truth. Great joy can elicit a thankfulness that stimulates a desire to know its origin and to search for other *knowingness* as well. But, we would never know that great joy if it were not an unusual experience. Also, some of us need to descend into the "pit of hell" before we can begin to think and act positively. We have to reach bottom before we ask for help or gain a foothold that will help us climb out. Many people have found themselves or God at such depths.

Meanwhile, when you realize that the people in your life are playing their parts in your jointly chosen drama and through love are doing whatever meets your mutual needs, how can you not love them? Why not accept every act, word, and attitude, whether yours or another's, as the perfection it is? I know this idea is a hard one to understand, let alone accept, but hopefully it will become more clear before this book comes to an end. I don't ask anyone to accept any of my ideas, and this is probably the toughest one. I only want to give you some things to think about that could bring you the comfort and happiness that my truths have brought me.

APPLYING THE INSIGHTS

- Do you feel that you have had more than your share of adversity in your life? So much so that you can't believe that you would ever have planned to experience so much heartache, pain, and unhappiness?

- Have any of your adversities led to something better? Examine your attitudes and see if changing them might help your situation. See if you can't find a silver lining to at least one of your clouds of despair.
- Can you imagine a way out of your current conditions? Daydream; fantasize a wonderful life. Then look at it and your current situation and see if you can improve what you are and have right now, from the inside. Your life isn't our there in the world someplace, it is right inside of you. Accept the fact that your life might well be illusion and that all the people in it are truly loved ones helping you, as you are helping them.

11

OUR EXPERIENCE OF PAIN, DISABILITY, DISEASE, & AGING

While we are fast approaching our awakening and so much of life as we see it is changing, we each have our own Earthly reality to deal with now. For most of us, this life is far more real than that other we can only imagine, and is more important. Our physical bodies, in and of themselves, are major contributors to our Earthly experience, and of course, make it all possible. Our bodies are wonderful and complex mechanisms, whose conditions perfectly help us experience human life.

OUR BODY HELPS US EXPERIENCE

The changes our bodies undergo throughout our lives create a whole set of experiences, from teething and learning to walk and talk, through puberty, adolescence, and adulthood, to old age. Some of our bodies are afflicted by disease or injury. Some offer challenges throughout life. Others are harmed by substance abuse or are ravaged by rape or other brutality. Children are abused in every conceivable way. Elderly people, too, are abused, so are women, in particular. The physical differences between men and women alone create a great variety of ways in which our bodies are involved in our experiences, especially those of romance, mating, and procreation. All of these depend on and are vital parts of our individual scenario.

EXPERIENCING PAIN

Experiencing pain is an essential contrast to Reality we find especially valuable. For one thing, without ever having known pain ourselves, how would we ever feel sympathy and compassion for others experiencing it? We might even think someone expressing pain is being a baby, exaggerating how they feel, perhaps to gain attention. Can you see how such thinking would affect an otherwise loving relationship? If we had never felt pain, would we ever truly know what it's like to be pain free? Would we know when we've been able to put our mind over our matter and rid ourselves of pain?

AILMENTS AND AGING

Let's look at some of the many ways our bodies help us in enactment of our plays, examining first the ailment and aging aspects of human life. My all-knowing Self tells me there's no such thing as a purely physical ailment. It says every injury, every illness and every bit of bodily aging is self-induced but not without the ever-present purpose and perfection. We've either planned our afflictions ahead of time or we are now creating them through our thinking.

If, as science tells us, the cells in our bodies are constantly renewed and completely replaced every year, why are we not forever young and healthy? Both age and health are conditions of the material human body affected by the human mind, with those conditions playing a big part in our scenarios. They help us experience emotions and feelings we could not otherwise get. They also are affected by our beliefs. If, for instance, we believe an illness is hereditary and we are vulnerable, we're apt to let it, or even cause it, to become our reality. If we believe age brings physical and mental debilitation, those conditions are what we'll get. Our soul and our human consciousness, being spiritual, are ageless, and health is not an issue. Our material body alone is subject to age, disease, and injury, because we've wanted such conditions, or believe them likely.

Think about it; deep inside do you feel an age or infirmity? Do you remember ever feeling like a baby or even a child? Does the inner you seem any different from the you of ten years ago or thirty? Haven't you, inside, always been an adult and, as an adult, haven't you always felt younger than your years would suggest? Can the real you inside feel an illness or injury? Aren't there actually three aspects of the one human you: your physical body; your physical mind or intellect; and the aware, intelligent, loving, healthy, ageless you inside?

In addition to age and infirmity serving our experiential needs, collective unconsciousness has gathered and perpetuated expectations concerning injury, disease, and age, and we continually tap into it. We accept such expectations as parts of our adult belief system. Is there physically any reason why the older we are the more easily our bones break, the more slowly they mend or the more likely we are to develop physical ailments? Children haven't yet become conditioned to expect a decaying process in the body, and are less likely than adults to take their infirmities seriously or to dwell on them. The older we are, the more concerned we are about our health and aging. We are less active and often less social, so have more idle time and less to occupy our attention. While idle, we feel the slightest discomfort, so we spend more time dwelling on our bodies and their infirmities. Once our body reaches maturity there's no reason for it to continue the aging process. But, "as he thinketh in his heart, so he is" (Proverbs 23:7). And the more time we spend on negative, sickly thinking, the more firmly we are those negatives.

Have you ever noticed that a person's face appears younger and more serene while asleep than when they're awake? Cares of the day show on our faces as aging. If we could always be as serene as we are when sleeping, our bodies would show no aging, inside or out. Apart from satisfying our scenario's needs, aging is primarily a function of our absorption of and obsession with the negative states and emotions, the stress of everyday living.

We each have the power to stop, or at least slow, our own aging process. When we learn to live by inner guidance, in the now, and less judgmentally, we are more serene and no longer feel the tensions of a frenetically stressful life. We don't so easily trigger the aging emotions of fear, guilt, anxiety, envy, resentment, and self-pity. And by releasing the hold our expectancy of aging has on us, we don't unduly concern ourself with the condition of our body. When we're not concerned and are at peace with ourselves, there is little to cause age or its infirmities. When aging and sickness cease being core parts of our experience, our body can be renewed naturally, inside and out. We can expect our body to remain agile, healthy, and strong. The fountain of youth is within each of us.

BODILY PERFECTION

Our bodies are fully capable of maintaining good health, when that is in our best interests. To medicate symptoms or permit surgery for a perceived aliment can actually inhibit the body's natural health process. If good health is what we and our soul want for us, we're better off letting our bodily processes do their thing. If ill health is what we want for our experience, that's what we'll get, regardless of whether we let the body do its thing or we hinder its involvement. So, it seems to me, that the less we interfere with our bodily functions, the better off we'll be. We'll be naturally whatever we and our soul want to experience.

Our body, like our human consciousness, is an expression of our soul and is perfect, regardless of its shape, wholeness, or health condition. Also, it is in total obedience to our mind, doing whatever we require of it. The mind to which I refer is not the physical brain, but part of our spiritual consciousness. The brain is its physical instrument, the computer through which our consciousness functions physically; rather like a TV set, which is not the pictures, the stories, the music, the programs. The TV set makes possible our physical viewing of those programs. Our brain makes possible our physical use of our awareness and whatever is in the ethers: those insidious collective unconsciousness programs of which I speak.

I remember being taught in school that the muscles of the body respond to impulses from the brain (I now say "mind"). To learn to walk, in a sense we had to think "move" before the muscles would act. As we grew up, moving became automatic and has long since required no conscious attention. Although they've never required our conscious effort, every bodily function is run by our mind, spread throughout our body in our cells. Science has discovered that each cell has its own pure intelligence and knows its job in support of its body's life. Each and every cell in our body is an extension of our spiritual consciousness and has a role to play in the life of its body, and single-mindedly pursues its agreed-upon task. Part of its task is to respond to instruction from our mind. When something in a person's body is not working as originally designed, or as we think it "should," it is because the person's mind is directing it otherwise, either in conformity with a planned scenario or in response to thinking that is going against the person's best interests.

Our body doesn't in itself feel pain, discomfort, hot, or cold. Our nerves send information to our brain where our mind can then use it. When, for instance, a harming accident occurs, the body lets the brain know something abnormal has touched it. The mind, then, decides how to respond and transmits the appropriate reaction back from the brain through nerves to the spot of abnormality. Pain, bleeding, itching, cell destruction, or amassing(swelling) may be reactions selected by our mind, chosen to best serve our needs. Or, no physical response may result. Whatever happens is neither automatic nor by accident.

Sometimes, to serve specific purposes, our mind transmits pain impulses through nerves to specific locations to cause discomfort. The purposes are never to punish or of mal-intent; no judgment is involved. Our needs, desires, and fears, whether conscious or unconscious, are unbiasedly fulfilled. Our mind transmits pain, cell destruction, and cell amassing, expressing and sustaining the discomfort or abnormality. This process is what manifests inflammation, deterioration, tumor, flu, and disease.

REASONS FOR INFIRMITY

According to my Self, our bodies serve us perfectly, especially in infirmity. Our mind brings about the infirmities, whether age, illness, disease, pain, or merely discomfort, primarily to serve one or more of these five purposes:

1. To gain us some desired Attention.

2. To provide an Escape from something we don't want to face.

3. To act as a Flag, letting us know our thinking, actions, or emotions are out of balance or not in alignment with our best interest.

4. To provide a set of circumstances we want to Experience and/or to help loved ones experience, for expanded awareness and spiritual growth.

5. To provide Death, in a humanly acceptable means for departing from this life.

The first three cause what are often referred to as psychosomatic conditions. They are both physiological and psychological in nature or physical manifestations of mental or emotional problems.

No matter the reason or purpose for any malady, it is nonetheless real; our mind makes it so. These illnesses or injuries range from minor to critical, depending on their cause and their purpose. The physical response to the fourth is usually more severe and often disabling in nature. It impairs mobility, one of the senses, or our ability to fend for ourself. It has the potential to radically change a life, while also having a great effect on others, especially immediate family. The fifth is the most severe and needs no introduction here. The following are examples of why and how we use infirmities in response to life's difficulties and in enactment of our chosen scenario:

ATTENTION

Attention is usually thought of as a need of children or of the lonely elderly, yet not one of us is above using an infirmity to gain someone's concern or to be noticed. Rarely is it a conscious act; we may not be aware of our need. Its cause is fear, loneliness, or lack of self-confidence. When we rely on the attention of others for our happiness, we also have to rely on whatever means are available to get it. A broken leg from a skiing accident makes a person the center of attention at work and socially. We usually let someone know when we have an ache, a pain, or illness; maybe not in words but with a grimace or other gesture, such as rubbing our temples or neck or limping. We, on some level, hope these will bring sympathetic attention.

There is absolutely nothing wrong with having used such a ploy. When we've done it, we've needed to for our own, likely subconscious, reasons, but rarely to hurt or unduly upset anyone. We aren't maliciously trying to hurt another, and most of us aren't very fond of physical pain, so wouldn't consciously inflict it upon ourselves for any reason. The sad thing is that we use something negative hoping to create a positive. While a negative ailment might get us attention (our positive), when brought about in this way it is more apt to worsen our situation in the long run. Children of all ages, especially lonely ones, will take attention any way they can get it.

AN ESCAPE

Many people spend a good part of their life watching television, reading, gambling, surfing the web, playing computer games, texting, and unconsciously do so to escape the realities of life. The most obvious examples of escape are those who abuse substances to hide from life and people in mental institutions who have cut themselves off entirely from reality. Less obvious is to become temporarily ill or injured to escape something we don't want to face. We've all done it.

Many years ago, while still in Los Angeles, I was scheduled to bowl a match game with a friend. Other friends were taking sides, many betting on me to win. I realized later that the pinched nerve in my lower back I got a week before the match, preventing it, was my way out. I had felt responsible to my friends and feared I'd let them down. I lacked confidence in my ability to perform well and was afraid I'd lose. This way I was able to avoid the issue. *Hurting my back just happened, it wasn't my fault.* But all

I really did was cause a fun time to be canceled and myself considerable pain. I was taking myself and the situation too seriously. I couldn't just relax and enjoy the fun of it. I had to stop bowling entirely for a few years and was plagued with a painful back for many more years. Oh, the things we do to ourselves. Life would be so much more satisfying were we to put our energy into overcoming our fears rather than trying to escape them. I *know* that now, but didn't then, and hindsight is always effective.

We all run away at times, because we unconsciously think we need to. Rarely are we aware of it at the time. We can become aware, though, and see problems arising when we look for and recognize the kinds of situations that cause us stress. We can change the situations, avoid them in the first place or learn to react differently to them. Most of us are perfectly capable of doing anything we want to do. We just need to want to badly enough and then accept our abilities without limitation, believing in ourselves. Think about people's superhuman feats in emergencies, done in response to an urgent need, without thinking. They act before their intellect can tell them they can't do it.

We place too much importance on winning. The outcome is never as important as the doing. When we fill an activity with self-imposed stress, we miss enjoying the best part. Competition, contrary to what many suppose, often keeps us from performing to our peak of ability. It invites stress and fragments our focus, distracting us from our performance. We have to be superhuman to overcome such obstacles, and when we can't we're disappointed. The more we enjoy doing something the more apt we are to do it well. Enjoyment is usually stronger when we concern ourselves with only our own performance and leave competition out of it. The less seriously we take ourselves, the more enjoyment we'll get out of life and the healthier and happier we'll feel. Winning truly is not the important part of any activity; participating is; the journey is.

A Flag

Our mind produces pain and illnesses to warn us of some mis-thinking. Minor aches and pains, cuts, bruises, and colds are such flags. Nagging and more serious illnesses or discomforts, such as asthma, sciatica, migraines, or ulcers are flags to more chronic mis-thinking.

Negative emotions all have their effect. They can cause us to act and react in ways contrary to our best interests. When we are depressed, full of self-pity, guilt, or resentment, we set up conditions that perpetuate that state. Our true nature is to be happy, loving, and caring. Contrary emotions, if not parts of our scenario, can cause conflict within us. Our mind wants peace and harmony, so warns us of such conflict. It gives us a headache, a backache, or some other discomfort. In effect, it hits us over the head to get our attention.

One of the many ways in which we mis-think is striving to make events come out as we want them to or think they "should," rather than going with the flow: letting them happen as our director Self intends. We've been programmed since birth to believe that we have to make things happen, and become frustrated when our efforts go unrewarded. What we don't realize or forget, is that all events work out for our highest good, and efforts to direct them have little or no effect on them, only on us. Our mind causes our body to tell us with pain or ailment when we're going against the current of our highest good. By that I mean trying to achieve our desired results, attempting to fix something that isn't broken, or stewing over negative possibilities (*what-ifing*).

Afflictions of the flag type may also cause us to back off from whatever we're currently doing and take a second look. Or they may cause us to take a needed rest, enabling us to gain a fresh perspective—vacations are important in this regard. A break from everyday activities may enable us to address something else simmering on the back burner. These flags can sometimes forewarn us of the conditions discussed under Escape and Attention. By effectively responding to our built-in early-warning system, we may obviate the need for one of those other, often more drastic, measures.

EXPERIENCE

Crisis, disfigurement, loss, and chronic pain are producers of extreme emotion, helping us expand our awareness and raise our consciousness. Some of us chose a birth "defect" as a part of our play scenario, others chose a disabling or physically challenging illnesses or an "accident" later in life. Still others involve childhood abuse and lifelong emotional dis-ease resulting from it.

Ted, a friend of mine, was born with one arm considerably shorter than the other. As a child, he was laughed at and made fun of by other kids and was bullied. His father, wanting perfection in his son and feeling he didn't get it, rejected him. Ted's self-esteem was low, and he found it nearly impossible to make friends. He couldn't participate in most of the usual school sports, a fact that he felt worsened his situation with the other kids. He was unhappy and withdrawn. Fortunately for Ted, during the summer before entering high school he decided he didn't want to wallow in self-pity any longer and wanted instead to do what he could successfully do without the use of two arms. He realized that his limitation extended to neither his intellect nor his legs and feet. He got heavily into the physical sciences and mathematics, and eventually earned a Ph.D. in quantum physics and became a university professor. Throughout high school and college, he took track, and set records in sprint running and in hurdles. These skills helped others to see him differently, allowing them to forget he had a deformity and accept him as a friend.

We can allow infirmities to consume us, making us bitter, resentful, envious, self-centered, hateful, and distraught. Or, we can choose to rise above them, being happy, loving, kind, good-natured, and enthusiastic. Either response is perfect, serving its own purposes. But one is more pleasant than the other and leads to greater happiness.

Most people with the loss of a body part or sense or with an emotional or disabling injury or disease have compensated by strengthening their whole self. They have developed talents and capabilities, using other aspects of their body and mind. We all have ways of masking or contradicting feelings about ourselves we built as children. Some of us excel as athletes; others in business or a profession, in the arts, or as a parent and homemaker.

Some people, like Helen Keller, recognize their afflictions as blessings and are thankful for the opportunities afforded by them. A saying attributed to the last Incan ruler seems applicable in Keller's case: "A wise man must blind his eyes, cover his ears and trust his heart to know the truth." It's easier to go within to know oneself and maybe become enlightened when one doesn't have the distractions of a three-dimensional material world. Experiencing affliction of any kind provides an impetus to become better acquainted with the individual we are and to seek enlightenment. It may cause us to ask for spiritual guidance, improving our communication with our God within and improving our overall spiritual awareness. It may make seeking and finding truth easier. It might help us go with the flow and allow our highest good to manifest.

The experience of an extreme infirmity or incapacity is rarely ours alone; we share it with at least our loved ones. Our experiences, particularly our reactions to them, offer growth experiences for us and others. In some cases we are dependent upon others for care or companionship. That dependency is an experience for them, as is our treatment of them in the process. Sometimes our infirmities cause us so much discomfort we become mean and nasty, unleashing our anger and frustration on those close to us. Our treatment of them is part of our joint play and for our mutual benefit. Physically challenged people frequently serve as inspiration to the rest of us. The good humor and positive attitude of a person confined to a wheelchair inspires others to good humor. Amputees who ski or run on one leg or on prostheses, the blind golfer, and the quadriplegic who paints holding the brush in her teeth don't allow themselves to be handicapped. They inspire awe.

Death

For each of us there comes a time when the purposes for which we entered this life have been served and—on the soul level—the desire to leave arrives. While serving as a vehicle for departure from our current incarnation, death also serves as a growth experience to others, and often it's the time and manner of our leaving that serve that purpose. A premature death may be especially valuable in providing a loved one an opportunity for growth. Someone we know, or in most cases a stranger, is also afforded a growth experience by being the instrument of seemingly accidental death. Occasionally the primary or only reason for a birth is an early death. That particular act of love might, in that way, provide a parent and/or sibling exceptional growth. A child's ability to cope with a terminal illness can be an experience to witnessing adults that gives them more than the expanded awareness of the experience itself.

These measures may seem drastic, but sometimes severe shock and loss create our most valuable experiences. Although of immense value while we are in it, our body is only temporary. It is a vehicle for our Earthly experience only and magnificently serves that purpose.

Finding cures for existing life-threatening diseases will not stop deaths. It will merely cause other diseases to spring up or what we refer to as "accidental" deaths to increase. As cures are found for current diseases, natural and human-made disasters will replace diseases as the main producers of death. Diseases are necessary as means for leaving Earth life that are acceptable to our human ways of looking at life. Terrorism and war provide other means.

NO BLAME

It would be easy to conclude from the foregoing that we are to "blame" for our afflictions. While we are responsible for them, no one is "to blame." No judgment need be associated with that responsibility. Everything we do and everything that takes place in our lives is for our highest good. It has loving purpose behind it. Don't allow yourself to feel guilty about anything, and never wallow in self-pity, unless you really want to. You are led to think and behave as you do by a truly loving part of yourself who has only your best interests and spiritual growth intentions in mind. Your soul-Self is allowing you to experience conditions and resulting emotions that you on a soul level have wanted and agreed to experience.

PAIN AND AFFLICTION ARE NOT BAD

We are programmed to believe that pain, anguish, sorrow, or frustration, disability, disease, and death are all bad. They are not, but are perfect, serving loving purposes. Our attitudes toward them and our reactions to them don't have to be negative. We don't have to buy into the old programs. We can love whomever or whatever helps us in this spiritual journey and can thereby transmute any negative effect they or it might otherwise have had. Sometimes we have to be hit over the head to compel us to stop and pay attention to ourselves. What better attention-getter is there than pain or suffering? Pain is not bad. It is trying to tell us something. Neither ignore it nor fight it. Accept it for the good it is and try to understand it. Embrace it in gratitude, then release it.

We would have no basis to appreciate pain-free, healthy, youthful bodies if we had never felt pain, discomfort, disease, or aging; nor would we understand and feel compassion for others who have them. Most of us appreciate the glorious beauty and warmth of a sunny day far more after many dreary days than we do after continuous nice days. Only by experiencing pain, too, can we know when we are able to control our emotional reactions and conquer the material. When we see the pain for its perfection, release it and never again experience it, we have conquered our subservience to the outer, unreal world. In the interim, it might help you as it does me to think of discomfort as *God making God aware of God.*

As spirit beings, we can see, hear, smell, and taste with our spiritual senses, and when we created material forms, we wanted to continue enjoying those capabilities, but in different ways. We made it seem that we see through eyes, hear through ears, smell through noses, and taste with tongues. But, in truth, we still use our spiritual senses to perform those physical senses in materiality, and use the brain to interpret them in physical ways. Then we apply programmed expectations and health conditions to our use of our physical instruments. So, if we were to realize these truths and make them our own, we could use our always healthy and workable spiritual senses to see or hear perfectly, regardless of our bodily conditions.

LOVE HEALS

In my truths, the major component of the ethers is love—the one and only true force in existence. It is our energy. We are literally surrounded by love, supported, nurtured, and embraced at all times by love. And it resides in us. That love makes everything possible, including good health, well-being, youth, and strength. It only awaits our receptivity and use of it.

Put maladies in their proper perspective. You give your infirmities whatever power they have. And, every moment you dwell on them is a moment lost from your day—a non-productive, or possibly counterproductive moment. Take back the power unto yourself. Let your Self experience human life in physical form through you, expressing its highest nature in the form of vibrant good health, strength, and vitality. Take yourself less seriously, and allow yourself to have fun. Life can be enjoyable; you can enable it.

APPLYING THE INSIGHTS
- Do you see your body as the perfect vehicle for your sojourn on Earth, and do you recognize how wonderfully it was designed?
- Think back over the last few months—or longer if you remember something significant—and try to honestly determine if you have used any or all of the three psychosomatic conditions. Make a list of each, one you can refer back to.

- They are:
    - Attention
    - Escape
    - Flag
- Keep in mind that we all use them at various times in our life. But ask yourself why you felt you needed attention, and see if you still do. This usually stems from loneliness and/or low self-esteem. Have you outgrown those feelings or do you still feel the need for attention? If yes, you don't truly need others' attention, you need only you own inner attention. Get in touch with your inner being and you will never be lonely again. And if you make your spirituality, Oneness with all, and the perfection of everything, your truth, your self-esteem will rise accordingly to conform with your belief.
- Ask yourself if you've become ill or in pain to escape something you were afraid to face. Be honest! Think about what you could have done differently if fear hadn't controlled your thinking and behavior.
- Do the same with flag conditions. Did you learn anything from such flags?
- If you've suffered some debilitating or life-altering condition, give some thought to its purpose(s) for yourself and/or for one or more loved one(s). Look for benefits to you and to others. Appreciate it. Love it. And make the most of those benefits in good humor and an upbeat attitude.

12

HEALING

Although both prayer and healing are very personal, we tend to pray for healing of our loved ones more than for ourselves. When we pray for others, we nearly always impose on them our own idea of what is good; we want for them what would make us happy. When one we love is disabled or threatened with a loss of a body part, eyesight, or hearing, we want to see them whole. We think of wholeness as perfection and find it hard to deal with the vision of our loved one in an imperfect body. When the life of someone close is threatened, our prayers reflect our desire to keep them alive and with us. We tell ourselves we're praying for what they want or for their good. We pray our heart out that our picture of what is good, right, and perfection will prevail. We pray that God will let them live, return their sight, leave them whole.

IN OUR BEST INTERESTS

Some people say God intends everything in our life to be good and only because of mis-thinking on our part is anything bad. They say God intends us to be healthy, free from pain, happy, and carefree. I say we each are the gods who intend (not consciously, but on a soul level) one thing or another for us, not a supreme Being outside of us. Also, while our thinking has its effects, our planned scenario carries the greater influence, and conditions of good health and prosperity may not be in the best interests of our soul growth. Good to serve us best may very well be adversity, affliction, heartache. After all, we joined this play of human life to experience unfamiliar conditions. There's an anonymous saying which I particularly like: "No man is more unhappy than the one who is never in adversity; the greatest affliction of life is never to be afflicted." Also, a tragedy or severe affliction now may lead us in a direction that will one day provide love and happiness beyond our current dreams. Afflictions also offer us understanding and compassion.

Regardless of prayers and how we as humans view life, our souls, knowing what's best for us, are the deciders of our fate. We each have preplanned our infirmities and when and how to leave this life, and our souls direct us toward those planned events. We learn some things only through loss, hardship, pain, deformity, malfunction, or challenge. When we pray such challenges away, we may rob ourself or loved ones of opportunities to experience and grow. It may be that one of those seeming negatives is the impetus to bring us or a loved one immeasurable joy or to set us firmly on a spiritual path. Possibly, too, our prayers to bring a loved one back to life may influence their decision. They may postpone what they want to do to satisfy our selfish desires.

A friend, reading that last point, asked, "Isn't that contradictory to your concept of preplanning? If we've preplanned our lives, can we change our plans? Can someone else's desires cause us to modify the play, the script?" I answered that our preplanning is not so specific. My idea of an outline is that it only covers intent, not detail. In the case above, if the intent is served by our staying awhile longer, we do so, and lovingly I might add.

Arthur Ford, in *Unknown But Known*, discussing out-of-body experiences, tells of a young man who was

> ...terribly ill and in coma, whose mother formed a prayer group and prayed for his recovery. He got well—and made his mother promise never to do such a thing again. The land he had seen in spirit, he said, was far more splendid than the one he returned to.

No one has any right to attempt to affect the well-being of another without their desire and permission. I don't mean we shouldn't pray for the safety and health of our loved ones, just not attempt to impose on them our idea of their safety and health. We can pray that all will be for everyone's highest good, in "divine right order." We can mentally send loving energy to help our loved ones do what they want or need to do. Love helps us all deal with the outcome.

HEALING WITH LOVE

Love is the most powerful force in the universe. When we send love from our heart to others, we enlarge the force field of love surrounding them and support them in whatever is in their best interests. That love can quiet negative thoughts and can help those others be more receptive to their good. The love we send out also returns to us and abundantly so.

Be supportive of the plans and desires of another soul by letting love flow. Respect their rights, their individual needs and their decisions. Do whatever you and they together feel can help them; but it has to be their choice, without coercion. If they want to go through chemo treatment for cancer, for example, support them through it. If they turn down chemo, radiation, or dialysis, support them in that choice too. Accept the outcome as fulfillment of their wishes and of the highest good for all. Pray, if you wish, for you both to have the strength and courage to face the consequences. This will help you approach the situation most positively.

Dwelling on negative aspects of a situation shuts off the love flow. You also run the risk of turning those negative thoughts into creative forces, giving them strength, possibly making them real. Focus attention on your own love and acceptance. Be happy and share with loved ones, especially when ailing. Our attitudes are always our own choice and they determine how we view our world. In effect, they create our world, what we see as our experience.

DOCTORS AS HEALERS

Western medical doctors view themselves as healers, special, even God, and most people have come to see them the same way—not realizing that we all are God. Doctors are prone to believe medicine is an exact science. They seem to feel that when they accurately diagnose a patient's symptoms and decide on treatment, the end result will be what they expect. The patient expects a cure from the doctor. Western medicine is based solely on our old ideas of how the body works, so is limited in its results. So much of what Western medicine does to treat a condition is nothing more than a band-aid, applied to a very specific symptom. That medicine focuses on the body in its parts and essentially unrelated to the mind, and spirit not at all. We are not our bodies. But our bodies, as whole, material systems composed of intelligent, interactive cells, are completely dependent on our spirit mind, and are affected by the beliefs and attitudes of our intellect.

Doctors are no more or less special or capable than the rest of us. Their role is that of facilitator in our experience of physical and emotional ailments. For that they are specially trained. They aid our souls in creating a great variety of conditions through which we and our families gain important emotional experiences, both positive and negative. Those experiences are the only consideration in the outcome of treatment, the only determining factor along with our personal beliefs. I'm sure it's perplexing and frustrating to doctors when two people with the same aliment respond differently to the same treatment. That's bound to be the case, because the treatment is neither the cure nor the killer; enactment of the preplanned scenario and our beliefs are both. And both sickness and healing are individual conditions, personal in nature.

This is not to say doctors needn't be consulted. As facilitators, they play vital roles in the scenarios of patients and their families. We mustn't relinquish our power to doctors, though; they are no more God than the rest of us are. It's important for each of us to listen to and follow our own body, regardless of and sometimes contrary to advice from a doctor.

OUR NATURAL BODY HEALTH & HEALING

Our body was designed magnificently to naturally protect all of its parts, to cleanse it of any ailment we do get and to quickly heal us. Each and every cell is intelligent and knows its job. To treat one part or symptom at a time denies the body's holism and perfection and its inherent ability to heal itself. If left alone to do what comes naturally and in conformance with our play scenario, our body will take care of itself. Our beliefs, though, often keep us from allowing our body to do its work or they impose conditions on it which counteract its efforts of protection and healing.

ALTERNATIVE HEALING

While chiropractic is a widely popular alternative to conventional Western medicine, other ancient practices are also finally coming into their own here in the United States. Although for thousands of years Native Americans have effectively used "alternative" practices, most others of us know little about them. Asians, Indians, and indigenous people worldwide have enjoyed the benefits of various practices since the beginning of time, viewing our bodies, their health, and healing work quite differently than Western medicine, under a different set of premises. They, in the main, apply the premise that the body/mind/spirit is a whole unit and anything that shows up in one part affects or is an expression of the whole.

Some practitioners assume the body is fully capable of healing itself, given the freedom to do so, and they work at providing that freedom.

Many such practitioners believe physical ailments are caused by body energies being out of balance or blocked as a result of physical or emotional trauma, stress, or cell memory of old trauma. They see their job as helping the body regain its natural balance and a smooth flow of its energy. They may use one or a combination of any number of techniques such as: various types of massage therapy, acupuncture, acupressure, reflexology, biofeedback, breathing exercises, visualization, yoga, and T'ai Chi. Some prescribe nutritional supplements, macrobiotics, herbs, plant and flower extracts, and natural aromas. Some use diet changes. Some use natural crystals to help the body's energy flow evenly and smoothly. Wellness can result naturally. Such holistic healing practitioners rarely treat a specific symptom. They often move the body focus from the symptomatic spot, and concentrate on the body holistically, aligning the body energies.

FAITH HEALING

Some of us facilitate healing through faith or the "laying-on-of-hands." Any healing technique can work, when the parties involved believe in it and healing is part of the script. When it comes to healing another, however, a "healer" must be certain the other truly wants bodily healing and their help. Healing, as we think of it, may not always be bodily or in a person's best interests. And, if not sought, efforts at healing could be interference in others' affairs.

Without going into the mechanics of healing, I'll relay to you what my higher Self has made clear to me. If you perform energy, psychic, or prayerful healing, be sure to detach yourself from any outcome. Be an open channel only, through which loving, healing energy can flow freely, unobstructed by your thoughts. That energy will seek out physical disease or emotional dis-ease and aid in its cure, if that is in the best interests of the person. Kosmic energy will support whatever is in the best interests of all concerned—what each Self wants as part of its planned scenario. You as an instrument or channel of healing must remain detached. It's not your position to influence the process. But then, if you are involved in healing, I'm sure you know that.

The outcome may or may not be physical healing. Mental and emotional healing is often more important than physical. Since physical pain or disease is only a symptom of a deeper problem or purpose, surface healing without inner healing would be only a band-aid. The problem, to gain the attention it wants, might have to manifest somewhere else in the person's body, and that could be more serious, more painful. Sometimes healing takes the form of clarity of purpose or some other understanding. It may be an ability to cope with something currently causing stress. Whatever the outcome, it is perfect just as it is.

MY FRIEND'S EXPERIENCE WITH HEALING

A friend of mine—let's call her Sue—found in her hands a sensitivity to the energy emanating from people, and was learning to use wonderful healing powers. Sue could pinpoint a spot of disorder or pain by feeling different temperatures as she scanned a person's body with her hands. After locating a dis-eased spot, she would lay her hands on or near it to focus loving, healing energy to it. Her family members and friends enjoyed such treatments and often felt considerably better afterward. The love Sue focused on them reinforced and aided the body's natural process. But she was too new to this healing process to understand how healing really works.

She volunteered her healing help to a co-worker afflicted with cancer. Certain she could cure the woman, Sue spent hours giving healing treatments. When the woman was no longer able to work, Sue went to her home, doggedly believing she could help. When the woman died, Sue was distraught. She gave up healing, feeling she had failed her friend, that she couldn't heal after all. What my friend didn't see at the time was that she never was *doing* the healing herself, only facilitating it. She also didn't realize that she had helped heal the woman, just not in the way she expected. The woman had originally been terribly afraid of death but by the time her death came, with Sue's help, she was at peace with herself, no longer afraid. Sue had talked with her for hours on end and had added loving energy to the woman's own energy. The woman was healed in the way her Self wanted her to be.

Because it was not the physical healing she had expected, Sue initially almost blamed herself for her friend's death. She became disillusioned with healing, and because she concerned herself with an outcome and had failed her own expectations, she became ill herself. Sue suffered for years with severe back and sciatic nerve pain, as unconscious self-inflicted punishment. She now understands what happened, and occasionally gives healing treatments again. I think her own healing became more rapid as she quit blaming herself and opened to channel loving energy. Sue won't again concern herself with results, but give treatments unconditionally and lovingly, getting personally out of the way and letting a person's Self and natural bodily healing processes work.

SELF HEALING

The most effective form of healing is self-healing, which can also be preventative. Louise Hay is famous for her use of self-love as a healing method, especially for AIDS and cancer patients. I believe self-love to be the real miracle cure, not just of our physical ailments or even emotional hurts and scars, but of humanity's problems throughout the world. I believe it to be so important, I devote a whole chapter in the next part to the subject of self-love.

VISUALIZATION

Visualization is a technique widely used in self healing. By repeatedly picturing in their mind a perfect, healthy, strong body, people actually make it so. This technique has been most effective in the treatment of cancer in children. The children visualize minute creatures—Pac-man comes to mind—devouring cancerous cells and then rebuilding strong, healthy cells in their place. Children are better than adults at such visualization because they are freer with their imagination and aren't so programmed with doubt as we are.

It's clear that mind can prevail over matter and that our body responds to dictates from our mind. Visualization is merely another way for our mind to tell our body what to do. It helps our intellect see what's possible and gears it to accept a new reality. Besides, it's fun to each day see in the mind's eye what is taking place in the body as cells are removed, repaired, and created. This picture can be as detailed and as colorful as one wants. It might make visualization most effective if the tiny Pac-men were seen to carry love to work and let the love do whatever it needs to do.

Our body goes through a repairing, sloughing-off, and recreating process constantly on its own. Since each cell is completely replaced in the normal course of the renewal process, we might ask ourselves if the new cell has to be replaced with the same conditions as the old one. Or, does it depend on what we believe?

Through visualization we help our body's cells release old beliefs and accept new ones. We tell the body what we want it to do and we focus its attention on it. The body can easily handle both projects, so focusing its efforts on particular healing does not distract it from its normal, on-going cell renewal. It merely produces more healing cells to perform the added task (if healing is our highest good). The body is programmable and responds to mental instruction, which is most effective when accompanied by a mental image and love. The body then knows specifically what we want. Visualization leaves no room for doubt or ambiguity. It works.

Don't Fight it, Join it

Here's a method I've found helpful whenever I feel pain or even discomfort rearing its uncomfortable head: I close my eyes and consciously relax all of my muscles. Then, with my awareness, I concentrate my mind on the affected area of my body. I feel the pain or discomfort as completely as possible, embracing it, almost enjoying it. I ask it what it's telling me, listen, then I tell it I love it and thank it for its help in drawing something to my attention, getting me to stop and relax a moment, or just being a part of my life. (It is, after all, only energy and neither good nor bad.) Then I release it and visualize it leaving me, going into the ethers to fulfill whatever other mission it might have. I continue focusing my awareness in that area without thinking anything in particular until the discomfort subsides. It will, rather like when I put my hand on the arm of my chair. At first I am conscious of the texture and temperature of the fabric I'm touching, but I soon stop feeling it. The pain, too, quickly goes on its way, leaving me feeling comfortable and at ease. That area no longer has a physical sensation. I stay relaxed in body and mind, letting my mind merely rest there, just being, like the hand on the chair arm.

For over 25 years, I was plagued with severe migraine headaches, and I sought help in both Western and alternative medicine. As I was getting rid of the headaches, but not yet fully, I told my body to disperse what toxins had gathered to cause discomfort. I asked the toxins to scatter into my body's elimination systems, and they usually responded pretty quickly. My sinuses would drain post nasally as one of the many paths of elimination. I also inhaled and then explosively exhaled through my mouth several times, providing another immediate elimination path.

MY SELF-HEALING MEDITATION

I came to use the following self-healing meditation, one I created with help from an alternative practitioner, and which set me finally on my healing path. (I still use it occasionally to relax and dissipate stress): I get comfortable and as relaxed as possible, *cleanse* my aura, and *center* myself, mentally balancing my energy. I then imagine walking to the edge of an imaginary deck where a flight of ten steps leads down to a special spot. My spot is a wonderfully magical combination of glorious flower garden, forest, and stream running from a placid, deep greenish-blue pool. This spot itself is a collection of love and harmony, serenity, joy, and bliss, where animals, birds, and insects share in its beauty and create a microcosm of a lush, peaceful Pacific Northwest forest setting.

I count backward from ten to one as I slowly descend the steps, and my body and mind become more and more relaxed, more comfortable, more at peace and filled with feelings of well-being. With each step, my body feels more vital, energetic, and strengthened, yet relaxed and my mind is more quiet. As my body eases it feels heavier and seems to sink deeper into my chair. As my mind becomes increasingly more stilled, I become ever more one with my Self. My intellect easily relaxes into a comfortable stillness. The closer I come to complete oneness, the more open are my chakras (energy centers) and the more smoothly vital energy flows throughout my body and my aura. All of my bodily functions go about their business in harmony and perfection. My awareness is acute of every detail in my body and in my imagined surroundings.

As I reach the bottom step, I sometimes visualize a round or oval opening there, rather like a "stargate" leading to another dimension, brilliant with light. Dazzling, radiant golden white light is on the other side, reached through that portal. I pass through and into unbelievably loving energy. There, I talk with my mother, brother, father, my aunt, a special friend, or my Self.

Usually, as I reach the last couple of steps, I begin to notice the sounds, scents, and colors of my flower garden. Once on the path, only a couple of paces take me through the garden and into the forest. In that short distance I notice roses, gardenias, gladioli, dahlias, asters, tuberous begonias, and so much more. Since it's magical, my garden is always well watered and nurtured, weeded, and pruned without effort on my part, and my favorite flowers are in full bloom all year. There are no rows, only a profusion of color, texture, and perfection in detail. Wonderful fragrances mingle in the sun-filled, yet crisp, clean air as I glide through the garden and into the forest.

The fresh scent of pine needles envelopes me there along with the musky odor of loamy earth and other recycling organic matter. A doe and a cottontail greet me. They are soon joined by birds, insects, and animals of great sort. A bear cub tumbles over a tree root to land at my feet and grins sheepishly up at me. My wonderful shepherd/collie-mix friend, Stormy, long passed over, sits in front of me wagging her whole body, while my beloved Punkin stretches tall and healthy between Stormy's paws, purring loudly. I reach down and pick her up and hold her to my breast. She purrs even louder and stretches a soft paw up to touch my face, then rubs her chin against mine. I am so filled with love, surrounded by it as I am. Looking around, I realize each being, scent, and sound comes alive only as I focus on it, not existing until I activate it with my attention.

I take my perch atop an ancient tree, fallen on its side across the clear, swift-running stream, my feet dangling just above the water's surface. The stream is created by runoff from the pool just ahead, formed by a small yet majestic, cascading waterfall tumbling down from a height of about twenty feet. The roar and splash of the falling water somehow aren't audible until I focus on them—they wouldn't want to take away from my enjoyment of the other forest sounds. Stormy and Punkin—who dearly loved each other in Earth life—sit there with me, one on either side. I look around, noticing the glorious contrasts of colors, shapes, textures, scents, and sounds, with a sense of quiet and serenity prevailing over all. I am filled with awe and wonder and overflow with love and a great sense of Oneness with it all.

I spring from my log into the pool, becoming a frolicking dolphin. As I swim, leap, roll, *walk* on the water, and do loops, I find myself grinning. I feel other beings swimming along side me and look over and see my brother has joined me as another dolphin. Together we frolic as if still children. Our fins momentarily touch, and he, only wanting to say hello, moves on. I swim deep into the green-blue water and surface to suck in a large noisy inhale of nurturing, cleansing air. I notice the air move through my blood to every cell of my body, energizing and renewing as it goes. I see the air absorb toxins and other no-longer-needed elements as it returns to my lungs, where those are turned into gas and expelled. I then exhale forcibly, a slow, lengthy, satisfying breath, creating a misty spout rising out of the water. Repeating this rhythmic breathing several times, I feel free; I feel filled with a splendid combination of serenity, joy, and love: bliss. I come back to the present directly from that dolphin state, so that I continue to enjoy those glorious feelings. I go on about my business, renewed, strengthened, rejuvenated, calmed, and pain free.

I fell in love with the dolphin imagery, not just because it works so effectively, but because the dolphin is such a perfect symbol. I see the dolphin as free and at peace with its world, serene, and yet at the same time truly fun-loving and playful. I see it as supremely intelligent, not with intellect but with pure intelligence, and the epitome of unconditional love. When I am swimming in my imaginary pool, I am the dolphin, and I am all that dolphin is.

HEALTH IN THE FUTURE

Eventually we will no longer need ailments to help us experience and grow or to help us make the transition home; we'll come and go with ease. But we'll likely get there in steps and will want healing practices as we proceed, commensurate with our progression. Holistic and energy healing practices will be the first main health care of the future. After that we may periodically go to a practitioner to help us maintain clear, free-flowing energy and avoid ailments altogether. Eventually, we won't need that.

Your Self is experiencing this life through you. It knows what it wants to experience, and its perspective is not only broad and all-knowing, but is based in pure love. It is in control of your body, your life and your interaction with the other actors in your play. Whatever illness you experience serves your joint purposes. The end result, therefore, whether death, incapacity, or healing, is what you want for those purposes, as always known and pursued by your Self. Rather than concerning yourself with healing, therefore, you might be better off letting go and letting God (your Self) take care of whatever it wants to accomplish. You might go with the flow by saying and meaning, "Whatever will be, will be," or singing "*Que Sera, Sera.*" Rather than interfering in the process, you might trust your soul to effect what is best for you.

If healing is best, it would likely be accomplished more quickly and certainly more comfortably without your interference and worry. If death or incapacity is best, it too might be more easily effected with your more open attitude. The result is probably going to be the same regardless of what you do and how you treat the situation. The more relaxed, trusting attitude on your part, however, will make the whole process easier on you and those who care about you. You need not be fearful. You need only trust; let go and let Self.

APPLYING THE INSIGHTS

- Thinking first about praying for loved ones, do you do so often? Examine your prayers, and see if they are based on either (1) your idea of what is best for them or something they want for themselves, or (2) something that could happen (what if) in the near future, or some good you doubt will occur. Keep in mind that we are each unique individuals who have chosen a particular journey for this life that includes some specific experiences, and that our plans are nobody's business but our own. So don't try to influence others' plans, experiences, or life direction. Whatever occurs in their life is truly in their best interests, and not yours with which to interfere. Do you see that most of your prayers are either about someone else or are based on fear? Make you prayers ones of gratitude and love to support the perfection of everything that occurs, and you will find them much more satisfying and more apt to be fulfilled.
- Do you believe that your body can heal itself, can give itself good health and if allowed to do so would to perfection? Do you believe, though, that if ill health is something you've chosen to experience, your body will do what your spirit consciousness, your mind tells it and will be in your best interests?
- If you are experiencing an illness, dis-ease, or physical challenge of some sort, do you *know* you can be relatively comfortable through self and bodily healing? Do you realize there are several different types of healing that can occur and that they aren't necessarily physical?
- Your Self-Healing Meditation—do you have a special imaginary spot where you can go whenever you feel pain or stress or just want to relax? Go there, and thoroughly enjoy it. Or, create your own mental spot, in the mountains, at the sea

coast, or in the desert. Soar through the clear blue air, swim through placid water, lie in the warm nurturing sun, or ski down a beautiful white mountain, whatever is most attractive and restful for you. Such a spot is a wonderful thing to retreat to whenever you feel any pain, discomfort, or dis-ease of any kind. It dissipates stress, wonderfully.

13

OUR EXPERIENCE OF DEATH

Whether a sudden tragedy, release from a lengthy painful illness, or quiet passing after a long active life, the death of a loved one is our experience too. In fact, our experience of it usually lasts well past their death and often affects in some way the remainder of our life. The sudden, unanticipated death is apt to have the greatest impact on our remaining life experience, while the lengthy illness is more often a shared experience before the loved one leaves. The nature and quality of that sharing create many of the memories we live with for the rest of our lives.

Although we can all expect to die sometime, a relative few of us knows very far in advance when or how that will be. We often hear "we could go tomorrow," and are told we'd be better off living each day as if it were our last. But seldom do we follow such sage advice.

NOT TALKING ABOUT AN IMPENDING DEATH

For a variety of reasons, not the least of which is that it's an unknown, most of us don't talk about death. Most of us prefer to not even think about it. It used to be common practice for the doctor and family of a terminally ill person to not tell them they were dying. Advising someone they're dying must be difficult at best. And, since death was never discussed ahead of time, the subject was easier to avoid than face head on. Fortunately, we've come a long way since then, thanks in part to changes in some of the practices of care givers and even thanks to television. Terminally ill people usually know or sense they are dying, so there's no point in hiding the fact.

Elizabeth Kubler-Ross devoted her medical career to working with dying children and their families, and she wrote books and lectured on the subject of dying. She was very vocal about saying the dying usually want to be able to talk about it. More than anything, they want their family to be natural with them. They don't want small talk, and feigned gaiety, or pity; nor do they want their illness and impending death skirted around in conversation. It's what is happening with them. It's real and unavoidable. It can't be wished away nor should it be covered up. The dying want their last days with loved ones to be filled with shared love and expression of genuine feelings. Kubler-Ross also said that a dying person, often more accepting of their situation, can be of help to others in facing their impending loss. Sharing of feelings about the experience can ease tension and enable closeness to soothe the pain felt on both sides. Open sharing in itself is a balm.

I don't mean to oversimplify the issue. Broaching the subject with someone who is dying is anything but easy. Most of us have done little in-depth thinking about death and likely aren't eagerly awaiting an opportunity to discuss it. Even when we have thought about our own death or that of a loved one, when it happens or is near everything changes. Often because we don't want to give up hope, we cling to the possibility that a mistake has been made and our loved one isn't dying after all. We may think talking about it will make it real. Maybe you want to be strong for a loved one, and believe that the only way to show strength is to avoid the subject of death altogether. That is false strength, stemming from self-absorption not love. If you truly want to be strong, face the issue of death with your loved ones. Do it together.

Of course, dwelling on the subject is no more helpful than not facing its reality. Sometimes very little need be said. A willingness to share may be all that's needed. Such willingness is a demonstration of love and strength and is comfort and support to someone facing death.

For some, the impending death of a loved one can be so painful that talking about it is virtually out of the question. When devastated by the imminent death of someone precious to them, many men, especially, find it impossible to talk about. When a person is used to hiding emotions and is unaccustomed to sharing their feelings and thoughts, the personal tragedy of death can be overwhelming. When people who never face their emotions and feelings are engulfed by them, they don't know how to deal with them. They either go totally to pieces or shut themselves further off from the world and the pain of it.

We all want to say goodbye to loved ones when we or they die, but obviously that's not always possible. Even when it is, we don't always do it, often because we don't know how; we don't know what to say. But, if you avoid spending time with your dying loved one because you can't handle it, I guarantee you will regret it the rest of your life. It's better to be with them and say nothing than not see them. Just being together can be quietly saying goodbye.

WONDERING ABOUT DEATH

When we learn of the death of someone, whether known to us or not, our immediate reaction is, "I'm sorry." We view death as a tragedy, especially when it seems unnatural. I've heard people say things like, "What a tragedy that he should lose his life. The poor thing; I feel terrible for him." We usually feel especially sorry for the family in their loss. We empathize with them in, their sorrow, imagining how we'd feel in their shoes.

When a loved one dies, we may grieve about our loss, but we also may be uncertain about their fate. Even those of us who talk about eternal life are hesitant to accept it, because it isn't a part of our experience. We are slow to trust what we've not experienced personally. Blind faith does not come easily. We may have been taught that we'll one day join our loved ones who have gone on before us, but wonder if it's true. We can't imagine what death is like, and we're apt to fear what we don't know and understand. All we do know is that death ultimately brings ashes through decomposition of the physical body or its cremation. Since we can't see it, we don't know what happens to consciousness. Is there nothing but blackness after the cessation of this Earth life?

> Either the soul is immortal and we shall not die, or it perishes with the flesh and we shall not know that we are dead. Live, then, as if you were eternal.
>
> ~ Andre Maurois

Either way, why be concerned?

Some of us may be less concerned about the after death state than we are about how we may die and a period before death. I know some of us fear the suffering of a lengthy, painful illness, becoming a burden to loved ones, or having to spend our last years in misery and loneliness. Whatever the case, it's part of our chosen scenario and perfect. Besides, we don't have to let our condition make us completely miserable, unless we want to.

My aunt recently died, only two months after her 100th birthday. She slept through most of the grand celebration. She was thoroughly crippled by arthritis, incontinent, legally blind, and all but completely deaf. She hadn't been able to watch TV for a couple of years, replacing that with reading one large print book after another, but then had trouble reading anything. As before, she thoroughly enjoyed listening to classical music through high-powered earphones, but then could no longer hear it. She had COPD and was dying of congestive heart failure; with a pulse rate of 41 when normal is above 75, she was slowly drowning. Ah, the "golden years." Although her body was rapidly giving up, her mind remained sharp. When asked about her quality of life, she said "I'm happy; I get good, loving care—in the assisted-living facility where she lived—and don't mind sleeping all the time." She remained cheerful to the end, but that was her nature. So, you see, it's all in our attitude. She finally went into Hospice care, ready to die, then did.

NEAR-DEATH EXPERIENCES

Many people are afraid of the act of death itself. They fear they may possibly experience the pain and horror of a violent death. I've been convinced, though, by reports of "near-death experiences" (NDEs) that no matter the conditions surrounding it, we generally don't experience either pain or fear at death. People worldwide have reported that they floated out of and above their body at or before the cessation of their heart and breathing, then watched rescue and revival activities. From their out-of-body observation point, they watched with detached interest and no sense of either pain or fear.

Materialist skeptics insist that remembered experiences in the near-death state are hallucinations brought on by oxygen-deprivation, dreams, religious fantasies, or subconsciously programmed expectations. But, millions of people in the United States alone have reported having similar experiences. NDEs have been reported throughout the world by atheists and people of every religious denomination as well as people of different cultures, economic background and with varying levels of education. Most have reported very similar experiences.

Neurosurgeon Eben Alexander wrote *Proof of Heaven*, after his own near-death experience, to try to convince his fellow medical professionals that the experiences reported by people after briefly "dying" were actually real, not the hallucinations science believes them to be. He somehow contracted a rare and usually lethal form of meningitis, which put him into a coma with absolutely no neo-cortical activity for seven days. He writes that without that brain activity even hallucinations are impossible. He describes a beautiful, peaceful, and completely loving experience. And, although a fully typical materialist non-believer of anything supernatural or spiritual before his NDE, he now is just as fully convinced of life continuing on after death. In fact, he says his experience over there seemed more real than anything here in his human life.

Although I am certainly a believer, I found Alexander's book very convincing, more so than other similar books, possibly because he is a medical professional, a brain surgeon no less, and had before been a materialist skeptic of the most rigid kind—clearly closed to any consideration of an afterlife or spirituality. I highly recommend *Proof of Heaven*—in book form or in a You Tube talk—to anyone who remains unsure of life after death.

NO PAIN OR FEAR AT DEATH

Some people, near death as a result of an accident, have reported being disassociated from their body at the point of impact and in no conscious pain. For example, Doctor Raymond A. Moody, Jr. in his book *Life After Life*, cites the following from one of his cases:

> I said to myself, "I'm in an accident." At that point, I kind of lost my sense of time and... I lost touch with my body... My being was suspended above me and the car was over the embankment; it seemed that it took the car a long time to get there, and in that time I really wasn't too involved with the car or the accident or my own body only with my mind.

And from another case he reports:

> At the point of injury there was a momentary flash of pain, but then all the pain vanished... all I felt was warmth and the most extreme comfort I have ever experienced.

Some people, who have had a close call with death through sudden trauma, have no memory of the event. Possibly, they experienced something similar to the above but don't remember. Also, when we break a bone or severely cut our skin, what we first feel is numbness. We don't feel pain until we've had a chance to think about it and then react. If our mind doesn't say "pain," we don't feel it. If our mind finds no reason for fear, we don't experience that either.

Those who are near death and not lucid are truly "not all there." Any outward response comes from their physical brain and body; their human self (their awareness) is out of body, perhaps reviewing their life, the current circumstances, and their effects on others, maybe considering whether or not to return. These conditions are true also of people in comas as well as mentally ill people who have become comatose and people with advanced Alzheimer's. Occasionally—usually just before death—a person in one of these conditions will suddenly "wake up" and be very lucid. This clarity occurs when, for a reason of their own, their awareness returns momentarily, possibly to convey a message or to let someone know that on some level they are still aware and mentally healthy.

No Experience of Death

Reports of NDEs—and affirmed by my Self—tell me there is no experience of death, because we don't die. In the case of sudden death, we may not even be aware immediately that we've left our body. In *Unknown But Known*, Arthur Ford tells of a British soldier hit during the fighting in 1917:

> 'My body,' he later related, 'was blasted from me so quickly I was not aware of its falling. I went on without it, feeling alive and free. Then I realized I'd have to go back.' After his recovery he said the experience made him realize, 'My body is not really me, but only a cloak or skin I wear.'

Our awareness is the only real and eternal part of us and it is not physical, so does not feel pain. When our awareness is outside the physical, we are not connected to suffering; it isn't our reality. Without its awareness, the body has no feeling.

SEEING INTO THE SPIRIT WORLD

After the death of our material body, our etheric body survives and can sometimes be seen. On occasion, and for their own purposes, discarnate beings have materialized to people still incarnate, making their presence seem very real. Ordinary people over the centuries and around the world have seen such discarnate beings—likely the origin of at least some ghost stories.

A couple of years before my ninety-six-year-old great aunt died, I visited her for the first time in several years. Although she was very frail, neither age nor infirmity seemed to have dimmed her characteristically sharp wit. Having lost her son in the Second World War and her daughter to a fatal stroke many years ago, she was living with her granddaughter and family. While we chatted, she frequently glanced up to a point over my left shoulder, where someone's face would be if they were standing behind my chair. She included that someone in our chat, referring to her as "Teen": her daughter's nickname. It was obvious to me Teen's presence was a normal, likely frequent, if not a constant, occurrence to my aunt. Including Teen in our conversation was as natural for her as it had been the last time the three of us were physically together. I don't doubt that Teen's presence was real to my aunt, but I do doubt it was a figment of her imagination.

This kind of occurrence is not uncommon with very old, very sick, or very young people. Children often have imaginary friends, who may not be imaginary at all. There is a spirit world all around us, usually invisible to our limited human eyesight. Children may not yet have lost their spiritual sight, and those near death may regain it. From reports of NDEs, I gather that usually the dying person is met on the other side by a loving guide, often someone they knew. Maybe on occasion the guide arrives early, maybe to help in their transition. Or, if we could see clearly around us, we might see many loved ones here all the time, perhaps helping us in some way.

THE ETHERIC BODY

Some people have seen the etheric body of a dying person leave their material body and float above it just prior to or at the moment of physical death. The etheric body is the prototype of our human potential. It's like the physical one in detail, except that, because it is of a higher vibrational order, it isn't subject to physical deterioration or mishap and doesn't age. It's a young adult, regardless of the age of its physical body and is ever healthy, strong, and whole. Disabled people have joyously reported after an NDE that their limbs were whole and completely usable. Moody tells of an accident victim, an amputee, who spoke of his out-of-body experience at the time of his accident, saying, "'I could feel my body, and it was whole. I know that.'"

RESTORED SIGHT AND HEARING

NDEs of unsighted and non-hearing people also help us accept the concept of the wholeness of our etheric body and our use of spiritual forms of our physical senses. While temporarily near death and out of their bodies, people without sight have *seen* everything occurring about them. They later accurately described in colorful detail things about their near-death scene they would have no way of knowing without actually seeing. People unable to hear have accurately related conversations taking place during their resuscitation. Some have reported things said outside in hallways or in waiting rooms. These kinds of experiences make it clear that our body is not us and that what we truly are, the Real living us, functions with all of our senses and without any of our body's limitations.

THE OTHER SIDE

If death is to be feared, why do so many people have a smile and look of serenity on their face when they die? Millions of NDEers have reported that what they saw on the other side was beautiful and love-filled beyond description. Nearly all have reported a pleasant experience with an extreme sense of well-being and love. Moody reported in an interview by John White, for *Science of Mind* magazine, that people who have had a near-death experience "...feel as though they are very different people and become more loving." With the NDE experience in their conscious memory, their contribution to the faith and comfort of others can be substantial.

Some NDEers have said they wanted to remain where they had gone, rather than return to their Earthly life. Many have said their life flashed before them so they could judge for themselves what they had learned, accomplished, and contributed. Some saw their purpose was not yet completed, so decided to return. In *Life After Life* Moody reports one such case,

> 'I was out of my body, and I realized that I had to make a decision... for me then it was perfectly clear—I knew that I had to decide whether to move on out or to get back in.
>
> 'It was wonderful over there on the other side, and I kind of wanted to stay. But knowing that I had something good to do on earth was just as wonderful in a way. So, I was thinking, "Yes, I must go back and live," and I got back into my physical body. I almost feel as though I stopped the bleeding myself. At any rate, I began to recover after that.'

Our real life off-stage is apparently far more love-filled and beautiful than whatever we experience here in our human roles. So we lose nothing and sacrifice nothing when we give up Earth life. Only bereaved survivors are sufferers, and then only to the extent it serves their purposes.

SPIRITUAL BENEFITS FROM THE DEATH OF A LOVED ONE

There are untold numbers of spiritual awareness-expansion purposes served by the death of a loved one, especially when seeming untimely. While often devastating, deaths of loved ones are our experiences, parts of our chosen scenario and of growth benefit to us as spirit beings. Some of us, when confronted with the death of someone close or are scared by a near miss, personally rethink our life and conclude that our relationships are more important than power, success, and material possessions. We value life more and take ourselves less seriously.

For some, shock caused by the untimely death of a loved one is instrumental in directing their attention inward. The death of a loved one more than anything else, may serve as an open door to survivors' spiritual journey. A sudden death, in particular, can cause someone close to question their own existence, the point of it, and its direction. It may cause some to question the existence of God. Such questioning, whether caused by bitterness or gratefulness, is worthwhile. For when we question, we get answers. Those answers or how they come may surprise us, but they will surely lead us in the best direction for us.

Such benefits of death may seem callous and not attributable to a loving God. However, while our worldly happiness may be shattered by apparent tragedy, the joy available to us through our inner real Self far exceeds any happiness we may experience through Earthly attachments. Our attachments are vehicles only; for our happiness most assuredly, but also for our experience of other emotions, all directed at expanded awareness and higher consciousness.

EMOTIONAL REACTIONS TO OUR LOSS

When a loved one dies, our sense of loss may be enormous. We may feel a void, accompanied by deep depression, as if some part of ourself has left us. We humans usually need to share our love with someone; and when that someone leaves, is no longer able to accept our love, we're temporarily empty of that love. We've lost something of ourself, so the loss is magnified.

We may feel it unfair of our loved one to leave us or for a so-called just God to take them from us when we needed them most or when life was just getting good. When death is sudden and unexpected, it always seems ill-timed, and often elicits reactive emotions. Anger, resentment, fear, and even hatred may arise, sometimes from thoughts of abandonment, loneliness, and helplessness. Sudden death can have a stunning and bewildering effect on those left behind, especially if death has never been discussed or in any way prepared for.

Guilt feelings, too, are not unusual following a sudden, unexpected death of someone we love. If death is by accident or other violence, there are always thoughts like, "If only I'd been with her, I could have protected her," or, "If I hadn't been late he wouldn't have been in that spot at that time." Then there are the thoughts about angry words last said or loving words unspoken. Today with drugs, drinking, and gangs so heavily involved, parents may feel they must have messed up in some way. I personally believe we can't mess up, that everything serves an ever-loving purpose, so no one is to blame. Guilt, then, while natural in our society, is unnecessary, but when experienced is still perfect as part of our awareness expansion through this physical experience.

It's often particularly difficult for youngsters to understand and cope with the loss of a loved one. Children are apt to take the death of a parent or sibling very personally. Knowing inherently there's a reason for everything and at the same time being naturally self-centered, children are apt to assume their parent left because of them. They may feel anger for having been left or guilt, blaming themselves for the death, especially if they had ever said, or even thought, "I wish you were dead." Or, they may think their parent would not have gone away had they truly loved their child. So, the earlier parents and their children talk about death, the better.

MY BROTHER'S DEATH

My brother, Chuck, my only sibling, died in 1990. He was just a year older than I, so growing up was a shared experience. After college he spent many years wandering around the world, first in the Navy, then in the State Department, and I moved to Oregon only three years after he resettled in Los Angeles. A bond between us withstood the many years of separation.

To me, his death was sudden, because I wasn't expecting it. He'd had pneumonia twice in the last year and a half, never regaining strength and health. I wondered about its debilitating effects—I hadn't thought of pneumonia as life-threatening in this day and age. But, he was on the mend, gaining weight, he had told me over the phone from a thousand miles away; all he needed was some rest and relaxation. For that, he went to Europe to spend a month. Only a few days into his vacation, he worsened and died while I was traveling to get to him. I experienced many emotions after he died. At first I was angry he didn't wait for me to arrive—he knew I was on my way. Maybe he didn't want to talk about his death, couldn't share it. What mattered most, I learned over there in Spain that my brother had died of AIDS. And I hadn't known he was HIV positive.

I mourned for a while, not for him in death, but for him in the last few months of his Earthly life; he had been so alone in his illness. But that had been his choice. I mourned for me; he hadn't shared his dying with me or anyone. There's no doubt in my mind that on some level he knew he was dying and went to his beloved Europe to die, alone. That non-sharing is what hurt the most. I miss him—his dogmatic way of arguing his point of view, his teasing, sharp sense of humor and his almost embarrassed show of caring without wanting to be obvious. I was angry, too, because putting his final affairs in order was something that fell on me. I got to share that part of his death, without benefit of intimately sharing that other, closing part of this Earth life together. I think "cheated" expresses best how our parents and I felt, and probably his closest friends too. We felt left out, excluded from one of the most important parts of a person's life. He chose to not share any of his ill-health and dying with his loved ones; why, we've all wondered. I'm sure, again on some level, he had good reasons, maybe more for our experience than his. Perhaps partly so I could write about it for others to read.

Although he was a very private person and generally unable to share feelings, there may have been more to his lack of sharing on this issue. For one thing, he may have been embarrassed—in the early years of AIDS it carried a stigma difficult to overcome. Later, I reached the conclusion that Chuck likely felt that talking about his illness and possible death, would be accepting it and would somehow make it real. Such thinking may have stemmed from our Christian Science Sunday School background, the only religion he'd ever known.

Obviously, though, his denial did not forestall his death. Instead, it only separated him from life and love with his family and friends. It put us far apart. I'm even more convinced now of the importance of open sharing, of life as well as death. How much more comforting, satisfying, and completing it would have been for my brother and for those of us who love him so much to have shared that part of our mutual experience in openness and love.

OUR RESPONSIBILITY FOR AIDS

If our society were to look hard at itself and take responsibility for its role in, for example, the spread of AIDS in America, it might see where change needs to be made. If society were to stop its bigotry and accept people as they are, no one would need to feel worthless and outcast. What society has done is the disease, and within society is the cure. Religious fundamentalists are largely responsible for such discrimination and bigotry. But they could serve humanity—and themselves—so much better were they to work on curing their own dis-ease: their homophobia; their bigotry regarding prostitution and drug abuse; their prejudice and persecution against people of other ethnicity, color, religion, and mental and physical acuity. They could follow Jesus' admonition to love everyone as themselves. Jesus said "judge not, that ye be not judged" (Matthew 7:1). They could be less judgmental.

One of the purposes served by AIDS in America and the mission carried out by those afflicted with it is to raise our society's consciousness to its own culpability and to help us be more loving and accepting. Haven't we had the judgment, bigotry and persecution scenarios long enough? Isn't it time for love and acceptance to take over? All the wonderful people dying of AIDS in Africa, I believe are parts of a mass consciousness-raising effort to help humanity more generally rise to a higher level, toward greater spirituality. Children infected with the HIV virus are certainly part of this consciousness-raising effort. Both children and adults are teaching us some vital lessons. We would do well to observe, learn, and respond from our hearts. Compassion is one of the most effective ways of raising our consciousness.

SHARING THE EXPERIENCE OF DEATH

Sudden death often leaves business unfinished, loving words unspoken, harsh words un-softened, questions unanswered, mysteries unsolved, experiences unshared. When we freely share thoughts about both life and death with our loved ones, we may prevent those later feelings of bewilderment, anger, remorse, and guilt. Concern and grief are honest emotions nearly impossible to hide. Why try? When facing the death of a loved one, share your heartfelt thoughts frankly. Your last days together might be more comfortable and even enjoyable, for both of you. They may bring a new closeness you will cherish forever.

The loss of a loved one to age or a lingering terminal illness gives us time to prepare ourselves, at least to the extent that's possible. It also allows us after the person's death to be thankful our beloved is no longer suffering. This thankfulness is soothing to our sense of loss, sometimes enabling us to better cope with it. Guilt feelings can creep in, though. We may think we shouldn't feel so angry, so abandoned when the other person is much better off. We think we're being selfish or self-centered, and feel guilty for seeming not to care more for the benefit of our loved one. Don't feel guilty. Those are natural feelings, and we have no good reason to try to control or deny them. We have no reason to care what anyone else might think of us, including our dearly departed. Those on the other side of life see us only with love. They don't judge us for anything we feel or do. They want us to do only what we want to do in our best interests.

While never easy, openly sharing a dying is easier for survivors to cope with than a sudden death. I think this means we ought to share each day fully with those closest to us, making time to do and be together. Nothing is more important. Those of us who can would be smart to express our feelings and emotions as they come along or change. That might help others get in touch with their own emotions and learn to express themselves more openly.

DEATH IS A TRANSITION

Death is a transition from one life situation into another, no matter how it comes. Our consciousness transcends the Earth plane into a spiritual level of existence, while our body changes from the human form back to its original elements.

Whenever I hear someone speak of death as a *tragedy* or say that someone was "*saved* from death's clutches," I ask myself why death is considered such a terrible thing. The 1994 euthanasia law, passed by Oregon voters was quickly struck down by the courts as unconstitutional, to the great relief of the majority of Oregon doctors who would be required to help administer the law. Health professionals will usually do anything to keep a patient alive, no matter the conditions or resulting quality of life. Oregonians had to overwhelmingly pass the law a second time to let lawmakers and doctors know we were serious. It's still under dispute.

I won't argue who has the *right* to take a life—the individual, the state in execution, a soldier in war, or only God—I will argue, though, that death is not the worst thing that happens, not for starving or diseased children any more than it is for miserably pain-ridden octogenarians. William Mitford, an English historian of the late 18th and early 19th centuries, wrote: "Men fear death, as if unquestionably the greatest evil, and yet no man knows that it may be the greatest good." Death is actually a release, freeing the actor from pain, discomfort, and limitation, as well as the confines of the physical body, the restrictions of its role and play scenario, and the haze of the human condition. Death is clearly a transition from one part of our life to another.

It's one thing to feel sorrow for surviving loved ones in the wake of a death, but another entirely to mourn the *loss* of their life. Both our life here as humans on Earth and our life after we leave here are parts of our continuing life as spirit beings. They are equally important, equally valuable to our awareness-expansion, and equally enjoyable to us as spirit beings. Life on both sides of the veil is to be revered, glorified, and enjoyed.

If you are living the aftermath of the death of someone very close, miss them, but be grateful for the time and experiences you shared. Move on with your life and let yourself learn from your experience of loss. I believe your loved one would not want you to pine your life away, unless you truly want to. Know there are no accidents; every event in life serves a loving purpose. Know that each of us—including both the villain and the victim—is an expression of a loving God, and that we voluntarily participate in each other's plays of life. There are no real victims and no villains. Know that every being that departs this life goes into a wonderful place and state. When a loved one dies, you are bound to feel loss and grieve for that, but don't grieve for them. Be grateful for them. Death is not an end, but a change, and always for the better.

Know that you won't be separated completely from your loved one(s) at death. When death comes, the being's consciousness continues to live in spirit. You and they are never really separate. Even now, when you sleep, you play together in other dimensions. Your actor self, your awareness, continues to meet loved ones in the spirit plane while your body and intellect sleep. There is no separation except in the human mind, and that too is for good reasons.

It seems clear to me that at bodily death, life—consciousness—continues uninterrupted with a far different perspective. According to Rocco A. Errico, the word "death" in Aramaic, the language Jesus spoke, means "not here, present elsewhere." And Chief Seattle said "There is no death, only a change of worlds." As Henry Scott Holland so eloquently put it in the *Readers Digest*:

> I am standing on the seashore. A ship spreads her white sails to the morning breeze and starts for the ocean. I stand watching her until she fades on the horizon, and someone at my side says, "she is gone." Gone where? The loss of sight is in me, not in her, just at the moment when someone says, "she is gone," there are others who are watching her coming. Other voices take up the glad shout, "here she comes," and that is dying.

APPLYING THE INSIGHTS

- Can you see how talking with loved ones about death will make acceptance and conversation at the time somewhat easier? Can you see also that sharing emotions at any time is a good thing? There's little point in dwelling on what to do when facing death, yours or a loved one's, because most likely when it occurs everything will change, but when faced together the process can be healing..

PART FOUR - MAKING THE MOST OF OUR EARTHLY EXPERIENCE

He who knows others is wise, he who knows himself is enlightened.

~ Lao Tsu

14

AWARENESS *vs.* JUDGMENT

The chapters in this part are all introspective in nature. In some, using my own self-reflections and their benefits, I encourage you to honestly examine your own thinking. I believe it is our own personal thinking which gives us our view of life, and I try to show how that works. Would you like to see your life as I do? Would you want to make the most of this wonderful experience?

Our adventures here in Earth life consist of experiences made possible by interaction with other beings and by participating in or observing events as they occur. According to my truths, our responses to what we encounter throughout life form those experiences, not the people and events themselves. We humans have been endowed with intellect in order to judge, react, and emote. Without emotional reactions we would remain always serene, unperturbed by anything in life. Since that is our natural spirit condition, without the judgment of intellect and our emotional reactions, physical existence would contribute very little to our awareness. We are in this Earth life to know our spirit Selves and Reality through the contrasts of physical separation and everything else we are not. Neither our spirit consciousness nor our human awareness could have evolved to where they are without this process.

PROGRAMMING INTELLECT

When born into Earth life, our intellect views a clean slate. As we experience, we fill our slate, using the positive and negative dualistic forces of the world in which we live. Our immediate environment and society further program our intellect to judge and react. We program intellect to judge everything it experiences and then react from that judgment. For instance, our intellect learns to associate certain features, characteristics, actions, and words with good, desirable, attractive, nice or with bad, objectionable, fearsome. We overlay those dualistic criteria on our experiences to form value judgments that further program our intellect. We then unconsciously compare each new person and event with past similarities and judge them accordingly. This process becomes ingrained and automatic, what I call "conditioned mind action," or "conditioned intellectual programming."

We perform conditioned mind action in subtle ways on a daily basis without realizing it. Nearly everyone we meet gets unconsciously evaluated by intellect against images from our past and our conditioning, so do we (our own physical characteristics, thoughts, talents, and behavior), so do our experiences. Emotions are stimulated by this automatic application of a conditioned mind.

> There are some minds, like either convex or concave mirrors, which represent objects (people, things and events) such as they receive them, but they never receive them as they are.
>
> ~ Joseph Joubert, French moralist

What we thus see in new acquaintances and situations, if they seem similar to a prior experience, is apt to be completely inaccurate. Our impression has little or nothing to do with them and everything to do with our memory of a prior experience, and could not be a true representation of the thing or person itself.

JUDGING

The more apt we are to judge people and events (condition our intellect) and the more experiences we accumulate on which our intellect can base prejudged reactions, the more likely we are to react automatically to later similarities. The less inclined we are to judge in the first place, the fewer bases we have for future automatic judgment of people and conditions that seem similar. If we accept people and events as they are, without evaluating them as positive or negative, we won't later compare others to them and react accordingly. We'll have no basis for comparison. And we can enjoy people and events as they come to us.

DUALISTIC STATES

The dualistic states, the positives and negatives we set up to experience, are only seemingly opposing, for they're really complementary. Positive and negative are merely two views of the same thing. We made things seem dualistic so we could know perfection more thoroughly, to better appreciate what we already had. Just as shadows give depth to form, negatives provide us a depth of experience in which positives alone would be flat, uninteresting, probably unrecognizable, and of little value. Rather than thinking of positive at one far end of the dualistic teeter-totter and negative at the other end, it would be more accurate to view the seesaw as a continuum of values from one end to the other. There are degrees, in blending gradation, all along the way.

BEING LESS JUDGMENTAL

The less judgmental and more aware we are, the more we see of the degrees. In a sense, the more beautiful each multifaceted state is. We eventually see the continuum without emphasis on any part. One segment is no heavier than another; the teeter-totter of duality is balanced. Without judgment, awareness strengthens. By experiencing life with less judgment and greater awareness, we gain so much more than just experience. We see more than just one side of a situation, and are appreciative of experiences for the sheer joy of doing, being, living.

Besides, each of the opposing states is circumstantial and subject to interpretation, relative and a matter of judgment. Isn't it true that what one considers poverty may represent wealth to another? What is ugly to one is beautiful to another. What is justifiably right to one is unconscionable to another. No two people judge things exactly alike. Also, our judgment is fickle, it changes. Our assessments of people change as we know them better. Our values and priorities change. What we think appropriate one day may be all wrong to us the next.

Dualistic states are part of our Earth experience, and have made possible our evolution to this point. Now, though, we must overcome their control over us so we can evolve further, back to consciously aware spirit beings. It's time to learn to balance the dualistic teeter-totter. By stopping the ups and downs of our thinking, we establish a balanced awareness of life. We live in the now filled with serenity, joy, love, and beauty. We see everything more clearly in its continuum. We can balance the teeter-totter only by lessening the force behind the unbalanced state: judgment.

AN EXAMPLE OF JUDGMENT'S AFFECTS

Although not always what may be described as a typical Virgo, I possess the very Virgo trait of analytical, often critical, judgment. I have always been confident in my use of "good judgment." My natural way of functioning has been from intellect rather than from heart or feelings. Early in my search for truth, however, I read William Samuel's *A Guide To AWARENESS and TRANQUILITY* and learned how judgment affects our thinking and emotions in our everyday life. I gleaned many insights from Samuel's book, but nothing he said was so effective as a story he tells from his own experience with regard to judgment.

In military service during the Korean War, Samuel commanded a rifle company in close contact with the enemy. He tells of one machine gun that every few minutes hurtled bullets just over his company's heads. It went on day after day and night after night, not doing any actual damage, but making his nerves raw. That gun became an obsession with Samuel. Repeated attempts to destroy it failed, and he finally gave up "completely, utterly, in hopelessness and helplessness." When his intellect surrendered, Samuel was filled with light, "...an instantaneous block of knowing." He relates:

> It was as if an inner and outer Presence absorbed me suddenly and violently to force my attention. It seemed to ask 'What is bothering you so much?'
>
> 'The bullets from that ungodly gun,' I answered.
>
> 'But, those bullets didn't hit you or anyone else,' the Voice within spoke. 'Thousands of them have passed overhead and not a one has touched you. They are falling harmlessly into the valley below.'
>
> 'It's the sound!' I almost shouted. 'The incessant sound is cutting through me like a knife.'
>
> 'Listen to me carefully,' said the Light. 'A sound is just a sound. What is the difference between the sound of thunder and the soft sound of rain? What is the difference between the sound of the gun and the sound of music? Aren't all of them simply sounds within Consciousness you are?'
>
> 'One is good and one is bad!' I answered vehemently.
>
> 'The sound that has you at your wit's end is a bad sound?' the Light asked me.
>
> 'Yes! My God, yes!'
>
> 'Has the sound a power of its own?'
>
> For an instant I seemed supra-conscious of sounds of every tone and intensity. Then the Light asked again, 'Has the sound a power of its

own to make you call it good or bad? Tell me, has the sound the ability to make you detest it?—or love it?'

'No,' I nearly whispered.

'Has someone twisted your arm and forced you to call that particular sound bad?'

'No.'

'Then tell me,' the Voice asked, 'if the sound has no power of its own and nothing external has forced you to make a judgment, who determines that what you hear within yourself—within consciousness—is good or bad to you, tranquilizing or upsetting to you? Who is the sole judge who has decided the sound of the gun is bad?'

'I am,' I answered.

'Yes, but Awareness is your identity; the Awareness-you-are simply 'hears' the sound, and Awareness is not a judge! Judgments are made by judges, and judges suffer from their likes and dislikes, from their 'good' and their 'bad.' That is the one who suffers, at his own hands from his own foolishness, but Awareness does not suffer. Dear Bill, you are Awareness voluntarily playing the role of judge, reaping all he has sown.'

...Suddenly I knew! I alone make the decisions I like or dislike; I alone am the master of such notions of the sights and the sounds. The sound making me so miserable was my own judgment that powerless sounds were bad and I didn't like them.

A great story, isn't it? Samuel's experience, reinforced by my intuition, left no doubt in my mind as to the cause of such as fear, stress, and much of our unhappiness.

THE EFFECTS OF SAMUEL'S STORY ON ME

Samuel helped me see that I alone—my thinking, my reactions—affect how I perceive my world. With joy, I realized that I never again *have* to feel frustration, anger, inadequacy, guilt, or any other negative emotion. Such were only the results of my own assessments of the situations I encountered. Negative emotions resulted from my making value judgments on people and events.

I also realized that this situation might have to be true of positive emotions, too. In being less judgmental, would I lose the ability to enjoy life? I thought about this a long time, and finally decided it didn't matter. I could live with fewer emotional highs if it meant lessening the lows. Since

I longed for tranquility, I chose to change my way of looking at the people and events in my life.

Modifying my normal life-long pattern of judging has demanded great effort and perseverance, but was made easier by Samuel's illuminating tale and my strong desire to change. I found a whole new way of viewing life, which is infinitely more pleasing and satisfying than the old emotional ups and downs associated with judgment. I have, for the most part, replaced judgment with awareness, with which to merely observe life, its people and events, without applying either the positives or negatives of dualism and judging them. And, I can let myself judge anytime I want. I can actually enjoy an occasional low whenever I want. My life is in my conscious control. It also helps to know that we are all ONE, equals in consciousness, and that everything happens for a loving reason and is perfect. No judgment is necessary. But I didn't know these "truths" back then.

This change in my thinking has had a great influence on my life and its relationships. I now know that both unconditional love and tranquility are impossible in a judgmental environment. Just as surely, I know that one can see so much more and so much more clearly through the eyes of awareness than through judgment, no matter how "good."

I not only made every effort to lessen judging, but consciously sought to know myself better and to become more aware of the world around me. I began observing myself and the people with whom I interacted. I found I could actually see how my reactions affected me and then how those effects were mirrored back to my environment for my subsequent reactions. These observations helped me to be still less critically judgmental of myself, others, and events. It's a strange and fascinating process. I often have two lines of thought going on at once. One is interacting with my environment while the other is observing and taking it all in. I watch myself and others enacting our parts in the play and have improved my ability to control how people and events affect me. Often now, I can respond rather than react to them.

RESPOND OR REACT

The choice here is between reacting with intellect and its judgments or observing with awareness and responding consciously, determinedly. Webster defines respond and react as follows (emphasis added):

Respond: To act in return or in answer. To react *positively* or cooperatively.

React: To act in response or *opposition* to... To be *affected* or *influenced* by circumstances or events.

We can either *respond* or *react* to each person, place, and event in our life. When we react, we are (convincingly) making believe that life is happening to us, that control is outside of us. When we respond, we know we control our life and we dictate what affects us and how we are affected by it. Events take place around us and people say things to us throughout our day. It is our choice how we receive them, whether we react to them, giving them control and power or respond to them from a positive, in-control, happy frame of mind. Another response is to ignore whatever it is. When we're in a bad mood, our responses are more apt to be reactive and negative than they are when we're in a positive frame of mind, our attitudes are self-perpetuating.

IMPROVED RELATIONSHIPS THROUGH SELF-AWARENESS

By seeing how I am affected, I can empathize with others as they react to their environment. By better knowing myself, I am more apt to accept myself and automatically am more accepting of others. I think I'm more caring and thoughtful, too. Also, I find I now seldom burden others with expectations, and I don't place expectations on myself as much as I used to either. I feel freer and I think maybe my loved ones do too. They may even feel more loved.

A wonderful thing about self-awareness is that, while heightening my self-acceptance and sense of worth, it actually has made me less self-absorbed. I am more aware of the needs, moods and interests of others. And, although I am more likely now to consider my own happiness and do what I enjoy, I am more considerate of others. I am more flexible in my likes and dislikes, too, not as picky or demanding. Little things aren't worth arguing or being upset over. My values have changed; I'm not as materialistic, not as superficial as I once was. I feel I'm more true to myself.

In general, my relationships are more satisfying, less troublesome, less argumentative. Not only am I better able to discern the needs of others and respond accordingly, but I can recognize mis-communication at the outset and avert misunderstanding. I am less likely to be disturbed by how others behave and less likely also to do those things which are apt to disturb others.

Expanding My Awareness

My self-awareness has intensified my general awareness, too, and made it more positive. I see beauty all around me now, where before I either was too busy to see it or didn't recognize it. Because my mind and emotions are no longer controlled by petty sensitivities, negativity, and judgment, I'm aware of so much more. I see patterns in clouds and colorful details in flowers, trees, and birds I was too self-engrossed to notice before. I see so much more of what is going on around me.

Awareness is a marvelous thing. The more I use, the farther it reaches and the more I want to use. The more acute my awareness becomes of my own emotions and their causes, the more I become aware of higher guidance in my affairs. The greater my awareness is of my environment, the more I recognize God in its beauty, and the more clearly I see the Oneness. I feel closer to the trees, animals, birds, spiders, and snakes, because I realize that we all are expressions of God.

ABATE JUDGING

If you choose to become less judgmental, tell your intellect that its past judgments were necessary to your past experience and your growth but that now you no longer want to continue judging so much. Thank it. Tell it that what you observe in others is not yours to judge. After all, you've no idea of the background or needs of others. You're really in no position to judge them, ever. Besides, since we're all enacting plays, what's to judge anyway? It's all relatively unreal!

I don't know that we can eliminate judgment entirely—or that we want to—but we can lessen our critical judgment. Through self-awareness, we can become aware of when our judgment is influencing our behavior in self-centered or negative ways. Then we can decide if that's how we want to be. The more we become aware of our own thoughts and feelings, recognizing the judgmental factors involved, the better we know ourselves. The less judging we do, the more apt we are to accept ourselves. The better able we are to know and accept ourselves, the less apt we are to judge others. As judgment recedes, overall awareness expands.

EXPANDING AWARENESS

Expanded conscious awareness is essential to your transformation, your Shift and your awakening. Perfect awareness is appreciation in the absence of judgment. Observing people's actions without right or wrong assessments of them enables you to be aware of the people for themselves. Observing without like or dislike decisions gives you freedom to enjoy everything. Without judging whether something is pretty or ugly, you become aware of beauty itself. You can know perfection by not judging anything as good or bad. Without conditioned mind action, you can love everyone, yourself included. Your new mission is to experience physical life without judging it as heaven or hell. By minimizing judgment, you are free to be, in full awareness.

APPLYING THE INSIGHTS

- Look back a few weeks and try to see what effects your judging has had on you. You may need to examine only the last week or merely a few days. Be sure to include judgments you've made of yourself, and keep in mind that the conditioning of our youth is the most ingrained, especially pertaining to ourselves. Ask yourself if your thoughts generally are judgmental or your emotions the result of having made judgments. When you can think of an opposite for what you are thinking, you're using dualism and being judgmental. When you think "should/n't," or when you watch someone's actions and think them wrong or right, you're judging. Don't feel guilty when you realize you're judging; that, too, is judgmental.
- Are there certain kinds of experiences you don't like and avoid because you once had an unpleasant time with that kind of experience? Are there certain people you prefer not to be around because they remind you of someone in an earlier part of your life by whom you felt betrayed, scared, or hurt in some way? Would new experiences or people possibly be more likeable if you hadn't had the earlier experiences with which to compare them?
- See if you can't find some way to make those earlier people and experiences acceptable in your mind. Then see if you can't look at new ones without comparing them to the prior ones. See if you can't enjoy new people and events as new experiences.

- For a couple of weeks, notice your judgments and do your best to lessen the critical ones. At the end of each day, think over the day, counting the number of critical judgments you made and enter them in a simple log. See if you can't make the number smaller each day or at least the ending day when compared to the first couple of days.

15

GETTING TO KNOW AND LOVE OURSELVES

Do you sometimes feel that everyone around you is better than you? Do you wonder if you can do anything really well or successfully, or if you're doing right by your children? Do you worry that you're not attractive enough, sexy enough, interesting enough to attract or hold a partner, not just any partner, but your ideal partner, your soul mate? Despite appearances of poise and self-confidence, everyone has such feelings.

I was a business executive from the late 1950s to the mid-1970s, during which time I took an MBA program for women executives offered at the UCLA School of Business. All twenty-some of us attending were sponsored by our respective companies, all capable executives, in or destined for upper management. The program covered every subject, from business law, economics, and accounting, management and personnel practices, to public speaking. The psychology professor drew an admission out of each of us privately to the effect that we felt inferior to everyone else in the class. Then he revealed that, without exception, every one of us had admitted such feelings. He said that the same was true of every man he'd ever taught in the similar program for male executives. That revelation greatly surprised me, and impressed me more than anything else I learned in that program. I found it comforting to know my self-doubts were "normal," that in them I was far from alone.

We've been programmed since childhood to believe we're inferior, imperfect, sinful. We've also been programmed to judge ourselves and others and to expect certain behavior and achievement of ourselves and others. That programming has been wrong and needs to change.

OUR SOCIETY'S LOW SELF-ESTEEM

While we all feel some inferiority or insecurity at times, many of us seem to live with a low self-image. This is partly because our society has discouraged self-esteem, equating it with vanity and egotism, and because fundamentalist Christianity—so dominant in our society—views us all as sinners, causing us to feel guilty. It's also due to long-time, rampant child abuse. A great number of people have a history of abuse, whether sexual, physical, or emotional, which has left many of us with deep emotional scars and a low sense of self-worth.

Usually because they were abused as children, most of the people who violate the established laws of our society have little or no self-esteem. They, therefore, also have no regard for anything or anyone else. They are angry with the society into which they cannot seem to fit. They detest themselves and are able to show the world only their anger and hate.

The same is true of so many of our youth. Many children take to alcohol or drugs to hide from a low self-image. Teenagers join gangs in search of self-esteem. Some fall easily into a life of crime, expressing their anger and lack of regard for self, others' lives, or property, and the law. Some gain temporary independence as a result of their life of crime that enables them to stand tall with their peers, until they get caught or killed.

HIGH SELF-WORTH

In sharp contrast, happy, self-assured people with high self-esteem view their conditions and the events in their experience with a positive attitude, so their happiness is perpetuated. It's also infectious. They exhibit happiness for the world around them to reflect, and they attract other happy people to them. Happy, self-satisfied people are our favorite loved ones, friends or associates, because they can give of themselves freely; they have nothing to lose and can only gain by giving. They can afford to be generous, caring, and loving; for the more they give, the more they have to give. They have nothing to hide or fear, so don't get caught up in possessiveness or other petty jealousies. They aren't constrained by inhibition, limitation, or pretense. They act, not selflessly, but because they want to for their own pleasure and peace of mind.

SELF-LOVE

Christianity has convinced our society that self-love is sinful and that selflessness is a virtue. It's taught us to think of ourselves last, only after the needs of everyone else have been seen to. Failure to live up to this altruistic standard of virtue has caused guilt complexes and produced hypocrites. While, philosophically speaking, it might be nice, it's not realistic.

What is self-love? It isn't vanity, pride, or selfishness. It isn't self-absorption. It's more an acceptance of yourself as you are and of your talents and capabilities as they are. It's respect and confidence in your ability to successfully do whatever you put your mind to do. We all have love inside awaiting our attention and acceptance. You are love. Knowing that you are as much God as everyone and everything else, you can extend some of the love you are to yourself. Then, also knowing that everyone else is as much God as you are, your love can flow out to everyone.

The only way to truly love another, I believe, is to feel the love that is inside. Self-dislike and self-contempt extend outward to others just as love does. When we emit a distorted view of self to our surrounding world, it reflects back to us with a distorted view of life. If we don't first love our self, the only love we extend to others is demanding, smothering, or superficial. It can't be unconditional and deep-seated without the self-respect and self-confidence that are part and parcel to self-love. Oh, I know, sometimes it takes another's love to give us the confidence to accept and respect ourselves. Honestly, though, it's a lot easier the other way around. We are much more likely to attract another's love when the love in our heart has surfaced.

Why do we fight the idea of self-love? Probably because it inspires a mental picture of egotistic, vain, selfish people, who never give a thought to anyone but themselves. Such people don't love themselves. Their facades are designed to hide inner fears and insecurity. The term "self-love" causes such reactions in us because of negative conditioning by misguided, self-righteous people who lack understanding of both people and love.

NONJUDGMENTAL ACCEPTANCE

While the various forms of love may differ from one another, they have one thing in common: When we genuinely love someone, we accept them as they are. Oh, sometimes we make allowances for shortcomings, but, in general, we don't pay attention to shortcomings. Love truly is blind; not in the sense of hiding the truth from us, but from a critical perspective. We see the good, beauty, strengths and overlook or minimize the weaknesses; they just aren't important. When a loved one is criticized, we may rush to their defense, likely thinking ill of the critic. When made unhappy by a loved one, we're quick to forgive. As the saying goes, they "can do no wrong." These are natural reactions.

Because of this common denominator, I like to think of love as *nonjudgmental acceptance*, meaning strictly that: acceptance without judgment, loving unconditionally. Of course, there's also more to it than that in the deep feelings we often get with love. But maybe we can say that those feelings are the inner spiritual expression of our Self, while the unconditional acceptance part of love is our outer human expression of love. We are so used to judging ourselves and seeing only what we think of as our shortcomings and flaws that self-love doesn't come easily. So it's important that we stop judging ourselves.

If you want to love yourself and quit judging yourself, be willing to accept yourself as you are, with whatever flaws you see, no matter how you look in the mirror, whatever "stupid" things you do, or how you compare to others you admire. Quit telling yourself you aren't as attractive, outgoing, smart, talented, or fortunate in comparison with others. When comparing ourselves with others, we invariably choose to look at only the features, characteristics, and conditions we find attractive or would like for ourselves. We overlook the compensating weaknesses, flaws, or disadvantageous conditions that make them balanced human beings like us.

Each of us is a unique being, physically, mentally, and emotionally designed to experience just what we're experiencing to serve specific purposes in our awareness expansion. You are worthwhile, contributing to the growth experience of many, many other beings and are absolutely necessary in their lives. Accept this truth even though you can't see how it could be, and feel good about it. Besides, we each chose our own background and costuming before entering this play, so they can't be less than perfect for our purposes.

No Reason to Judge

Since people are only enacting their role for loving purposes, they and whatever they do aren't ours to judge. We don't know what purposes or mission anyone is fulfilling, and it wouldn't matter if we did; none of it is our business. We can accept them as they are. The same applies to ourselves. We and what we do aren't ours to judge either. Although we probably don't know our purposes, we can be sure they are loving and beneficial to others. We've been guided to do everything we've done, and it has all been perfect. So we each need to accept our self unconditionally as we are. We *can* stop judging our self and selling ourselves short. We still need to evaluate our thoughts and actions, though, to see that they are heart based or maybe that they need to change to become more heart centered.

No one can make you feel inferior without your permission.

~ Eleanor Roosevelt

Maybe someone, a parent perhaps, convinced you at an early age that you were worthless, dumb, or foolish. Put those judgments aside; that person didn't know what they were talking about. They may have tried to make you feel low to make her/himself feel higher. People do that, and they unconsciously do it to benefit both parties. It doesn't matter why. Forgive them and release your judgments. Your reaction to them is what you are dealing with now.

KNOW YOURSELF

According to a web site entitled *Know Thyself, Man's Ancient Quest for Self Knowledge*, a legend relates that seven ancient Greek philosophers, statesmen, and law-givers gathered at the Temple of Apollo in Delphi to inscribe "know thyself" over its entry. While it isn't known when or where the adage originated, both the Hindus and the Egyptians taught it before the Greeks did. "The essence of knowledge is self-knowledge," said Plato, while the Hindu Upanishads affirmed "Enquiry into the truth of the Self is knowledge." And William Shakespeare wrote: "Of all knowledge, the wise and good seek most to know themselves." I believe there is nothing more valuable to our personal happiness and our individual evolution than *knowing our self.*

Watch, through the eyes of self-honesty, as you go through life, and reflect objectively on your reactions to others and the events around you. Honest and positive self-interest and self-awareness will help you achieve happiness. By knowing yourself, you will understand how you got to your present state. If you want to change it, modify your thinking away from past programming, reactions, and behavior. Take responsibility for your own life, not with guilt or regret, but positively, recognizing your own thinking as the source of both your misery and your happiness.

Your current state is the combined result of a lifetime of reactions. So getting to know yourself could help you decide what reactions to keep and which ones to release. Your responses to people and events in your life can tell you a lot about yourself, if you're willing to look at them honestly. Ask yourself why you reacted as you did. Ask how you felt about the situation or event and then ask why. Don't judge your reactions or the reasons for them; just be aware of them. Be as objective and dispassionate as you can. Use the information however you want. Let it help you overcome pent up resentment, a low self-image, or to respond differently next time. Or, if you prefer, use it only to better know yourself. I marvel at the ways our soul/director has of getting our attention and of teaching us.

You Do All You Can Do

Stop placing demands and expectations on yourself. Although you may think it isn't good enough, what you do is all you can do under the circumstances. We each do all we can do at the time, and it's what we're guided to do. If you could do better or differently, you would. That is, if your purposes would be better served in another way, that's what you would do. It isn't that you'll never do better. You'll be happier, though, if you don't think in terms of good, better, best. Those are relative terms and solely dependent on judgment and perspective. They contribute nothing to the moment, except frustration and demoralization, unless you are the best; and then, that's only a judgment and temporary.

HAPPINESS AND HIGH SELF ESTEEM

> The foolish man seeks happiness in the distance; the wise man grows it under his feet.
>
> ~ E. Phillip Oppenheim

Quit looking outside yourself for happiness. Truly only you can make yourself happy or unhappy. You can be happy as you are, if you quit trying to be someone you're not. You are a unique expression of God. You are perfect and wonderful now and always have been. Your Self guides you in everything you do; can you do anything, then, that is less than perfect? Love yourself, as you are. When you love (nonjudgmentally accept) yourself, you will be so filled with love it has to get out. You then can share it with others, resulting in an overwhelming feeling of bliss. Giving from your own love, only adds to your supply rather than depleting it. And, we are all ONE, so when you love yourself you also on some level love everyone else, and they love you back.

Along the way to this heavenly state of love, be thankful for every bit of awareness you experience. Each little bit opens you to far more. Be grateful for the experiences of your life that enable you to know yourself. When you recognize the benefits you have derived from your experiences—the people and events—and are grateful for them, you are less apt to judge, yourself or others. You can truly accept and love yourself, unconditionally, nonjudgmentally.

Let nonjudgmental acceptance give you self-esteem, and make your love available to everyone else in your life to help them raise their self-image. You already have the love within you; all you need do is recognize and accept it. Accept love for yourself; accept the healing, all-powerful love as your very being. Let it flow throughout your entire body and consciousness and through you to everyone you meet. Let the love that is within you join forces with the love that surrounds you and let it call forth the love from within every other person.

APPLYING THE INSIGHTS

- Ask yourself if you can honestly say you love yourself. Does the idea embarrass you or make you squirm? If so, there's a reason for it. Can you think of what that reason might be? Is it a legitimate reason? Really?
- How would you gauge your self-esteem? Are there reasons for your assessment of yourself? Are those reasons outside of yourself, and do they make a fair assessment?
- Consider what you can do to raise your self esteem and to love (nonjudgmentally accept) yourself as you are. Realize that love and self esteem don't come from outside yourself, they come only from within. Are you letting outside people and events affect how you feel about yourself?

16

IMPROVING RELATIONSHIPS

Emphasizing that our Earthly growth experiences come primarily through interaction with other people in our chosen play, my Self often focuses my attention toward relationships. It puts me into learning situations, then helps me make the most of them. While involving me in a variety of conditions and personal experiences, my soul has made me aware of the interplay of involved actors and their emotions and driving forces.

I feel fortunate to have been exposed to such interplay, but especially to have been made aware of it as it occurred. Observing human nature in action has been my great privilege and blessing. It has not always been comfortable for me, but is clearly valuable in retrospect. The experience of watching interactions of others has helped me in my own relationships, including with myself. And I'm sure it has expanded my awareness considerably, helping me to be aware of other people and their situations, helping me be compassionate. It also made me realize how truly valuable good friends are.

FRIENDSHIP

Friendship is possibly our most beautiful gift to ourselves. True friendship is the purest form of love. It is acceptance without judgment, expectation, or obligation. It's mutual loyalty and respect. Sincere friendship can endure through hardship, separation, and time and is unencumbered by demands, obligations, or pretense. It involves respect and freedom: mutual respect for the rights, privileges and "space" of each other and freedom for each to be him/herself, to live our own life in their own way. Ideally, we each have such friendship, not only with friends but with our mate.

A relationship with demands, expectations, obligations, pretense, or distrust is something other than friendship. It isn't love and it can't sustain happiness. True friendship is a sharing, caring, companionship, ,and a giving with no strings attached. Friendship can be offered anyone and can be accepted by them but it cannot successfully be demanded or taken.

DISCONNECTING A RELATIONSHIP

Our feelings about another often depend on the extent to which our views coincide or on the nature of the other's response to us. For example, when a lover stops responding in our chosen ways, becomes indifferent, or perhaps falls for someone else or leaves us, our picture of them no longer conforms to our expectations. We're likely then to view them as uncaring, hateful, contemptible, and all that we despise. Our love may turn to hate.

Many songs express feelings of betrayal, claiming the lost lover lied all along. They make us feel sad and used. But, just because a person's feelings toward another are no longer loving doesn't mean they lied when they once said "I love you." All people change, grow in some way, and sometimes two people just grow in different directions.

Also, and contrary to popular opinion, the person jilted is rarely an "innocent victim." A happy, satisfied person is seldom drawn away from their happy home, the source of their satisfaction and contentment. A person able to share him/herself with another—share their life, thoughts, dreams, disappointments, interests—is not easily lured away from that environment. People who are loved unconditionally for themselves and are allowed to love unconditionally in return have no reason to be discontent. They can be themselves, without pretense or airs. They aren't judged for their thoughts, words, or deeds, not held accountable to the expectations of their mate. For them to be attracted away is next to impossible, unless otherwise planned for in their scenario, which in this case is unlikely.

Sometimes by prearrangement on the soul level, one person dissolves a relationship to allow both parties to find new sets of interactions and more satisfying relationships or to find a new direction of life. This is a part of their script and not meant to be hurtful. Every relationship—no matter how lasting, how deep the emotional involvement, or how fulfilling—is a worthwhile experience. As human life may have it, the less happy experiences are often the best teachers. Isn't it true in this life that we learn the most from our errors and failures? We more often than not learn the "hard way."

BREAKING UP AMICABLY

Change is the nature of human life. And when two people change in different ways, go in different directions, there's no reason for either of them to feel rejected or to reject the other. There's no reason that people who once were close, whether in friendship or partnership, can't remain close. Maybe their closeness isn't expressed in the same way, but there's no reason for animosity; no blame or hurt feelings are necessary. A nasty divorce or break-up is never a good end to a relationship that was once loving. Each person can continue to give the other their nonjudgmental acceptance, and their split can be amicable. If they want to they can remain friends.

WHEN LOVE TURNS TO HATE

Since love is nonjudgmental acceptance, when we fall out of love, we also may become overly judgmental. We may lose our tolerance for personality traits and habits we once accepted with love. What we once thought cute is now irritating. What we used to accept as just part of the other's individuality is now a major flaw in their character. Little quirks we overlooked before become big annoyances. Unless we can maintain the nonjudgmental acceptance natural to love we're apt to be super-critical, belittling and deriding whatever they do. We magnify and find contemptible every flaw we see in the other's character, every difference between us, every mistake the other makes. It's likely, though, that the very things in them we now dislike the most are things we do ourselves. We're looking into a mirror, designed to help us better know ourselves. We can realize what in our own attitudes and behavior might better change if we want to find happiness.

EXPECTATIONS

Disappointments arise when we judge others to have failed us. Expectations of others stem from our falling short of our own desires and dreams. We look to others to satisfy our needs, to bring us happiness. They can't, and we do them and ourselves a disservice to ask of them the impossible. We may transfer our perceptions of our own inadequacies to them. We need to learn to love enough to let people, including ourselves, be as they are, without expecting anything from them.

We are virtually incapable of accurately foretelling the kind of reaction our words and actions will elicit from another. Our expectations are based on our view of our own actions, accompanied by the knowledge of our intent and biased by our underlying desires. We never know another's true frame of mind at any time, so we can never be certain that our meaning will be what they interpret. If the other knows all of the circumstances surrounding our actions, they aren't likely to remember or weigh everything the same as we have. They aren't apt to react or respond to them as we would or as we want them to.

Since it's clearly futile to base our feelings and behavior on what we think others' reactions will be, we would benefit from dispensing with expectations; they only frustrate us and get in the way of happiness. Without being indifferent or insensitive to others' feelings or needs, we needn't overly concern ourselves with the effects our actions may have on them. We can act in our own best interests and toward our own happiness and let others do the same. We can even assist them in their effort.

NEGATIVE GAME PLAYING

We sometimes attempt to control others through negative game playing. People who lack a sense of self-worth and confidence sometimes think they have to manipulate other people to give themselves a sense of superiority, false though it is. When hurt by others, left alone, or don't receive the kind of attention or response we want, we cry when around them, materialize asthma, a headache, or other illness. We'll use any means available to get what we think we need or want.

Games of control can be destructive to a relationship, bringing only greater unhappiness, never attracting love, affection, and attention. No matter how much they love us, people respond more favorably to positive, happy attitudes than they do to negative ones. Once we begin being positive, everything in our life will reflect the positive attitude, drawing more positives to us. We'll find it easier to be happy and love-filled. In addition to past experiences and programming, our present frame of mind governs our reactions to the people and events in our life. If our frame of mind is positive, we are apt to view the words and actions of others as relatively positive, despite their intent. Negativity works the same way, but doesn't bring the happiness we seek.

HELP OTHERS GAIN SELF-ESTEEM

Using that positive attitude, help others gain self-esteem. When a person lacks confidence, they interpret everything they do and what others says as reinforcement of that lack. Never tear down, deride, or belittle another, even in fun. That can't raise your self-image or spirit, only drag you down. Instead, say what helps others feel good about themselves. Stress their capabilities and assets, encouraging them in whatever they do. Sincerely compliment them on their successes no matter how small, and thank them for anything they do to help or please you. The better you help others feel about themselves, the better you feel about yourself and the happier your relationship is.

RAISING CHILDREN

All of the above points are important to all our relationships, and especially with our children. Since I don't have children, you might wonder who I am to try to say how people "should" raise their children. Although I certainly have uninvolved observations, I will relate only what my Self has told me it wants me to say. And, of course, like with everything I write, you can take it to heart of reject it. What you do with anything I write is always up to you.

Children need love that is accepting and nonjudgmental, not demanding, smothering, or protective. Respect your children as individuals. Love them for themselves, not for who or what you want them to be. Teach them by your example, but don't expect them to follow your dreams or your path. Don't place expectations of any kind on your children. They have their own way to make, whether you agree or disagree with it. Be supportive of your children's endeavors, without interfering. Help them when they seek help, but not by doing for them. Give them every reason for self-esteem and they'll automatically do their best. Their best may not conform to your idea of best, but don't define best and you won't impose your version on anyone. No one can fall short.

CLOSER TO SPIRIT

We consider children unprepared for life and expect them to mature intellectually and behaviorally as they progress in age. We equate knowledge, experience, and life's conditioning with wisdom, so give only adults credit for such wisdom. Children have to learn judgment and the dualistic criteria to base it on, what we often equate with wisdom. Children are not born with the judgmental intellect we value so highly, so we consider them undeveloped until they acquire it.

> A child's world is fresh and new and beautiful, full of wonder and excitement. It is our misfortune that for most of us that clear-eyed vision, that true instinct for what is beautiful and awe inspiring is dimmed and even lost before we reach adulthood.
>
> ~ Rachel Carson *The Sense of Wonder*

Children are closer to the natural, loving innocence that many of us adults would like to recapture. They haven't yet outgrown, thus forgotten, the wonders of the spirit world they've recently left to enter human life. According to my Self, the inner selves of children are not really of such youth and immaturity as their outer form would suggest. There's no such thing as new or old souls. All souls have always existed as aspects of the ONE. What are referred to as new or old souls is probably a reflection of the number of Earthly human lives they've experienced.

We Program Our Children

Because it's the normal way in most parts of our society, we stifle and inhibit our children. We impose our judgments on them, teaching them our dualism and programming their thinking and behavior. We expect them to accept as their own the limitations with which we have learned to live. We quickly subdue their enthusiasm and teach them to hide their emotions. We want them to accept our values as theirs, teaching them that material wealth and possessions are the measure of success. We impress upon them the importance of winning, that even second place is losing. How do we unteach them?

If you haven't already taught judgmental programming to your children, you have the opportunity to allow them to teach themselves, from within. Show your children love, truth, kindness, positive thinking, and the value of intuition and you'll have to teach them little else. They won't need to learn to prejudge everything as we did, nor will they need to be taught right from wrong, good from bad. With love in their hearts and truth in their minds, they'll instinctively do what is good and right, by no others' values than those of their own inner Selves.

With self-esteem they won't want to overuse drugs, alcohol, or any other addictive substance or activity. They won't abuse themselves or others in any way. Teaching them to accept themselves without judgment enables them to extend that same nonjudgmental acceptance, love, to everyone and everything in their lives. In particular, teach them to be kind to their peers and to never bully or make fun of another. Trust them.

Do everything you can to minimize your child's competitive nature and in the process reduce your own. Don't encourage your child to compete in anything they do: sports, the arts, grades, friends. Instead help him/her to enjoy those things as processes, for the fun or pleasure in them. Competition actually stymies greatness, and can hurt the child in the process. Enjoyment in participating in what he/she loves doing builds and enhances this capability.

Children are born unafraid. They are born accepting and open. Unfortunately, most TV cartoons teach our children to fear a boogie man who lurks under their bed or in the closet and reaches out to grab them at night in the dark. To counter this, remind your child of the comfort, warmth and peace of the dark womb from which they've recently emerged. Help them feel comforted by darkness, not by fighting the boogie man, but by loving it. Often those cartoons are violent and show beings killing each other, but then they have the "dead" one rise up unhurt to battle again. Such cartoons lead children to see violence as not truly harmful, and give them an unrealistic view of life. They encourage bully actions and violence as a way of responding to others. Check out the cartoons and other programs your children watch, and be selective of the ones you allow them to watch.

Children often have invisible playmates. But, just because we can't see them doesn't mean they aren't there. If kept as close to their original spirit world as long as possible, they won't lose sight of it. When you as a parent approach life from a positive mind set, you encourage your children to fill their lives with positives. And when you teach your children that they can do and be anything they want, you help them to achieve a rich, full, happy life.

LET YOUR CHILDREN LEARN THEIR LESSONS

Don't wish only the good, easy, and beautiful for your children, though, that's not how we humans learn. Besides, your idea of those conditions may not be what's best for them. Each individual must make their own choices and do their own living. Like you, your children have entered this life to progress toward awakening through expanded awareness by experiencing and helping others with their growth experiences. Don't do anything to deprive your children of their opportunity for growth, regardless of its form.

I have probably oversimplified all this about teaching your children. But, I hope you get the idea. I can't and don't intend to tell you how to raise your children. I can only suggest conditions and ideas for you to consider.

FORGIVENESS

Throughout our lives an occasional person does something that hurts or angers us. Some are loved ones or friends; others are or become enemies as a result of their actions against us. We're apt to remember their hurtful words or actions long after we've forgotten any nice or loving things they may have done. Hurt, anger, and hatred are emotions we've wanted to experience but may become counterproductive when allowed to fester and control our thoughts and behavior. For our own peace of mind and happiness, we would do well to make right those experiences and the people involved. Until we set ourselves free from hurt, anger, and resentment our relationships will be tainted by those emotions—if we even allow ourselves to be involved in similar relationships.

Nothing we or others do is bad, evil, wrong, or stupid. It's planned, coordinated, directed, and enacted to perfection to serve loving purposes. There is nothing, therefore, for which forgiveness is needed. But, since our vision is clouded by the veil of illusion, we can't see our own and others' actions for the perfection they truly are. So, we need to learn to forgive, although that erroneously presumes blame in the first place.

> 'I can forgive, but I cannot forget,' is only another way of saying 'I will not forgive.'
>
> ~ Henry Ward Beecher

If you can't forget, if you ever sadly or angrily relive in memory a hurtful experience, you haven't forgiven. So long as you harbor ill feelings, you haven't accepted the good afforded you by the experience. You can't forgive a person or circumstance by trying to bury the hurtful experience and saying, "I've forgotten it." The only way to truly forgive and forget is to look at the experience and make it right. It's bound to have been of some benefit to you; accept that benefit. Even if you can't pinpoint a benefit, know the event had love behind it and was one of numerous stepping stones to where you are now. Love everyone who has helped you along the way, and everyone has.

Look at and Release Hurtful Experience

Judgment creates the need for forgiveness. Only when you have judged and reacted negatively to someone's words or actions have you set up a condition in your own mind that requires forgiveness. If you allow people to do and be as they want without judging them and making their deeds offensive to you, you have no need to forgive them.

Sometimes a hurtful experience, especially in our childhood, is provided us to form a basis for strength or weakness which we will use later in life to help us act or react in ways we have chosen to experience. All circumstances are perfect and for everyone's highest good, recognizable as such or not. We would do better to actually make such situations right in our minds and release them. We make them right by accepting them for the love behind them. We might first let ourselves rant and rave, stomp our feet, throw things—get the venom out, all of it. When we've fervently released situations in this way, we can then fill the remaining void with love (nonjudgmental acceptance). The situations no longer have power to control us, they are no longer things we think about.

Think back to my recitation of William Samuel's story about the machine gun. Hurtful words of people in our life are very much like the noise of that machine gun. In and of themselves they are nothing, have no power to hurt anyone. We give them any power they have when we accept them as fact. We could just as easily ignore them, let them roll off our backs, or see them for the good that must truly have been intended (on a higher soul level).

LEARNING FROM MIRRORS

When another's words or actions, whether directed at us or not, provoke strong negative emotions, our attention is drawn there purposely for a constructive reason. Things about others which upset us are often problem areas in our own lives that we may not see. Occasionally a friend subtly points out a fault or hits a nerve with something they say. Our Self arranges such scenes as mirror imagery to show us something about ourselves that we would want to address if we were aware of it.

The negative game playing I mentioned earlier is one such thing I've observed people putting off on others. That is, a person who is heavily immersed in negative game playing, without seeing it in her own behavior, sees it all around her, and is disturbed by it. Another is being right. One person is terribly disturbed by what seems to her the fact that her husband always has to be right, when, from my uninvolved observation, it is she who has to be right. That's why, when her husband occasionally argues, it offends her. A friend tells me tearfully how nasty her husband is to her, but refuses to see that she treats him with contempt and derision. Recently on rare occasions he has begun to react to her negativity, and that is what she views as his nastiness. I guess she expects him to forever take her insults. The interesting thing is that she truly does not realize her contempt shows so she doesn't know what he is reacting to. She vehemently denies that she feel contempt. This sort of thing works both ways, of course. That is, we sometimes provide mirror images to which our loved ones and associates can react. It may only be their perception or their reading of an event or situation, but to them it is real as they see it, and they react to it.

Your world, everything you experience, is not only a reflection of your personal attitudes and beliefs but is a mirror of your own conflicts, fears, and cell-memory concerns accumulated over the course of your life. If you look around and see mainly conflict, fear, and deplorable conditions, that's because you have conditions inside you which are trying hard to get your attention. You may, perhaps unconsciously, harbor anger, hatred, fear, or frustration deep in your cell memory. And so long as it's there, you'll either see its reflection in your world or you'll feel it through pain or dis-ease or both. Anything you see out there in your world that strongly gets your attention is something inside of you. It's getting your attention because it wants to help you release it for your well-being and happiness.

You don't necessarily have to identify an incident or person as the culprit. And, it may not be one incident only. It could be a build-up of some way you see yourself, possibly instilled in childhood. It could be a combination of things. And that really doesn't matter. Just as your body is a whole enterprise sometimes needing holistic treatment, your mental/emotional being sometimes needs holistic treatment, too. Even when a condition can be isolated to a specific incident, your reaction to it affects the well-being of your whole person. So the whole person you are needs all the love and attention you can give it.

Assuming you probably have some residual emotion(s) hanging around from childhood, you would do well to get in touch with your inner child. You may want to let it rant and rave and spill its guts all it wants until it has exhausted itself and released whatever it was holding on to. Then you need to truly love the child and whatever memories its rantings stirred. You need to release all negativity, erase its power and appreciate its help in your experience of human life.

Were you to honestly and sincerely examine your own thoughts and actions, paying particular attention to the kinds of things in others that upset you or the things that most often provoke negative feelings, you might be able to improve your relationships substantially. The key here is "honestly." It wouldn't hurt to assume you do the things you don't like in others, then work at behaving differently. You may never recognize your own actions as being like that, but if you work at not being that way, you're bound to improve your behavior and your interactions. You won't subject people to such things, nor will others have to play mirrors for you to learn from.

I know, you may ask "Why bother, if everything and whatever we do is perfect?" Because it's perfect on a soul level, but not necessarily on this material level. And we came here to experience, and everything we each do adds to each other's experience; we don't want to escape or avoid any of it. Although your behavior doesn't *have* to be improved, if it is, you and your loved ones will be happier.

We also need to understand what it is to be self-centered. We can love ourselves and realize that we are the only one we can ever truly know and affect by our actions, emotions, and attitudes. We are the center of our own life, and that is intended. We can be self-centered without being self-absorbed or selfish. In being heart-centered, we can't be selfish or self-absorbed.

Sometimes people act from their own personal hell that has nothing to do with us. We are involved for our own benefit, which may have nothing to do with them. We may misunderstand someone's words or intentions, and harbor hurt feelings solely of our own making. Even if that's the case, there's been good reason for it. Maybe we want to learn to accept ourselves without judgment for the pain we caused and accepted to ourselves; who knows? We don't have to know.

Although you see no good reason for hurtful events having taken place, you can still accept that each was in perfection, because everything is. You can know that each other person involved was functioning under inner guidance, so could not have done anything bad, wrong, or mean; there had to have been a loving purpose for each hurtful action. And it wasn't yours to judge anyway. Any pain you feel is brought about by your judgment of another's words or actions. Only you can hurt yourself; only you can give yourself happiness and feelings of well-being. Although intellect may fight this idea, you can use your heart and accept it as fact. You can accept the love of each wonderful person, and love—nonjudgmentally accept—them just as they are.

ACCEPT AND LOVE YOURSELF

Accept and love yourself for ever having been hurtful, short-tempered, or sarcastic with others. Know that each such event was part of the play scenario, likely for yours and others' mutual benefit. Look at each such situation dispassionately, without guilt, then release it. My friend, Ishvara, used to say, "I'm guilty, I'm guilty, I'm guilty; so what?" Sometimes just saying that aloud helps. Never dwell on hurtful memories, letting them cause you pain. That gives them undeserved power over you. Instead, be grateful for both the events in the first place and your recollection of them so you can deal with them.

Love Is Behind Every Act

Know that love is behind every act, whether it hurts or stimulates happiness. Use your knowledge of that love to wash away any ill feeling you have. Love is the most soothing balm there is. With all your God-given power, love (non-judgmentally accept) any person and circumstance that ever seemed to cause you pain. Love, and you will open yourself to ever so much more love. By erasing hurt, anger, or resentment, create a void for love to fill—accept, then forget the incident.

Your relationships are the focal points of your play of Earth life. They provide the experiences through which you expand your awareness and thus your spiritual consciousness. They are, therefore, perfect and, regardless of appearances, formed and enacted in love. So, accept every person and every event as an outer expression of inner love, and you will be far happier in all your relationships. Be the love you truly are.

APPLYING THE INSIGHTS

- Have you disconnected a relationship, whether with a friend, or lover, partner, or spouse? Was it amicable; that is, did you part friends? Think about what you could and might have done differently had you known then that whatever happened between you to break you up was done for good, loving spiritual reasons and that the other person is truly a loving friend.
- Do you expect certain behavior from your loved ones? Make a list of your loved ones, then next to each name list what you expect of them. Think about each one, and see if your expectations are fair. Think what each relationship might be like were you to not expect anything of them, let them be their natural selves.
- Is there someone in your life whom you feel did you wrong, hurt you, betrayed you? Do you harbor ill feelings toward them? What if you were to look at the circumstances differently, seeing the true love behind what was done? Has your life been better in some way since then? Have you allowed it to be? Could you benefit from making the incident(s) right in your mind? Do it. Forgive and then forget the whole thing. You can, if you truly want to be happy

17

CREATING OUR REALITY

I believe that it is by our attitudes, thinking, and beliefs that we create the reality of what we experience in life. And William James, 19th century philosopher, seems to have believed the same thing, saying: "Human beings, by changing the inner attitudes of their minds, can change the outer aspects of their lives."

I believe that each of us has created our life just as it is and will continue to create the rest of it in two ways: by participating in the planning, casting, and staging of our play and by the way we view and react to the conditions, people, and events that make up our life. The latter is how we exercise our human freedom of choice and see our world through our beliefs and thinking. What we see in our world is not necessarily what's there or what anyone else sees; it is a reflection of our personal beliefs, thinking, and attitudes. We unconsciously superimpose our beliefs on our world and see it from that perspective. Our thoughts, then, are our own creative forces.

So, if we want to change anything about the world as we see it, we have to change our personal beliefs about ourselves, other humans, other beings, and Earth life generally. I probably make that sound easy when it isn't easy at all. Our beliefs are entrenched from life-long development and programming. But we can ask ourselves if our beliefs are our own or what others have taught us and we have accepted as ours. Most importantly, we each need to be certain that our beliefs are heart based and not self-indulgent, negative, or materialistic. Do we care about people who are different in some way from us? Does it matter to us that other species are endangered because of our human self-absorbed, indifferent behavior? Are our creature comforts, wants, and tenuous lofty status more important to us than the plight of starving and oppressed people throughout the world or the fact that polar bears are dying because global warming— regardless of cause—is destroying their habitat? But then, you are reading this book for some reason. Maybe you are already seeing yourself and all other Earth life a little differently than you did before you began reading about my beliefs. If that's the case, don't just switch from old beliefs that belonged to someone else to my beliefs. Be selective. Get your own beliefs. That's truly the only way to create a new reality for yourself.

FOCUS

Everything yet unmaterialized is in etheric form in the energy surrounding us. Our focus pulls it into manifestation for us to experience; such as those different people and endangered species everywhere. Our focus is determined by our state of mind, our thinking, our judgments. Our world reflects whatever is in our heart and that reflection is what we focus on. Perhaps by focus we animate the world around us. Does the world outside exist—live, move, and breathe— without our seeing it? Is there sound without our hearing it? Is there warmth or cold or pain, without our feeling it? Are you sure? Maybe nothing would exist at all if we were unable to focus our attention. By our focus, our world is beautiful and happy or it's ugly and sad. By our focus we direct our attention, expand or limit our awareness and create the reality we expect to experience.

For example, some friends had enjoyed a visit to Mexico, but said the poverty and squalor there were depressing. Later, Mauri and I went to Mexico, where we found relative prosperity and impressive cleanliness. We noticed women sweeping or mopping everywhere we went. We saw tidiness and beauty inside thick, sheltering exterior walls of homes and businesses. There were few sidewalks, streets were dusty, exterior walls were paint-chipped, and windows were barred and dust-encrusted. But inside were central courtyards lushly planted with greenery and splashes of bright colors, with clean glass doors and windows facing inward for people to enjoy partial sun, lots of shade, quiet, and privacy. Courtyards and rooms alike were protected from the harsh Mexican elements and the curious eyes of passers-by. They were cool, comfortable, cheerful, clean, and relatively prosperous looking. There is often a marked difference between the exterior facade and the real interior, whether in Mexico or here in the United States, whether a place, thing, or person. Focus, judgment, and expectations determine which we see.

By focus we see what we expect to see, based on our beliefs and what we've been taught about a place or person. By focus we live in the now, in the past, or in the future with the past and future moments influencing our now moments. By judgment we see around us ugliness, misery, poverty, and crime, or love, prosperity, and beauty. Also, when our thoughts are fragmented or scattered, the outer manifestation of them can be no more cohesive. We empower our thoughts to be forces by focus and conviction. This is so regardless of our awareness of it and whether we would consider our thoughts positive or negative. We create our own reality, good or bad, by our thoughts and attitudes and our beliefs behind them.

CHOOSING POSITIVE OR NEGATIVE THINKING

Focus is a choice. We choose what we see. How we see anything, while a matter of focus, stems from an attitude created by choice; for instance, happiness. Well-being also is a choice. So is misery. They all result from a single choice: to think positively or negatively. This one choice affects our entire life from the moment of choice, on. It affects how we approach life and how we view every condition, situation and event in our life. It affects how we view ourselves. This choice determines whether we tell ourselves "can do" or "can't do." It forms the basis for unconditional love or for guarded, controlling, jealousy-ridden, and unfulfilling half-love. It provides us a life of misery, drudgery, and poverty or a life of prosperity, joy, and bliss.

If we believe in negative concepts, like can't, shouldn't, limitation, fear, they will dominate our life. If we feel certain that unhappiness, ill health, poverty, or misfortune are ours, we can't avoid them. It's important to accept negatives and recognize the thinking that causes them. Our reactions to events in our life, stemming from programs based on our past experience and limited by judgment, create negativity in our minds. This conditioned consciousness is the only way and place we can experience negativity. Yet, if we wholeheartedly believe that love, happiness, good health, and prosperity are ours, we won't avoid those either. They are abundantly ours, by choice.

By choosing to think positively and by controlling our focus, we can create a positive reality. By focusing on love, peace, abundance, happiness, and good health: the positive side of life, we can literally turn away the negative side. Fear, anxiety, ill health, misery, and even poverty do not have to exist in our lives. I don't mean deny them. That has the opposite affect; it holds your attention on them. Instead, say to your intellect that while those negatives were parts of your reality yesterday, you choose to create a new, positive reality today, right now. Each moment, you can choose by your focus what you want to feel, think, and actually create as your reality, your world.

One day in our designer jewelry shop, Mauri and I had been talking with a visitor about how friendly the people were in our town. I went out and started up the street to go visit someone, smiling at other strollers and getting smiles in return, when I ran into a friend. Her head hung down sadly and she looked forlorn. I hugged her and cheerfully asked, "What's happening?" "I've got to get out of this town!" she said. "People are so nasty, so unfriendly here. I'm miserable here." We were viewing the same town and the same people, but from different perspectives. Our respective attitudes actually gave us quite different views of the same thing. Moving to another town would not solve my friend's problem. She will find all towns unfriendly until she chooses to view them positively, to be positive. Only a change in attitude will help her.

IMAGINED REALITY

Another way we create our reality is with our imagination. Some of our experience is day-dreamed rather than actually occurring.

THE WHAT-IF SYNDROME

Rarely are the outside happenings what frighten us; we scare ourselves by anticipating something happening to hurt us or a loved one. We what-if. Mark Twain, in his usual eloquence, said: "I'm an old man, and have known many troubles, most of which never happened." We seldom just let things happen as they will in full knowledge that everything is perfect. Instead, we anticipate what will happen. We create our own dramas in our minds. We imagine (what if) either the worst or the best, and rarely get either. What we do get is tension, anxiety, fear, and often disappointment. So long as we anticipate the future in this way, our reality will never be one of serenity. And spending our time what-if-ing is ruining our enjoyment of now.

When I went through the process of examining my thinking and attitudes, I found that any underlying fear I had was based on something that *could* take place in the future—what I what-if-ed. It was a figment of my intellect playing its part in my experiential growth. Once I realized this, I could laugh at it and love it.

Some years ago, I drove Highway 101 along the southern Oregon coast in a small pickup, pulling an ungainly travel trailer. Ordinarily I think that area from Port Orford to Brookings displays some of the most beautiful scenery there is. High wind gusts there, however, can be treacherous. That day the rain was horrendous and the wind fierce; gale warnings were out for gusts up to 60 mph. Even with the windshield wipers going at full speed, visibility was minimal. My shoulders were tense, my knuckles white as I gripped the steering wheel. I leaned forward as if I could see better closer to the windshield or because leaning into the wind would help get us through it. We were approaching an area just north of Humbug Mountain, which I knew to be especially dangerous. I was aware that wind gusts had blown heavy semi trucks off the road there. It was not the place to be pulling a trailer. I was anxious, to say the least.

I began talking to my Self, as I've always done in stressful situations. Soon I relaxed, remembering what my Self had impressed upon me: There are no accidents. I realized that either nothing harmful was going to happen or, if it did, it would serve a loving purpose for my higher good. I knew that my Self was in charge of my life, so I had nothing to fear. As we got past the critical area without a single gust, I allowed myself a small sigh of relief and a "Thank you, Self."

> That which is not to be, shall never be; that which is to be shall never not be;—why dost thou not drain this draught which will eradicate the poison of anxiety from thyself.
>
> ~The Upanishads, Vairagyasataka

It truly is comforting to know that nothing can occur by happenstance; that every event is purposeful.

DAYDREAMS

Our world—by that I mean our experience, our reality—reflects our thoughts and beliefs. So, when we daydream, we tell our world what we believe is true. Since we create our reality through thought, it's likely that whatever is in those daydreams, those thoughts, will be our reality. In most cases it is only our interpretation of our experience. Then we act on it or daydream further, and often compound our situation. If our original imaginings were negative, we will have created a whole negative scenario in our thoughts which we believe to be true, and everything that has been said or has occurred has reinforced that belief. We make it so. By creating the negative scenario, we are imposing that picture on the people and events in our life. We've created it as our reality.

If you have something going wrong in your life or some great frustration, think about your thoughts on the issue. Are your thoughts, your imaginings, positive about it or negative? Did you set the issue going in the "wrong" direction in the first place, perhaps by your judgment of someone or some circumstance or negative reaction to something said or done? Have you compounded the issue by focusing your energy and attention on it in negative ways? Are you preoccupied with it? Do you talk about it with others, in complaining ways? Has it grown worse as you've focused on it?

The only way to now improve the situation is to realize what effects your thinking has had on it, accept your responsibility in bringing it about and *know* that your thoughts can now change it. Since negative daydreams created the situation as you have been living it, by changing your daydreams to positive imagining, you can reprogram your experience. Create in your mind a wonderful fantasy about the issue to daydream. Make it believable, realistic, and see it happening, not in the future but right now. Believe it. You and you alone can improve your life. All you have to do is think positively, *be positive*. Daydream all you want, but don't let negativity into your dreams. Know that your dreams are as true as you can believe them to be. If your life can reflect your negative thoughts and beliefs, is there any reason your positive thoughts can't be believed and be your reality. Again, it's all up to you. Be positive in all your thoughts and your life will have only your positivity to reflect.

LOVE YOUR INSECURITIES AND RELEASE THEM

You might love your negative experiences and emotions as they come along and release them, without either ignoring or hiding them. By repressing your fears, insecurities, and other negative emotions, you push them deeper inside. They seek freedom so will reappear in some other form, including illness, until you set them free. Acknowledgment, love, and gratitude set the negatives free. Appreciate them for the opportunities they give you. Love them for their opportunities. One way to express love for negative emotions is to resolve them. Look behind them for their root cause. Ask yourself what in your life seems threatening in some way. What are you nervous about? By seeking out the underlying fear, you give the emotion its due. Then you can release it.

CONSCIOUSLY CREATING

If you believe your thoughts are creative, you can do anything. You can have anything or be anything you wish, so long as you focus your attention on the specifics of your needs and desires and believe in their fulfillment. Are you skeptical? Do you need proof before you believe that something will work, at least for you? All right, since believing is the crux of this matter, test it for yourself; don't take my word for it. Make this theory work for you.

Parking Places

One simple demonstration is to create a parking place on a crowded street or lot as you arrive at your destination. Many of us exercise this easy and practical capability regularly. But we don't necessarily realize the power it demonstrates, so don't think to apply it to other aspects of our lives. If you've never tried it, do so the next time you head somewhere that parking is apt to be limited. Just say to yourself, "I'd like a place to park near the entrance of...." Be specific, state your destination and whatever conditions you want met. Then relax and know your parking space is awaiting your arrival. Visualizing where you want the space helps. See it awaiting your arrival.

If this doesn't work at first, it's only because you don't trust that it really is a power or that you have it. You may think it only coincidence anytime it works. For your own enjoyment, give it a chance. Experiment with it a few times, just for fun. Try to put your doubts aside and let it work for you. Exercise your power every time you'd like a choice parking spot. Get your intellect to accept the fact that it truly is a power you have. Prove it by repeated demonstration. Get your intellect used to things working out as planned and get used to thinking in specifics.

I'm sure you've sat in your car at an unsignaled highway or intersection unable to get out or make your turn because of never ending traffic. Next time, as you approach the cross street, ask that a break in traffic let you out quickly, easily, and safely. See it as fact. That will be your reality.

Desired Weather

Another demonstration of your power is to dictate specific weather conditions. Yes, you can. Believe it and do it. Whenever you are planning a vacation, outdoor party, weekend camping trip or just a day working in your garden and want the weather to be nice, ask for it. Again, be specific. State the conditions you want met. State the type of weather and the duration you want. Be sure to be specific to the extent it matters to you. If you don't want a heat wave, don't say you want hot, sunny days. If you don't want a cold snap, don't just say you want cool weather. Don't use general, nebulous terms. Define what you want. Be sure also to state where you want this weather to exist. You probably would rather not drive from your perfect weather at home to the beach where it's foggy. In being specific, we focus our intentions and empower them.

When I first became aware of this power, I learned very quickly how specific I needed to be. Mauri had a beautiful one-acre vegetable garden, but faced an inordinately short growing season. Tomatoes were nearly impossible to grow, they didn't have time to ripen. Her corn also was in danger of dying still green on the stalks. It just wasn't hot enough. We confidently asked for warm weather to ripen both the corn and tomatoes. The following day began a terrific heat wave. The temperature went from the sixties to over 100 degrees. For nearly a week the temperatures wavered during the days between 102 and 108 degrees, setting daily records. The corn ripened, some of the tomatoes did too, nearly everything else in our garden bolted, and we wilted. Other than being enlightening, it was not a pleasant experience. Of course, like much of life, it had to be drastic and somewhat unpleasant to be the perfect teacher.

If you don't succeed immediately in one of these efforts, keep trying until you do. The only thing holding back your desired results is your doubting intellect. I exercise my power on a regular basis, because I know I can. You can, too, whenever you wish.

I'll never forget the first time Mauri alone applied her creative power to weather conditions. Four of us friends had gone to Hawaii on vacation. We had driven up above Waimea Canyon on the island of Kauai to what I had promised was a fantastic view, not of the canyon, but of lush green mountainsides fingering down to a verdant valley, a narrow sandy beach and turquoise sea. We found the mountaintop shrouded in thick clouds, however, allowing no view at all. Aware of my convictions in this area, my three friends asked me to dissolve the clouds. I had quickly busied myself taking close-up pictures of gorgeous flowers, so suggested that Mauri perform the necessary magic. Reluctantly, Mauri agreed to do it. She then confidently said, "If it doesn't interfere with any other plans, clouds please disperse so we can enjoy the view."

Although we'd been told by another sightseer that the clouds had been there for at least an hour, Mauri had hardly finished her request when the clouds parted. Not only was the view as I had promised, but golden rays of sunshine spotlighted the valley down to where the white sand met the green-blue sea, emphasizing its beauty, and wild goats scampered playfully on the nearby mountain side. We reveled in the majesty of our scene, snapping pictures to preserve it for posterity. Then the clouds returned like a curtain dropped on the stage, again obscuring the view. My friends were in awe of more than the beauty of Kauai. The clouds' parting and returning had been so specific, so sudden, so complete, no one doubted the cause. Mauri, because this was her first demonstration of this power, was more than a little shaken. Our friends were impressed, but I've yet to convince either of them of their ability to do the same, if only they believe. I don't always get the weather I ask for, but usually. When I don't, I'm philosophical about it. I think, *Oh well, there must be some good reason I didn't get it.* Usually the reason eventually becomes obvious.

BE CAREFUL HOW AND FOR WHAT YOU ASK

Practice materializing parking spaces and weather conditions until you are fully aware of your power. You'll see there's no limit to what you can accomplish. Then apply this power to other conditions in your life. After all, if you can control the weather, you certainly ought to be able to control your own life! Be careful, though, how you use this power. Use it in perfection and without interference or harm to another. Don't be selfish in your desires or in your means of effecting them. Don't insist on continuous sunny, warm days, for instance, because some rain or winter snow for recreation and summer water, is needed; a drought is not what anyone wants. Likewise, rain to provide water for crops and livestock is better limited to as necessary, to avoid destructive flooding. Don't insist on getting something specific if another party now has it. Be prepared to accept an alternative. The results will please all concerned. Whenever I make a request using this power, to insure that I'm flowing with loving energy, I begin with: "If it doesn't interfere with any other plans for higher good, I would appreciate...."

Be careful, also, how and for what you use this power. Keep in mind that God—the Kosmos, or Self—in responding to your request, doesn't judge but merely fulfills. Be sure you select what you truly want. You are apt to get it either way. Actually, you are telling yourself what you truly want, and, since this life and the materiality of our world are illusion, you are making that illusion fit your thinking. And when you get what you've asked for, don't forget to express your gratitude.

Leave Some Things to God

It might help to specifically list those things or conditions you really want in this life. Take a careful look at your list and determine those items about which you can do nothing. Leave those to God, your Self. Concentrate your efforts on those things over which you have control or which require effort on your part to bring to fruition. When you've turned over to your Self certain of your listed items, forget them. Know they're in good hands and will be yours when the time is right. Don't try to determine how; does that really matter? The ways of God are many and wondrous. Don't be afraid to use them and don't limit them in the process.

Focus on What You Want Not on How to Get It

If some of the items on your list would need purchasing, don't just list money as one of your needs or desires. Money is a means of acquiring some of the things you want, but not necessarily the only means. Deciding exactly what you want takes time and careful thought and consideration, focusing your thoughts.

If your wants include a new home, new car, or a trip to the Orient, list the details you want satisfied. Don't concern yourself with the means of getting them, and you won't limit your achievement. Don't think your limited income will have to be miraculously and substantially increased to provide for your heart's desires. You will probably doubt that possibility and block it. Leave it to Self. Your potential source of supply isn't regular income alone. You may inherit the home of your dreams, win an all-expense paid trip to the Orient, or receive a new car as a gift. You may win a lottery or find gold or oil in your back yard. The IRS or some other agency or public utility might find they made an error many years ago through which they overcharged you; now you're entitled to a refund, substantial with accumulated interest. Stranger things have happened.

THERE'S NO LIMIT

There's no limit to your potential supply. Only your doubts, feelings of unworthiness, lack of imagination, and adherence to conventional means (which you think are all that's possible) cause your lack or limited supply. Relax. Let go, let Self do it. You didn't tell Self how to find your parking spaces or how to go about changing the weather, did you? Know there's unlimited abundance in the universe and as much of it is yours as you want to create and believe you are worthy of. There's no finite amount of anything. We create our own abundance, and it's infinitely creatable. Seeing what you want already waiting for you and behaving as if you have it helps. Also expressing your gratitude even before you have it helps too.

PRAYER AS FOCUS

The value of prayer is that during prayer our mind doesn't wander, so our thoughts can't scatter or fragment. In prayer we identify clearly what we want and thereby open our way to receive. Prayer is not a case of our telling Self what we desire; it's making our desires clear to us. There's no need to tell Self; the all-knowing God within each of us knows our needs and wants, our every desire, much better than our conscious mind does. Our Self knows what's best for us and for others as well, knows what we planned for this life.

BELIEVING

No matter how strongly you desire something, if you fear it can't be yours or have the slightest doubt about your worthiness, need, or God's ability to deliver, you're wasting your energy praying for it. If your prayers lack conviction, it's obvious you haven't convinced yourself you should get what you want or that you truly want it. And until you're convinced, your thoughts can't be creative forces. When you desire something and know without any doubt it can be yours, it is yours.

In his teachings, Jesus stressed believing, such as: "...and all things, whatsoever ye shall ask in prayer, believing, ye shall receive." (Matthew. 21:22). When we're sure of positive results, we feel no need for help in attaining them, so aren't apt to pray for them. We probably don't think to pray for them. We're more apt to pray for something about which we have doubts or about which our feelings or desires are ambiguous. If we think ourselves unworthy of the objects of our desires, we'll probably pray for them, because we feel the need for help. As long as doubts or ambiguities motivate our prayers and remain to haunt us, those prayers will not be fulfilled.

If you ask in prayers for only those things you're unsure of, your prayers are actually self-defeating; they lack conviction, and can't be satisfied. As a result, you've likely become used to your prayers going unanswered. As long as you confine your prayers to those desires about which you have doubts or which concern others, you give yourself little reason for faith in God. You doubt God's willingness or ability to respond to you. You may even doubt the existence of God. What you've created is a self-perpetuating defeatist attitude and a no-win situation. Only you have created your conditions, circumstances, pleasures, and misfortunes. Your reactions to life are under your control. You can wallow in self-pity and live in poverty, ill health, and misery or you can make the most of life in success, abundance, and happiness. It's up to you.

Vain Repetition

Once you've set your sights on something, if it doesn't require action from you, you can set aside your thoughts on it. If you believe it can be yours, let it materialize. You can't force it. You've put the power of creativity into action by your prayer (focus) and your belief (conviction). Repeated thought or prayer would only emphasize a lack of confidence and be counterproductive. Again, in his eminent wisdom, Jesus said:

> But when ye pray, use not vain repetition, as the pagans do; for they think that they shall be heard for their much speaking. Be not ye therefore, like unto them, for your Father [Self] knoweth what things ye have need of, before ye ask Him
>
> ~ Matthew. 6:7-8

Once you've set the wheels in motion, your Self will produce the best possible results. It may not always be in the timing you want but will be when it's truly best for you, all things considered.

Positive Affirmations

There is one time when repetition is not only good but probably necessary. Your doubting intellect may not readily accept the fact that such as abundance, for example, is yours. Your intellect has only your past experiences on which to base its beliefs, so reprogramming for acceptance may be necessary. Repetitive positive affirmations may help you overcome doubts. Each day, tell your intellect that it's all right for you to receive your abundance, whether of good health, loved ones, joyful experiences, food, or the material things you want. Tell it there's an abundance for everyone. And advise it that you are now receiving that abundance. By repeating such affirmations, you replace earlier negative thoughts with more positive ones. Your intellect can then join in your receptivity rather than block it.

You can apply this technique to anything in your life. Use it to help you lose weight, quit smoking, improve your health, locate and obtain your dream house, become centered in your Oneness, attract your heart's desire. Be sure, though, to always frame your list of wants and your affirmations in the present tense. Through affirmation you put new data into your subconscious and reprogram your intellect. So, as you affirm that you *will* lose weight or *will* receive, the "will" is stored in your subconscious, and when intellect addresses the issue of your weight loss or your receiving, it reads "will" as sometime in the future. Your desired results will always be in your future, never now. When you affirm, "I am in good health and am shedding unwanted, excess weight at this very moment," it's true; it is a fact. When you affirm, "I deserve and am receiving my abundance now," that's a fact. Accept it. Receive your good now. Behave as though it's true, now, and it is. Cast out any old doubts, now. Open yourself to receive, now.

Consider What You Ask For

Be sure also, in addition to the material things you desire, that love, happiness, good health, serenity, and spiritual growth are high on your list. There's nothing wrong with wanting to accommodate the outer or material side of your life; do so with relish, but not at the expense of your inner, spiritual self. By accommodating first your spiritual desires, your list of material wants is apt to be shorter. Possessions are less likely to be important to you in a state of inner bliss. When you feel in your heart the joy of true love, material things lose their attraction. Also, once you've trod firmly on your path toward awakening, you're more receptive. You know the source of your supply and better understand your role in the creation of your reality. Anything you want is yours.

THY WILL BE DONE

When I say let God do something for you, that God is you, your Real, soul-Self. That God is the creator, implementer, and director of your life's play. When you pray, you are asking your Self to create for you the world as *you* want to see it. But your God-Self creates naturally toward your highest good, which sometimes may seem bad or unresponsive to you. A great deal of the time it is in your best interests that you either don't get what you think you want or get a circumstance to help you work through some negative thinking. Then you get all worked up when events don't turn out as you've prayed for or when your life isn't as rosy as you'd like it. You give up on God and throw your emotions into turmoil.

My point is that you don't know what is best for you, and can't do much about it anyway except compound the problem and further upset yourself. You don't have to work hard to get what you truly want, which I assume is love, happiness, good health, and prosperity. The problem comes from your deciding and trying to effect what will satisfy your desire for those conditions. Did you tell God how to create your parking places and ideal weather? Of course not, you don't know how. Well, you know even less how your loves, happiness, good health, and prosperity can best be created. Quit trying to do what you cannot do. Let go, let God.

OUR SELF AS CREATOR/CREATION

Our high vibrating, soul-Selves create our world for us to experience. As we each enact our play, our Self creates whatever fulfills our play's needs, whether it has to do with relationships, health, supply, job or career, or spiritual growth. While some of these creations are called for by the script, others are in response to our thinking, as I've explained.

When we create our reality through our beliefs, attitudes, and choices, we are our own creator, and we see the world around us in accordance with those beliefs, attitudes, and choices. Since the creator is its creations (they come from and of the creator and are the creator's thought manifestations), either our self or our Self is our relationships, our supply, our health, and our job or career. When we try to control those aspects of our life, they reflect only what we (our self) expect or wants them to be. By turning those aspects and their out-workings over to our Self, we allow Self to express freely. By identifying them with our highest possible imagery of Self rather than with our lowest self expectations, we free our Self to create the best, the most and the most fulfilling and satisfying conditions in our life.

Throughout the New Testament, Jesus is quoted as saying such as, "I seek not mine own will, but the will of the Father [Self] who hath sent me" (John 5:30). In three of the gospels he is quoted as praying: "O my Father, if it be possible, let this cup pass from me; nevertheless, not as I will, but as thou wilt" (Matthew 26:39). In prayer, Jesus stated what he wanted, but acknowledged that *nevertheless*, he would expect and accept the will of his Self, not his own human will to prevail.

GOING WITH THE FLOW

We have to learn to get out of the way and let our Self's will be done. We block our greatest love and happiness, our good health, and our prosperity when we try to make things happen according to our limited idea of what is good. We need to learn to go with the flow. The flow is the natural, unobstructed creation of our good by our Self. I know that my world is the out-picturing of *either* my limited intellectual thinking and emotions *or* my Self. It cannot be both at once. I also know from experience that the world created by my Self is considerably more pleasing and comfortable than that created as a reflection of my human thinking. I have found that I go with the flow best when I keep in mind that I am God and that everything else is also God. I put myself consciously back onto my path toward awakening by acknowledging that I am my Self's physical, human expression and that through me my soul experiences this life. My life is not mine alone; it is mine and my soul's—the whole of me—and it is for the benefit of numerous others. It is a joint venture. I realize that I am here only because my soul-Self wanted to experience itself in physicality. I try to let my Self do that as much as possible.

CHANGING ATTITUDES

What you show the world reflects your current thinking, whether fearful or loving, negative or positive. And, what you see may not be at all what's there, but is what's in your thoughts. Accept and never lose sight of the fact that through your beliefs and the use of judgment and choice you create your own reality, whether good or bad, ugly or beautiful. You have the power to consciously create your world as you desire it to be. Beauty, love, prosperity, happiness, and serenity are yours anytime you choose to buy into them and let your grand Self express its nature rather than what your little, human self thinks it wants.

APPLYING THE INSIGHTS

- Do you ever create daydreams in your imagination? If so, are they basically positive or negative?
- Do you see how your own thinking, attitudes, and beliefs create your reality, your life? Would you say you are generally a positive or a negative thinker? Does your life generally reflect your answer to that question? If you are more often negative in your thinking, do you want to change that? Do you think you can?
- For a couple of weeks, see where your focus is; make a list of your daily thought focus. Don't judge it, merely observe what you think about. At the end of the two weeks, look over your list and determine what you would like to change. You may find that as the days progressed, your focus, your thoughts became more positive. If that is the case, continue the process for as long as you want and see if your attitudes don't change substantially. What you are doing is giving your self and its attitudes their due; you are loving your self, so it is responding more positively. If your focus hasn't become more positive, continue the process until it does. Diligently doing the next exercises might help.
- Create your parking places, whether you think parking will be scarce or not and whether or not you believe the process will work. Do it anyway, again without judging the process or yourself. Keep creating them until you regularly get them, and don't forget to thank your Self—or the powers that be—for its help.
- After you've accomplished getting parking places, go through the process again with weather conditions. Give it all a chance.

- Once you've succeeded in these endeavors, go through the first exercise again, and see if you aren't generally more positive.
- Think of another area in your life you would like to change, such as your weight, smoking, whatever. Apply the consciously creating process of parking spaces and weather to whatever you've chosen to change, and do it.

18

CHOICES: HAPPINESS IS AN ATTITUDE & SERENITY CAN BE A HABIT

Ever given any thought to where your happiness comes from or, if the case, why you aren't happy? I mean really thought about it, not just giving credit or reproach. We all want to be happy, but that doesn't make it so. In fact, the more we want it, the more elusive happiness seems to be.

Despite appearances and a lifetime of programming, happiness does not depend on any outside conditions, events, or people. I see happiness as an attitude, and strictly an inside job. It depends on only our own perceptions and choices of beliefs and attitudes, and our reactions to the people and events in our lives: the emotions and worldly feelings we give ourselves. People and events help us experience so we can determine for ourselves what our life is to be like, the quality of our life. Happiness is in our heart, each and every one of us, awaiting our acceptance. Only our attitude determines our acceptance or not. Charles Swindoll, an evangelical minister, wrote:

The longer I live, the more I realize the impact of attitude on life....

The remarkable thing is we have a choice everyday regarding the attitude we will embrace for that day.

We cannot change our past.... We cannot change the fact that people will act in a certain way. We cannot change the inevitable.

The only thing we can do is play on the one string we have, and that is our attitude....

I am convinced that life is 10% what happens to me and 90% how I react to it.

Attitude is our most important daily choice.

CHOICES

We make choices constantly throughout our day. Those choices determine our perception of our world and our attitude toward it, which in turn, influence subsequent choices. Our responses to the people, events, and whatever we see, hear, smell, taste, and feel are the ways in which we experience life. Those responses are by choice.

External Stimulants

Millions of people of all ages use substances such as alcohol or drugs to help them reach and sustain some measure of comfort. Quickly they find it takes a greater quantity more frequently to achieve that goal and each trip is shorter than the preceding. Before they know it their life is out of their control. Misery for them is the only sustainable result, never happiness.

We can achieve happiness and even sustain it any time we want, by choice. No one has to wallow in self-pity, fear, sorrow, anger, or low self-esteem, although those, too, are choices that serve our purposes at appropriate times. Any time we want to, we can choose to feel good about ourselves and stand tall and face the world with confidence, good cheer, and a positive attitude. We can choose to be happy. External stimulants of any sort cannot in themselves provide happiness, temporary and superficial elation perhaps, but deep, lasting happiness is an inner feeling, coming from and existing only in our hearts. Even love, that which gives us our greatest joy and our severest misery, is in *us* not in that which comes or doesn't come from someone else. It is the feelings in our own hearts which comfort, thrill, and bring us bliss or depress us, and bring anguish.

Although you may not have a partner whom you feel is your soul mate, or your ideal job, or all the money you think you need, you can still be happy. Make the most of and enjoy your solitude, if that's what you have. Don't dwell on what you think is missing or limited in your life. Be happy with yourself. Your Self is your best company. Sai Baba, a wonderful Indian Guru, said: "The way to happiness is not to get what you like, but to like what you get."

ATTITUDE

Knowing little about the disease called depression, I'll allow that some people have to overcome huge hurdles to achieve some modicum of happiness. The rest of us have no such excuse. If we are unhappy, in some way and for some reason we may never consciously know, we have chosen that state. We have turned control of our emotions over to the negatives of life and react to them in like terms. We don't have to. They have no power of their own, only what we give them, and that is by choice. We don't have to give those negatives permission to affect us. Having at some point chosen unhappiness or depression, we can reverse our attitude to one of happiness by actively pursuing that state.

I was in high school when I tired of being lonely, listless, and generally unhappy. Realizing my happiness was entirely up to me, I made a conscious decision to change my life. I set myself some goals and decided what I needed to do to achieve them. It worked. So, I know from my own experience that happiness is one of those things we can all achieve when we put our intention to it.

Optimist or Pessimist?

Sure, some people tend to be optimists and, responding positively to their life, are generally happy. Many other people seem to be born pessimists, invariably looking on the bad side, expecting the worst, seeing only the ugly, and moping through their days filled with unhappiness. Such people are quick to blame others or outside influences for their plight, refusing to take responsibility for their conditions. I'm sure they would never view happiness as their choice. Yet it is. The pessimist, thinking something is three-quarters empty, longs for what's missing, while the optimist, seeing that the something is one quarter full, is grateful for their bounty.

As an example, let's say an optimist and a pessimist both sit down with checkbook and calculator to pay bills. Their economic situation is identical. The pessimist adds up the bills and compares the total with his checkbook balance. Seeing several hundred dollars more in bills than in the bank, he goes into a funk. After staring dejectedly at his debts he pays the rent, electricity, and phone bills, closes up the rest and mopes around depressed the remainder of the day. The optimist compares the same total debt with her same bank balance and, smiling, joyfully pays all the bills. Knowing that in a day or two payday will bring another several hundred dollars to add to her balance, she is delighted she will have plenty of money to cover food, gas, and incidentals the rest of the month, maybe even put some money into savings. Feeling a sense of accomplishment and comfort, she smiles and thinks, "Life's grand," then goes out to have some fun.

You can choose how you view anything. I know it's not easy for a pessimist to change attitudes, but with the desire to see the bright side, with careful attention to your way of thinking and responses, and with determined effort to change, you can do it. The rewards are many and great and well worth the effort.

People have said, If you don't like what you're doing (usually a job or career), move on to what you do like. I suggest *looking before leaping*. That is, look first at what you are doing and your attitude toward it. Is it your attitude that's keeping you from enjoying it? Is it salvageable? Is it worth the effort to salvage? If your answer to these questions is yes, ask yourself what you can do to change how you feel about the job. Then do it.

If your attitude is impairing your enjoyment, changing what you do probably won't help; you may just drag your negativity along with you and find yourself no better off, possibly worse off. Your attitude needs nurturing, bolstering, and changing. Having honestly and carefully examined your situation, if you still want to move on, by all means do so. But be sure to start your new life with a happy, positive attitude.

The same holds true for your current significant relationship. If it's worth saving it's worth some effort. Change your attitude and the other person may change attitudes also. Don't expect them to change, though. You control only your own life and attitudes. Show others your love, happiness, and positive attitude, and they likely will want some of the same. But they have to choose for themselves. Meet each challenge with a new attitude. Keep the power. Choose whatever you want. Choose to give into it if you want, but make that a conscious choice, and be happy about it.

I'm an optimist and don't like to have my picture of my world display other than the optimism I feel. As a result, I don't read or watch the news. It's almost always negative and exaggerated, sensationalized by the media. I somehow get a general sense of what's going on in the world out there, so don't feel out of touch. I see no point, though, in being depressed by events, especially since I don't see them as real. They are real to the people involved for their personal purposes and often for humanity more generally, to help us emote against them. I don't feel I need such stimulation in my life, so am quite happy without it.

REAP WHAT YOU SOW

As mentioned earlier in the discussion of karma, your thoughts bring conditions to you; we "reap what we sow," in attitude and behavior. Knowing this, why not control what comes to you, what you reap? By sowing positive, happy thinking with an upbeat attitude, returning conditions will surely perpetuate that attitude. They will perpetuate whatever is your attitude. So, by choosing the attitude with which you face life, you let it reflect back to you from your world, even causing it to do so. By consciously controlling your choice of attitude, you get more of what you want.

A great deal of our thinking is automatic, based on our environment, past experiences, and programming. By holding a positive attitude and actively doing those things that make you happy, you'll reprogram your automatic response mechanism to think positively, actually drawing more of what you want to you. By becoming an observer of your thoughts you can learn to keep from reacting with negative ones. You can choose the thoughts you want to act on and change the nature of the others. Once you become a regular observer, your heightened awareness will raise the nature of your automatic thoughts. When you make the conscious effort to become aware of your thoughts, you not only make possible a change in attitude, but you strengthen your conscious connection to your Self within. The more aware you become, the stronger is that inner connection and the more successful you are in getting what you want. One clearly helps the other. Anyone can be happy. We all have that option available to us. Happiness truly is ours for the choosing. We can each choose how we approach life, each new day at a time, actually, each new now at a time.

We draw to ourselves the people and events we need to help us create our experiences of this life. They don't just happen to us, so why react to them as if they do? Why not respond positively to them, happy to see them, happy to have them helping? When we're negative, we draw more negativity to us but when positive, we see and greet only the positives. Our happiness depends entirely on our own attitudes.

Let's think for a moment about what comes after happiness: serenity—or is it the other way around? I'm sure the vast majority of us would love to be serene, at peace within ourselves, no matter our life circumstances. The wonderful thing is that we can be. Serenity is something we can adopt as a habit. It, like happiness, is purely an inside job, not dependent at all on any outside influence. By being wholly positive in attitude and fully accepting of the truth of our spirituality and Oneness, we can be serene and can maintain that state as our way of living. The less judgmental we are the greater our chances for serenity. When we *know* that everything is perfect and purposeful, with love at the core of everyone and every event in life, we can be serene in the fact that there are no accidents or coincidences, no victims or villains, and no death. There's nothing to fear. Serenity is ours whenever we decide to accept the perfection and love of everything, and see ourselves as the creator of our experiences, by our attitudes as our choices.

What is the opposite of serenity, or what is it that keeps us from being serene? Fear, anger, distress, stress, sadness, anxiety, envy, guilt, greed. Actually, all the negative emotions are counter to serenity. So, to develop serenity as a habit, we have to get rid of negative emotions lurking in our minds. Actually, being an observer, not judging things, events, and people around us as either positive or negative, brings serenity. It's both the highs and the lows which keep us from being serene. We and only we can bring serenity into our life. It is peace of mind, it's being in the flow of divine love, it's having no quarrel with anything or anyone in our life. It's also Oneness, harmony, and bliss, all of which are naturally inside each of us. We have to recognize ourselves as the source of serenity. We have to love that in ourselves and allow it to shine through.

CHANGING CONDITIONS THROUGH LOVING, ACCEPTANCE, AND ALLOWING

It's not really that we change the conditions and situations of the world around us, but that we change the way we interpret and react to them, which changes the way we see them. The negatives aren't there if we don't see and accept them. The positives weren't there for us when we saw everything through the distorted vision of fear. Nothing is either negative or positive, it just is. We, by our choice of attitude, make it, impose on it what we expect to see.

There are three words which I feel we need to let affect our life, essentially to the exclusion of any others. They are: LOVE, ACCEPT, and ALLOW. Think on these, and see where they take you. While holding all three in your heart, can you entertain any negative emotion? It's all up to us. It's our choice to be the negatives or the positives. Or, we can be the observer of our life and not judge anything as either good or bad. We can accept and allow. Our love can be unconditional.

Keep in mind that this life is all illusion, and that we've—each and together— made it as it is. We've made its conditions and problems as they are, because these are what we wanted to experience, the background and scenery for our individual scenarios. But even then, how we individually view those conditions and problems depends on our personal beliefs and attitudes. In a sense, we each live in our own parallel universe, one slightly different from anyone else. We don't live separately; we are never separate from the whole, the ONE, so also are never separate from each other. We each are truly unique, though, so we see what suits us to experience.

You are here in this life to experience, and so much of your experience depends on your choices: your attitudes, your beliefs, your judgments, your reaction in the form of emotions. Your choices determine the course of your life. So choose wisely. Choose a positive attitude. Choose happiness. Be serene in your choices.

APPLYING THE INSIGHTS

- Think about your happiness or lack thereof. Is your attitude mostly positive or is it more often negative? If negative, does it bring you happiness? Do you believe that if you were to be more positive throughout each day (as worked on in the previous chapter) you could actually be happier? See your happiness as a choice in attitude, one you can make. Like creating parking places, create your happiness. It's up to you, your choice.
- Are you an optimist or a pessimist or maybe somewhere in between? Does it seem to matter to your happiness and general well being whether you generally think positively or negatively? If it does and you want to change, you can. It's your choice. Using the techniques of the insights applications in the previous chapter, make an effort to change your general attitude. Make a daily list of the attitudes you assume. With what attitude do you start your day? Does it change in mid morning, at lunch time, mid afternoon, dinner time, evening, bed time? Try to identify the causes of the changes you notice. Add those causes to your list. But, keep in mind that only your

reactions to people and events in your world are the actual causes of both your emotions and your attitudes.

- Notice each day's pattern; are they similar? That is, do you become either more negative or more positive as the day progresses? Do you regularly start your day positively and then does your positive attitude diminish or grow? Or do you start your day negatively, perhaps wishing you didn't have to go to work or do whatever you have planned? The negatives in your pattern are drawing your attention to something you might think about changing. But remember, don't change jobs in hopes that the new job will bring a new attitude. That doesn't work. Your attitude has to change first.
- Do you unconditionally love, accept, and allow? Or do you judge, expect, and easily get irritated or annoyed? Look at these attitudes throughout your day and see what effects they have on your happiness.

19

GOING WITHIN TO *KNOW* AND LOVE OUR SELVES

After decades of declining interest, religion in America regained popularity in the late 1960s, particularly the billion-dollar business of televangelism, despite its many scandals. Eastern religions gained notice, too, and began seriously affecting many Americans' approach to life. New Age metaphysical centers emerged, encouraging meditation and other, for most, introspective reflection. The number of books along religious, spiritual, occult, or metaphysical lines grew enormously. People began openly discussing spiritual and metaphysical subjects and paranormal phenomena.

We began to shift away from materialism, and our personal reflection and interest became internal. Our concerns became global and more compassionate, more caring for the well-being of all other humans and other species as well as the environment. Perhaps spurred on by the candid writings of Shirley MacLaine, an ever-growing number of us wanted to know about ourselves. Eastern meditation became a popular technique as a way of quieting our little self (intellect, ego) so we could be serene. Some of us used it in search of enlightenment to connect directly to the source of all knowledge within us, to get answers to our growing questions.

We wanted to understand who we are, where we came from, what we're doing here and what will happen when we die, our destiny. We wondered what our life here is all about. We couldn't help thinking there must be more to life than what we see every day.

About that same time UFOs and aliens drew our interest, with the Roswell incident and Area 51 taking center stage. People began wondering if we humans were so different from other animals because we had actually originated on some other globe in space and immigrated to Earth. Interest in Atlantis and Lemuria was renewed, with many books written using Edgar Cayce's Akashic readings to relate about our truly ancient, perhaps original, huge civilizations. Texts from ancient peoples began surfacing, being interpreted, and made public, providing new knowledge about our early ancestors' spiritual beliefs. To interest us even more, archaeologists began—and continue today—almost constantly locating and digging up ancient megalithic cities whose construction defied reason and made questionable science's fairly new notion of human evolution and its time line. We suddenly had a lot to think about, stimulating things, creating perplexing questions.

As I see it, all of this activity toward the spiritual and internal world occurred for one reason: because it was time for us humans to begin a concentrated effort to awaken. It was time for us to consciously Shift our focus, attitudes, and behavior. It was time for many of us to begin to remember our spirit Reality, the Oneness of our consciousness, our divinity. All of this was to help us awaken.

At the same time, beliefs and ideas became arguments, local conflicts and wars erupted, and the gap between haves and have-nots widened. Prejudices became focal points of dissention. Crime increased, as did abuse of women and children. Many government, corporate, and religious officials became corrupt, causing a lack of trust. All of this has grown steadily ever since the 1960s. But these sorts of things are in their own ways helping us raise our awareness to ever higher levels of consciousness.

ENLIGHTENMENT

One belief stood out for me from all else in those uncovered from our ancient ancestors: that we each have an internal connection to the divine, and that by going within we can access our divinity and be enlightened by it. By communing with our inner being, we can *remember* our Oneness, our spirituality, and all truth of our existence. This was the message of ancient Mystery schools as well as most indigenous traditions everywhere. As I explained earlier, I see enlightenment as a path toward awakening. It is finding ways of remembering our true spirit beingness and the Reality from which we came.

Our ancient ancestors are a great source of spiritual truth, to the extent we are able to uncover their texts and accurately interpret them. I believe—because of my belief that our human evolution is circular/spiral—that our earliest ancestors came into human existence on Earth still fully aware of their spirituality and Reality. They hadn't yet hidden their memory and knowledge with human intellect and programming—or only minimally had—so any texts or symbolism they left for us would contain truths we could confidently rely on, if we are able to accurately interpret them. And I'm sure that our combined Selves will help us interpret them when it's time for us to know.

While it helps to know what others believe, especially our ancient ancestors, reading about others' beliefs can take us only so far. Our Selves, always in Reality, know all of those truths and help us remember them when we're ready to do so. So, regular conscious communication between us and our souls brings us all the enlightenment we can use. With their help, we each will awaken, on whatever path is best for us. Solid conscious and constant communion with our Self is the most effective and important way of being enlightened, of remembering. Our search for answers is leading us back to our spiritual foundation. The greater our self-knowledge, the more we're drawn to the spiritual. Ultimately we find, as an inescapable truth, that our inner consciousness is spiritual. We are spirit beings.

> The whole world is Spirit, there is no thing else in Reality; ...Betake thyself to this view of things, and rest in peace, thus regaining thy real Self.
>
> ~ *The Upanishads*, Yogavasishtha

The Upanishads are commentaries on the Hindu Vedas, usually expressed as aphorisms: fairly brief sayings of great wisdom and truth. The Vedas are our most ancient written texts, their origin so old no one knows who originated them or when they were first spoken or ultimately written down.

THE ENLIGHTENMENT PATH

The increased activity along spiritual lines is because many of us have Shifted our consciousness and humanity in general is fast approaching such a Shift. Many of us are beginning to awaken. Those of us on the path of enlightenment, responding to more persistent prodding from our inner Self to seek truth, are questioning more and learning more, actually remembering. Many people who would be on the enlightenment path, however, are searching for truth in places and in ways which cannot fulfill their quest. No matter how spiritually aware preachers, lecturers, gurus, and authors may be, they can't give anyone the experience of knowing for her or himself. The teachers can help by starting the process, uplifting and encouraging them, by pointing them in the right direction, and by helping them remember. But until seekers stop relying on others for answers and begin seeking within themselves, their quest won't be fully satisfied. An ancient legend relates:

> The gods argued a long time, trying to agree where best to hide Truth from man. Some said, 'We cannot hide it in the mountains, for he would scale vast peaks to find it.' Others said, 'Nor can we bury Truth in the depths of the earth, for he would dig until he discovered it. Nor should we cast Truth to the bottom of the sea, for there too, he would search it out.' They were in a quandary until the wisest god proposed the answer: 'We will hide Truth within man, himself. He will never think of looking there.'

I *know* (intuitively) that each of us has all the answers we'll ever need right inside of us. We each have in our own heart our all-knowing, individual part of the Oneness. I believe it is that part, our own Self, with whom we must commune to gain enlightenment—to know and consciously become one with in order to reach our goal of awakening.

INTUITION

Those of us on a path of enlightenment toward awakening must *experience* truth. Just intellectually knowing, understanding, and accepting it is not enough. We must experience it with our *inner senses*, with our very being. We must feel it, see it, and know it in our heart, where it leaves no doubt. Only then is it our experience. I think of this as being enlightened through intuition. It's a case of lifting the veil over our memory of Reality so we can remember what as spirit beings we always know.

What are inner senses? They are some of the powers natural to us as spirit beings, powers we haven't lost, only hidden. They include what we call extrasensory perception, inner vision, hunches, *knowingness,* and spiritual feelings—those innermost feelings that originate within, not caused by outside influences. They are collectively, by my definition, what we call intuition. They are tools through which our individual soul-Self communicates with its human extension self.

> How do we know when we *know*? There is no question about *knowing*; there is something so far beyond the intellect, a vision so extensive that it has no horizon...
>
> ~ Ernest Holmes (italics added)

I *know* intuition to be our personal channel to Kosmic knowledge. Everything that has ever been or will ever be is available to us through intuition.

When we commune with our souls through intuition, we not only tap the experience of all time but of creation itself. We actually remember the truths of Reality. That's why our inner voice is so recognizable. It is memory. Don't you *know* when you remember something? There's no doubt, the answer that pops into your head is the one you're looking for. That's how it is when you tune in to the voice of your soul. You recognize it and remember its truths immediately and clearly.

INTELLECT

Intellect is the Earthly human side of our thinking, functioning only while we're alert to this plane. It is born anew with each new life and is the aspect of our consciousness that sleeps when our body is at rest. Our intellect has never known anything apart from this Earth life. Having no memory of its own, it bases its logic on data drawn from our subconscious memory bank—data generated by our own experiences, including the words and actions we witness or read of others. Intellect has been programmed since childhood to use dualistic criteria to classify everything into good and bad categories, then to make rational choices. By discrimination and logic, our intellect chooses which part of the dualistic teeter-totter it judges to best serve its immediate needs. It tries to separate us from all other life, from each other, and, most importantly, from our Self, our God. It sustains that separation, nurtures it, and insists that our possession of intellect makes us superior to all other life.

Our souls are not very forceful and rarely attempt to override intellect. Therefore, the more we consciously reason, the less input we receive from our Self through intuition. We are apt to have greater success remembering something, for instance, if we don't work at recalling it. Relaxing your thought process periodically enables you to receive more of what intuition has to offer. While seeking a solution to a problem, a hot shower can ease tension and be joyfully rewarding—a virtual fountain of inspiration. Meditating, daydreaming, or perhaps gardening or exercising, letting your thoughts wander where they will, all help. During these times, because intellect is still, Self can implant insights from the source of all knowledge and wisdom.

One who relies exclusively on intellect will never be a person of great wisdom. The truly wise recognize the validity and immense value of intuition (communication from Self) and have learned to rely heavily on it.

Mozart, for example, is said to have received musical compositions while "unconscious."

Many inventors, like Thomas Edison, have "slept on" a problem and awakened with the perfect solution. Albert Einstein said: "There is no logical way to the discovery of these elementary laws. There is only the way of intuition." It's been said that all great scientists become mystics, the wonders of this magnificent cosmos and life on Earth making them at least reverent. What's a mystic? One who believes that direct knowledge of God, spiritual truth, or ultimate reality can be attained through subjective experience (as in intuition or insight).

> The Self is not realizable by study, nay not even by intelligence or much learning. The Self unfolds its full essence to him alone who applies his self to Self.
>
> ~ *The Upanishads*, Kathopanishad

Only by deliberately going within can one's self establish a conscious connection with Self.

Our soul consciousness speaks softly through intuition, providing *knowing* without the use of rational process. It is our creativity, talent, inner beauty, source of inspiration. It is our wisdom. Our intuition never defies reason, although its information will probably be very different from what we've been taught and is seldom factually supportable in physical human terms. Our soul has no axe to grind, no fears, no desires, no sensitivities to be satisfied or hurt. Being infinitely impartial and nonjudgmental, it offers nothing but truth and sound advice. Carl Jung once said,

> We should not pretend to understand the world only by the intellect; we apprehend it just as much by feeling [intuition]. Therefore the judgment of the intellect is, at best, only the half of truth, and must, if it be honest, also come to an understanding of its inadequacy.

And in one of his last interviews Jung also said (italics added):

> I could not say I believe, I *know*! I have had the experience of being gripped by something that is stronger than myself, something that people call God.

We all use intuition much more than we realize. All instinct, insight, inspiration, and creativity come to us from our Selves through intuition; none is intellectually reasoned. Great ideas occur to us spontaneously, as depicted in cartoons by the lighting of a light bulb above the thinker's head. Intuited ideas usually inject themselves into non-related thoughts or blossom when our intellect is quiet. Seldom does genuine inspiration occur while the intellect reasons on that subject. Intellect often gets in the way of our inspirational thought process, though, sometimes persuading us to reject the perfect answer, leading us temporarily astray.

Intuition has gotten a bad rap from materialists. They have derisively referred to it as "women's intuition," and either see it as fantasy constructed by our human brain as wishful thinking, or something used by Satan to wrongly influence us. If it is either fantasy or evil, why do so many truly good, intelligent people, such as Holmes, Jung, and Einstein take it so seriously? Why have so many people benefitted so greatly from listening to their inner voice? I don't believe I could ever have come up with my absolutely wonderful, fearless, loving philosophy and understanding of life had I not gone within and listened consciously to my soul-Self through intuition.

If you are currently engrossed in intellectual exploration, you may be reluctant to diminish intellectual activity in favor of intuition. Fine. All of us have to be true to ourselves. Those pursuits which we enjoy most are the ones which are of the greatest benefit to us at that time.

A PARTNERSHIP OF INTELLECT AND INTUITION

I believe that a partnership of intellect and intuition is essential to a well balanced individual and to a pleasant human experience. Intellect and intuition need not be at odds, one against the other, one in place of the other. We can teach intellect not to jealously guard its place in our esteem and to accept the contributions of intuition. It needs to understand that each has its place in our life. We need to subdue our vociferous, limited, negative-thinking intellect if we are to hear the wisdom of our Self. Reprogramming our intellect is in order.

Earlier, we considered reprogramming intellect through positive affirmations, because intellect learns by whatever we feed it. While affirmations can be of immense help in redirecting intellect, you can also talk it into being a partner with intuition and helping you rise to higher levels of consciousness. Help it realize how exciting and fulfilling that would be. Talk with intellect; love it. Get it to help you rise to a higher level of being.

By allowing intuition to guide you more actively, you can demonstrate to intellect a happier, more prosperous, more tranquil experience from which to draw its conclusions. The pure love and supreme wisdom emanating from within will become evident to intellect. The more it sees of the positive experiences brought about by intuition, the less intellect will seek to control your thoughts and actions. Your Self, then, will have greater freedom to lead you toward wisdom and awakening.

COMMUNING WITH THE STILL SMALL VOICE WITHIN

Knowledge is gained by study, experimenting, and learning from others. Education from books, however, does not a wise man make. Wisdom is not learned in school, nor from reading what others have written, no matter how wise the source. Wisdom comes only from within one's heart, one's Self. The words of others often excite inspiration, but that inspiration has only one source and comes to us individually through intuition. The only way we will ever gain the wisdom to Shift is by communing with our wondrous inner Self, our "Still Small Voice Within." Communing is not difficult. It's simply conversing with Self through intuition.

A Process

If you haven't gotten in touch with your Self within and want to, maybe something from my experience will help you. Strong commitment and dogged persistence are necessary; sporadic, haphazard attempts at communication won't get the job done. To really succeed one needs to be open to and familiar with the inner voice and fully trust it. Select a period each day in which you can relax and be quiet. It doesn't have to be lengthy. Learn to do some relaxing, centering, and mind-stilling exercises. Then, if you have them, ask questions one at a time. Ask your Self as if speaking with another person, ask, then listen.

Beginning

The hardest part for me was beginning. I'd have had no idea where or how to start, if friends hadn't offered suggestions. They taught me to stand and ask my "guide" to rock me back and forth for yes and from side to side for no. I soon found, though, that it wasn't always convenient to stand and do it that way, so I changed this to movement within my mind as if it were my head nodding for yes and shaking from side to side for no. This works well because I can do it riding in a car, sitting in my chair, lying in bed, and I can do it privately, not making a spectacle of myself.

This practice got communications going, but slowly. I knew so little, I had no idea what to ask, let alone to ask in a way that could be answered yes or no. Then, at Terri's suggestion, I began asking for single words on which I could focus my attention and from which I could learn; not just any words, but meaty ones I could look up in the dictionary and ponder for meaning in the context of some spirituality. Focusing on particulars in this way kept my mind from wandering. I ultimately moved to phrases and finally began a wonderful communion—inaudible communication—with my voice within.

PRACTICE

Practice asking and getting responses to those yes or no questions until you have no doubt as to each answer and know from where it's coming. Ask everyday, mundane questions at first, and let your Self give you yes or no answers. Until you've got this part of the practice down pat, don't worry about asking spiritually profound questions—they'll come later on their own, through intuition. Being attuned to the *voice* of your Self takes persistence. Receiving even the simple form of communication, words, takes effort on your part to succeed. It's not easy at first to discern the right word. If your mind is sufficiently relaxed and quiet, the first word that pops into it is probably the right one. Sometimes, however, intellect, wanting to be helpful and also not wanting to be left out, puts a word into mind. Once you become familiar with communication from your Self (or your guide, guardian angel, ascended master, or however you think of your voice within), you can easily discern the difference. Until then, it might help you, as it did me, to ask for yes or no to each word, to see if it was given through intuition, not intellect, and is the correct answer. Practice words until they flow, then you can move on to phrases.

BE STILL AND KNOW

Don't dominate the conversation. Once you've asked a question, listen. Shut up and focus your attention on the subject of your question or on an inconsequential object. Some people stare at a pencil, others at the flame of a candle. Be at ease in both body and mind. Answers can come through only to a quiet or well-focused, yet relaxed conscious mind. Still the chattering of your intellect. You aren't listening for intellectual thoughts; you're seeking communion with your inner voice. You aren't able to hear clearly another's words when you're talking or thinking, and your inner voice is no exception. Learn to ignore intellectual thoughts, letting them float by without holding on to any. But don't expect to make your mind blank; that's nearly impossible and to try to do so could block out the messages you seek. Ask your question and be still.

There's a fable about a wise man who saw someone talking much and listening little. So the sage said: "Note the difference between your ears and mouth. The Holy One created for you two ears and one mouth so that you might listen twice as much as you speak." The Hebrew Bible tells us to "Be still and know" (Psalms 46:10).

Sitting quietly and stilling the intellect enables us to receive *knowingness* from within, as the wise have suggested. Listen for your inner voice. Listen intently, as you might when you thought you heard the baby cry or a kitten mew. When you listen intently for something in particular, you shut out all other sounds and tune in to the particular one you want to hear. When you focus your attention inward, extraneous thoughts can't easily come in.

What you receive is unlike anything you experience in any other way. It isn't easily described; you must experience it to *know*. Each person receives in a way appropriate for them. Some people speak of a voice, others feelings or internally seen pictures. Some people write or type automatically—that is, without conscious effort or intellectual interference For me it's an infusion of thought into my mind, as a deep inner sense of *knowing*. Regardless of how they arrive, truths come to us individually from our own soul-Self through our inner senses.

Attunement with our Self raises our vibrations and makes pin holes in the veil of collective unconsciousness enshrouding humanity. The pin holes provide tiny glimpses of understanding, Reality, light, love, remembering. When we receive thoughts from within we use our inner senses to glimpse true Reality through those pin holes. Since that Reality isn't physical, we may glimpse a total concept rather than a visual picture or word-for-word truth. We may be flooded with a beautiful sense of serenity, joy, love, or harmony. Since our inner senses aren't physical, the uninterpreted reception through them isn't physical.

TRANSLATING LIMITS MESSAGE

We usually translate into physical terms what we've received, because those terms are familiar to us. We translate them into words or pictures with which we can relate. Such translation, however, may dilute, distort, or limit them. It may even render them senseless. Sometimes, while writing my truths, I've become so entangled in words, the original thought escaped me. It's almost as if it wafted by, providing me a brief glimpse, then floated on. But I think it always returned. Some messages have been so deep or have come so rapidly that my awareness, used to the slower pace and limited scope of my intellect, has picked up only bits and pieces. I've had to ask that insights be sent slower and in smaller, more easily assimilated doses.

NORMAL, EVERYDAY COMMUNICATION

Once it begins, regular daily sessions will make this communication easier. Soon the communion you desire will flow and be well worth the time and effort you've put to it. Actually, receiving messages from within isn't limited to conscious solitary communion. It's frequent and a normal part of our everyday thought processes. My truth is that, without our being consciously aware of it, our soul communicates with us throughout every day. We don't realize it because we haven't learned to distinguish its messages from thoughts coming from intellect. Often when we receive an intuited message, we allow intellect to judge it and convince us to respond in contrary fashion. The gut feeling, hunch, first answer are some of the messages from our Self that easily get overlooked, ignored, or pushed aside.

You also receive subliminal guidance throughout every day from your soul-Self. You get ideas, suggestions, cautions, and feelings as you interact with others and go about your daily life. Because you don't know how valuable such communication is you may ignore it, then often later wish you'd paid better attention. This conscious communication practice will help you discern that guidance from your soul, so you will be more apt to follow it. And consciously allowing your soul to guide you will make life considerably easier and more satisfying. But if not, ask your Self to explain.

WHY SO QUIET?

You may ask why our souls are so quiet of voice and so subtle in their use of attention-getting devices. Like everything else, there's a good reason for that too. Learning to recognize our soul's voice and consciously communing with that Self is a vital part of our growth process. Until now, most of us weren't ready for the enlightenment and awakening phases of life, so we didn't want to be able to discern that voice. Many of us are now ready and will move rapidly into it. The beginning recognition of it is a thrilling, awareness-expanding experience that we wouldn't want to miss. I can't emphasize enough how wonderful this conscious communion is. Only experiencing it for yourself can give you that wonderful feeling.

Recognizing Inner Thoughts

Learn to recognize the thoughts stemming from your inner Self, differentiating them from those of your intellect. Through self-awareness, get to know your own normal intellectual way of thinking. Know your judgments, your reactions to others, and the pace and attitude of your wandering intellectual thoughts and daydreams. Be consciously aware of your feelings, emotions, attitudes, and prejudices, but don't judge them or yourself for them. By being familiar with your normal thought patterns, you can gain a vital knowledge of self and begin to recognize as different those thoughts emanating from your soul. Thoughts from your soul will never be judgmental nor involve or evoke fear or any other negative emotion. They may manifest as feelings or desires, but will never suggest you go against your best interests or do what you'd rather not.

Your Self is your own soul, that larger, higher-vibrating part of you that remains always in spirit. It will give you only positive, loving, and good advice, so you can always trust it. Having never pulled the veil over its wisdom and memory—as we humans have—it knows all things, so you can get any question truthfully answered, so long as your intentions are pure, fair, and loving. If your question infringes on someone else's privacy, the answer will be ambiguous or not available.

Eventually, your intuitive communication may be in another form than words and verbal thoughts. Your Self will communicate with you in the way most comfortable and effective for you. It may be in the form of feelings that tell you things or possibly mental pictures. It may come in whole blocks of thought, like a brick of insight put in place in a wall of wisdom. Some people visualize a shaman or other wise being strolling with them and telepathically speaking with them. Others communicate through what seems to them an avatar, ancient being, archangel, Jesus or other master, or a prophet of old. Other people still, just *know,* intuitively understand a situation, relationship, concept, idea, or the nature of reality, without going through this kind of practice.

With good conscious communication with your Self within, you will be far happier than ever before, will have fewer problems with others in your life and with life in general, and will be healthier.

BE A CONSCIOUS RECEIVER

You can be a constant conscious receiver of the messages from your inner Self. By persistently tuning in and increasing your awareness and sensitivity to your inner communications, you can learn to live *consciously* by inner guidance, as you truly do now unconsciously.

Once communion gets easy, try to stop your intellect from interpreting the messages you receive, and allow them to assimilate into your awareness in their raw state. Your awareness will expand accordingly, the wisdom will be forever available, for use whenever needed. It will be truthful, useful, and insightful, not distorted or weakened by intellectual interpretation. Unbeknownst to you consciously, this is the primary way you receive guidance in enacting the script of everyday life. To make it conscious, still your intellect and allow your inner Self to think, speak, and act for you. Do it persistently and you will be an open, perfect channel for spiritual expression. Unite your inner and outer self/Self in communion. Be whole and awaken to spiritual consciousness.

BEING ONE WITH SELF

Jesus was a perfect example of what I'm talking about. I believe his baptism signified his wholeness and awakening to spiritual consciousness. Separation no longer existed between his conscious mind and his higher, impersonal, loving inner Self, which he called "Father." The words he spoke were not the results of reasoned thinking by his conscious mind; his intellect remained stilled. His words were his soul's from within. The same is true of Siddhartha. Christ was the Self of Jesus, the Buddha the Self of Siddhartha. Probably the Prophet Muhammad or the Arch Angel Gabriel who spoke to him giving him truths was Muhammad's Self. Each of us can be consciously one with our inner Self. You already are one, you just haven't yet consciously awakened to that Reality. The steps are yours to take.

Throughout the last two parts I've suggested going within to get help in dealing with every-day life and in making changes in your attitudes and behavior, if that's what you want. While this chapter has primarily focused on getting answers to questions and being enlightened about your spirituality and this life more generally, communion with your inner Self will provide insights and loving help. It will give you conscious awareness of a constant companion to love, cherish, and enjoy whenever you want. The practice described below in 22 steps is the one I used to immense advantage. If you commit to it and follow the steps diligently, you too will find yourself in a whole new world at a new, much higher level of consciousness.

APPLYING THE INSIGHTS
Communication by Intuition with your Higher Self
Stage One:
1. Get relaxed and focused: still of body and quiet of mind;
2. In your thoughts, ask your Self to answer questions with a nod of your head for yes and a shake of your head for no;
3. Close your eyes and ask a question that can be answered yes or no, any question (it doesn't have to be profound; at this stage the simpler the better);
4. Feel your head move up and down or from side to side (it may not be physical movement but an inner sense of movement); determine what you think is the answer;
5. Ask if you have the correct answer, and again feel your head move, indicating yes or no;
6. Ask another mundane question, going through the same steps;
7. Continue asking questions until you easily feel the head movement and consistently get the correct answers;
8. Practice daily, making the questions deeper; get truly comfortable with the process and confident in the answers - at least two weeks.

Stage Two:
1. Ask your Self to give you a word to ponder; the first word that pops into your mind is usually the right one;
2. Verify the word you got with the yes/no head movement routine;

3. If you didn't get it right, ask again until you get the correct word;
4. Ponder that word throughout the day; look it up in the dictionary; see what message there might be for you in it;
5. The next day, ask for another word, and ponder it;
6. Continue this word practice for a couple of weeks, again, until you are comfortable and confident that you are always getting the correct word;
7. Ask your Self to answer a question with words, a phrase, rather than yes or no;
8. Ask a more complex question then the ones you started this practice with, but keep it fairly simple at first;
9. When you have an answer, check it out with the yes or no routine to be sure you got it right;
10. Continue regularly asking questions and getting answers. Soon you will be carrying on wonderful conversations with your inner Self;
11. You may find that questions you haven't thought of before just pop into your mind. That is your Self giving you questions it wants to answer on subjects or concepts it wants you to know about and understand;
12. Be open for messages, insights, feelings from your Self throughout every day, and when you get a message, pay attention to it;
13. Above all, enjoy both the practice and the wonderful wisdom you receive, and be persistent. Commit to making good, conscious, consistent, regular communication with your higher Self. Your Self knows all and eagerly wants you to know all too. Actually, you once did, eons ago, and now you are remembering those truths. So, the more you use this intuitive practice with your Self, the more you will remember more quickly and easily, and the closer you will get to reunion with your Self.
14. It's important to be able to discern the "voice" of your inner, higher Self from that of your intellect. That's why with each step you need to verify the correctness of each answer. Your intellect, not wanting to be left out, will try to butt in and give

you answers; but those answers are not necessarily true, and can mislead you. You want to communicate with your true Self, not intellect.

PART FIVE - THE SHIFT

The veil that clouds your eyes shall be lifted by the hands that wove it,

And the clay that fills your ears shall be pierced by the fingers that kneaded it.

And you shall see.

And you shall hear.

Yet you shall not deplore having known blindness, nor regret having been deaf.

For in that day you shall know the hidden purpose in all things,

And you shall bless darkness as you would bless light.

~ Kahlil Gibran, *The Prophet*

20

THE VEIL IS LIFTED

We've considered what we can do to change our world to a better environment for greater well-being and happiness by changing our own beliefs, attitudes, and behavior. We've also examined our afflictions, our health, and our daily human experience in light of my philosophy, in a sense looking at why I think "bad things happen to good people." In this final part we'll see what is currently going on to transform humanity and result in the better environment. We'll look at what all these eons of human experience have brought us to, why, and how. And we'll see what our awakening is about.

RELIGION'S INFLUENCE

Religions of the world have tried to coax us into virtuous living. They've taught of our judgment day to come, of God's wrath and castigation. They have defined justice as retribution or outright punishment. Threats and other coercive tactics to get us to live righteously and follow their tenets have made hypocrites of many of us and alienated others of us. Seldom have they succeeded. We humans are inclined to fight or act contrary to something foisted on us. We can't be forced by fear or any other coercion to do anything from our heart; we have to want to.

The sin-based tenets of Christian religion don't reflect the teachings of Jesus or any ancient wisdom. They were created by church officials to account for the nastiness we humans do against each other and to serve church interests. Yet this doesn't make them less godly, less purposeful, or of less value inwardly to humanity than they would be had they more closely followed their Master's teachings. Those tenets were created by God as they are in order to serve loving purposes. Because we are all God, every word in scriptures and every bit of religious dogma came from God to serve our highest good in some way and in their time.

For the same reason, we can say that the dogmas and doctrines of science have been presented by God, as well, in the way that the scientists needed at the time to believe and teach them. They, too, have served purposes of their own in this time.

NEED TO CHANGE

Our belief systems have been important parts of our human experience and evolution and always will be. But maybe it's time to change what they consist of, change *what* we believe.

The sin-based tenets and the persecution and vile acts caused by and for religion in the name and glory of God, have contributed greatly to our plays. The fighting between religions around the world serves the people involved and humanity more generally, although it's often hard to understand why fighting, brutality, and terrorism should ever be backed by religion. Religion has provided glimpses of truth, clothed in terminology and ideology needed by our human consciousness in its sleep-state condition. It has helped us immensely to enact our plays of human life. For many, religion likely also will play an important part in our up-coming transformation, our Shift, and our mass awakening. We've nearly completed the dark, strictly human phase of our evolution and can now increase our conscious awareness. We can now accept philosophies which are based in love and move away from other rationales for being and doing good.

Besides, it's not enough to live a virtuous life, stifling jealousy, lust, and greed. Nor is it enough to live righteously, being kind to our neighbors, self-sacrificing, and doing good deeds if these aren't genuine and sincere. Whatever we do must be our innate nature to do, an outgrowth of our love for God, for humanity, for our neighbors, for ourselves. We no longer require coercion. We can be good, kind, and loving, not because we think we have to, but because we want to. It is our intrinsic nature to be those qualities. We need only awaken to them. We are in the process of realigning in awareness with that nature, with those qualities. That's what the Shift is about.

Religion Can Help

Without a need for fear-driven, negative tenets, religion can focus on the positive, more true ancient spiritual teachings. Religion can help us to awaken, whatever our individually chosen path. I believe the less rigid religions will flourish once they get past their own fears and jealousies and learn to teach unconditional love and true spirituality. They will be needed, for seekers of truth and awakening need to come together, to share and help each other remember. As Buddha said: "The first law is to seek out the brotherhood of seekers." Religions can offer forums in which seekers can share and all can learn. We needn't feel alone in our enlightenment and awakening.

Religions will need to change, though, to meet changing needs of their congregations. Those that don't change will be left behind. Without the need to jealously guard their status, older religions can dig into their archives and make public their more spiritual scriptural texts. Thousands of ancient texts have resurfaced in only the last few decades, and all contain considerably more clear forms of spirituality than any scriptures currently used by Western religions. Those ancient texts—of the Nag Hammadi Library, the Dead Sea Scrolls, the Gospel of Judas, the Gospel of Mary—have been hidden and have lain dormant for up to two thousand years. So they haven't gone through the revision and copying processes that the more familiar ones have. Not corrupted by either time or political self-serving institutional devices, they surely now will provide more true original spirituality—if interpreted correctly—than the familiar ones. We are rapidly realigning toward greater spirituality. Now is the time for us to know. Now is the time for religion to help us realign or get out of the way.

WHY TRUTH HAS BEEN HIDDEN

You might wonder why truths have been kept such secrets. You might say you'd have found life easier to cope with had you known what I've been relating to you. That's the point. You likely would have lived differently throughout your many incarnations. You'd have known the unreality of your Earthly roles and would not have taken them seriously. You would not have been inclined to grieve over your losses or anguish over your adversities; all such emotions have been necessary to your awareness expansion. You might have opted out rather than stayed and seen the hard times through.

It's been necessary from the beginning for us to believe in our separation, to experience the results of it. Could we have experienced such emotions as fear, greed, hate, and envy without having first lost or hidden our knowledge of the Kosmos—our Oneness, love, serenity, joy, and the true beauty of it all? Without experiencing those less desirable emotions and conditions, what would we know of the more desirable ones? We'd have no basis for comparison, no perspective. The person born without hearing will not in this life know the joy of a child's giggles or the beauty of Beethoven's Moonlight Sonata, but also won't truly know what s/he is missing. Without hearing, perhaps the deaf can better appreciate sight and enjoy their intellect, emotions, and intuition more fully. Think how wonderful Reality, in all its glory, will be to them when they return Home and hear the lilting harmony of music and of pure spiritual love! Without the experience of lack or absence, we'd never know what we really have so couldn't appreciate it. The sets of dualistic opposites give us opportunities to see and discern the virtually unlimited variations and details between the extremes.

It's not that the negatives don't exist; it's that they aren't truly negative but are parts of the whole experience. Although not as pleasant, they are often more valuable to us than the positives.

Now that we've had all those dark experiences, there's no reason to repeat them. Many of us are closing out that dark phase of our human evolution, coming ever closer to seeing and appreciating Reality. We no longer need the veiled state. Subsequent phases of our evolution, instead, require en*light*enment and our awakening state.

EARTH ANGELS

We are not alone in our efforts to awaken. In addition to our ever-present soul group companions, beings I call "Earth Angels" are helping us prepare for awakening. They've been with us since our human beginnings to help us in many ways: Some to lead us, teach us, and show us how; many now to help us change our thinking, our attitudes, and behavior. Because this is a time of enormous change, time of Shifting, there are millions of Earth Angels living here right now. Most are human as we are, for the most part living as we do. They are beings who incarnate to serve the growth needs of others. Although some are helping individuals, most Earth Angels have incarnated into this time period to help humanity more generally. Most of them are not consciously aware of their difference. Few have previously achieved awakening from human life; yet, some are fully awake. Others, while slowing their vibrations to create human form, haven't fully veiled their spiritual consciousness with intellect and are consciously aiding humanity. Many have lightly veiled their consciousness enough to realistically enact their human roles alongside the others of us while remaining more awake. Their awakening has been faster so they might serve as examples and teachers to the rest of us.

Moses, Siddhartha, Jesus, and Muhammad were perhaps obvious Earth Angels, as were Lao Tzu, Confucius, the 14th Dalai Lama, numerous yogis, and native chiefs and shamans everywhere. But the vast majority are not distinguishable from the rest of us. The founding fathers of America may have been Earth Angels. All world leaders may be, and all major industrialists too; their impact on the lives of millions has been substantial. Also, the many great inventors, poets, artists, composers, philosophers, scientists, physicians, and other hugely gifted people, who have brought us culture, knowledge, improved health, entertainment, and convenient technology may have been Earth Angels.

Some Earth Angels aid humanity through beauty, and wisdom, while others deliberately commit vile acts to provoke fear, horror, and outrage. Some evoke moral indignation, others deep, heart-wrenching compassion, all designed to increase our awareness and raise the vibrational level of humanity's consciousness. As abhorrent as the idea may be, it's likely that Hitler was an Earth Angel. Their acts and influence don't have to seem good in our human terms. It's almost certain that the millions of human beings killed by the Nazis during WWII were Earth Angels. The millions of starving and AIDS-ridden Africans may also be, like hordes of extras in our play. The current ebola epidemic may be another aspect of the Earth Angel activity designed to help general humanity, while providing a way to leave Earth life that is acceptable to our human understanding.

When thinking about all those Earth Angels serving humanity in the form of famine- or disease-plagued people, know they only *seem* to suffer. Their suffering is what we need to see. It elicits sympathy, indignation, and outrage and it draws forth from us love, compassion, caring, and sharing. Their role in our plays is to suffer well, to make it look good, real. That they do to perfection. Take heart, though; they don't really know the anguish they exhibit or the pain they appear to feel from malnutrition and disease. The hoards of diseased and starving people may not see their living conditions as squalor. Without contrast for comparison they are unable to judge their condition; it just is. Teaching them, therefore, may not be kindness. It may actually hurt them by providing them a glimpse of that contrast. They also probably don't use judging intellect to the extent the rest of us do, and certainly not the programs that condition us.

The vast majority of such people probably have never taken on the intellect that makes the rest of us so human. They have remained children at heart and are still very close to their original spirituality. Their energy vibrations have remained more rapid than ours. Their time, therefore, is different from ours. Each day, month, year goes by more quickly for them, and their life span, too, is much shorter than ours—both blessings, given their seeming misery. Many children born in disease- and famine-ridden conditions never reach maturity, another planned blessing.

CHILDREN, IN PARTICULAR

You may have noticed how children seem to be more frequently the center of dire news or human-interest stories lately. In addition to starving and contracting AIDS in Africa, children are killed by gangs, drunk drivers, or their playmates here in the United States. They are kidnapped and/or killed by serial killers, or abusive parents. They are subjects of human trafficking. Children are running away from home, and taking to the streets, drugs, and prostitution; and children are contracting crippling and murderous diseases. Children are being born addicted to drugs or are subjected to abuse of every possible nature. Children are physically malformed or are autistic and they are dying in their cribs or in house fires. Children are orphaned. Children are going on rampages and killing classmates and teachers on school grounds. Children are committing suicide.

Children are stealing the limelight in every conceivable heart-wrenching way, and for very good reason. Nothing draws humanity's attention and raises us to higher consciousness as convincingly as children in trouble. Millions of children have entered Earth life in this time period to help in these ways to quicken humanity's progress to higher levels of consciousness. And, it's working. We are being filled with anguish, compassion, and outrage. Growing numbers of us are trying to help. In the process, our individual attitude is changing. Many of us are becoming less materialistically self-engrossed and more caring, loving, appreciative, and respectful of all life. We want children to be free from abuse and to be able to grow up in happiness and fun and with high self-esteem. The horrors against children are reported to us on television for us all to see, so we can be shocked by them. They are bringing out the higher in us. They are Earth Angels.

Similarly, elderly people are also drawing our attention and evoking heartfelt emotions. In growing numbers, elderly people are afflicted with the mental disease Alzheimer's or are being mugged, raped, conned, abandoned, and generally abused, or ignored in nursing and assisted living homes and hospitals.

The collective unconsciousness lightens a little each time one of us is touched by the plight of others. It lightens a lot when such touching makes a real difference in someone's approach to life. Our individual attitudes are reflected in general world conditions, governmental postures, and in the positions of warring factions. To change these, we must change our selves. Peace will one day prevail and love will replace hate and indifference, thanks in large part to Earth Angels.

Animals

Some Earth Angels play a more immediate role in our individual lives. Our pets are Earth Angels, here in that form to serve specific individual needs. They help us experience complete nonjudgmental love while serving as companions, confidants, teachers, and sources of joy. They help lighten our everyday burdens of life and soften our attitudes.

"Of all living creatures, only humans know that someday we will die." This anonymous statement is the sort of thing believers in Darwin's theory of evolution spout with great regularity. How does anyone know that, especially with such certainty? Many otherwise social animals uncharacteristically go off on their own into solitude to die, cats especially. If they don't know they are dying, why do they choose then to behave differently?

I believe that animals are considerably more aware of both life and death than we think they are. More aware than we are. I believe that in addition to heightened physical senses, they are able to use inner spiritual senses more than we normally do. They communicate telepathically and are more sensitive to feelings—each other's and ours—then we are. They are far better at reading our moods than we are, and most of our pets know ahead of time when their best human friend is ill or is returning home from being away. Some know when people are close to dying. Why shouldn't they know that someday their own physical body will die? We've all heard stories that tell of heroic rescues animals have made that clearly demonstrate not only intelligence but an ability to reason. Animals, too, are grabbing our attention lately, especially those whose habitat and very lives are endangered by the effects of global warming, human ignorance, arrogance, and self-centered stupidity, or the greed of poachers. News reports tell of abused and neglected animals, and more and more TV commercials use cute animals to get our attention. Clearly there's a lot going on at this time to help us humans raise our awareness.

WHY NOW?

If it's been for our benefit that truths be hidden all this time, why uncover them now? Why are we being given truths now? What's different about now? I believe that Humanity is nearing an attitudinal Shift in consciousness, and many of us are on the brink of awakening through enlightenment. We have lived our many lives experiencing and expanding our awareness. Some of us have accomplished nearly all we set out to do, save that ultimate goal of awakening. The time to wake up is fast approaching. By raising our awareness to higher levels of consciousness we have made ourselves more responsible and more able to consciously use truths with greater love. There is no longer a need for truths to remain hidden from us.

Truths have never been very deeply hidden, and many before us have known them. We once knew them. Many wonderful books, such as the Hindu *Upanishads* and *Bhagavad-Gita*, Hebrew Scriptures, the Christian New Testament and the Qur'an of Islam have offered truths. The messages in these books aren't always understood, their wisdom hidden among nontruths and interpretable in many ways. But truths are always there, often only slightly veiled. When the time is right for us, we'll each learn truths from the above scriptures and those other, newly uncovered ancient texts. More importantly, we'll learn from our personal source of all truth, our soul Self. The veil will be lifted and we will understand. We will remember.

Our ignorance has not been accidental. It has served many purposes as parts of the plan for our human evolution. At the times of the Mysteries and the Vedas and such teachers as Buddha, Confucius, Lao Tzu, Moses, Jesus, and Muhammad, we weren't ready to understand their messages, because we had considerably more to experience in our darkened, asleep state. The awareness-expanding experiences of the previous three millennia have been invaluable and necessary to our evolution. Those earlier teachers planted the seeds from which we have grown.

We are finally understanding the teachings of the ancient Mysteries from the Sumerians, Egyptians, Greeks, and nearly every culture of the two millennia preceding the common era. Their spirituality is being more accurately interpreted and made available to humanity now, because we are finally ready to use their wisdom wisely. The two most common teachings of those Mysteries are: We are all ONE; we must go within to know our Self.

Humanity lives under zodiacal movements of a little over 2,000 years, called ages, with each age centering on an emphasis in life experience and spiritual evolution. Over a period of 26,000 years, all these ages are completed and then a new cycle begins. The outgoing age of Pisces, while one of darkness, has prepared us, with the help of contrast and the above great teachers, for en*light*enment, awakening, and Oneness. The new age of Aquarius, one of light and love, will see awakening become reality.

With the teachings of the many great sages and other Earth Angels setting our stages, we've experienced every conceivable adversity, degradation, and carnal desire. We've witnessed blessed mixtures of good and evil and happiness and misery. We've been afforded choices not possible in the environment and under the circumstances of earlier times. Had we even partially comprehended the ancient teachings, we could not have experienced these events.

Ever notice how blindingly bright the sun seems when it first shines out of rain clouds, and how warm and wonderful it feels? When we awaken into Reality, we'll realize how blind, deaf, and insensitive we've been in Earthly human life. But we will be forever grateful for having been so limited, if only for a short while. We will be grateful for having believed in separation when we can see, know, and fully appreciate our Oneness. We are now preparing for a wonderful time.

Your awakening is taking place little by little at your own pace, serving your own purposes. No one is any higher or lower or more or less advanced than another. We are by choice on different paths and at different stages of both our human and our spiritual experience. Some of us have other missions to accomplish in this life before we can more fully enjoy the fruits of our labor. You may be one such, so will deny truths and not attempt right now to seek them. Everything is perfect, and what you're to see, you will when it's to your advantage to do so. The clouds of human life will disperse and the dazzling light and warmth of Reality will shine through. When you are ready to be still and know, the veil will be lifted and truths revealed. A quantum Shift in consciousness is yours to experience, and from there, awakening.

21

LIFE'S CYCLICAL NATURE AND EARTH-CHANGE PROPHECIES

I've written in several earlier places that I believe our human evolution is circular, or actually spiral, rather than linear as we've been taught by both science and religion. Many alternative archaeologists, Egyptologists, and historians believe that we humans are so different intellectually from our animal cousins because we didn't originate here on Earth. They say we emigrated from another physical world in outer space. I agree we didn't originate here, but that's where the agreement ends. I say the world from which we originated was not physical but was spiritual. I also say that's true of all life in the cosmos and that everything has life.

CYCLICAL/SPIRAL EVOLUTION

While I find every reason to believe that sentient extraterrestrials exist elsewhere in this universe, I find even more reason to believe that humanity began as very intelligent and very spiritual beings, and that our evolution has been circular rather than linear. Nearly everything in our physical universe is associated in some way with an essentially circular form. Our sun, Earth, our moon, and all of the other planets are round in shape, as are tree trunks and branches, our own trunks, arms, and legs. Our eyes appear round. Most cells and molecules in our bodies are basically round and the tiniest atom appears round. The orbits of planets and moons in our solar system are elliptical, and electrons move around the nucleus of an atom. A raindrop is round and light falls in a circle.

Cycles follow. Water runs down a drain in circular motion and the finite amount of water on this planet is maintained by the constant circular motion of cycles. Why then, would we presume our Earthly experience, our evolution, to be any different, an anomaly?

OUR NATURAL TEACHERS

So much we want to know about ourselves is available to us by observing nature. Our domestic animals and our own babies can teach us so much, if we're willing to observe them with our heart, maybe along with our intellect. Oceans, rivers, mountains, and deserts all speak to us, while trees, plants, wild animals, and insects all display examples from which we can learn. Look around. Doesn't nature project the cyclic pattern I contend exists in all things? Certainly the seasonal changes in deciduous trees and plants, the zodiacal phases in the precession of the equinox, and the daily sun rising and setting and our moon waxing and waning vividly display their nature of coming and going in cyclical patterns.

ANCIENT CULTURES KNEW OF THE CYCLES

The Maya, Aztec, and Peruvian calendars show four cycles of humanity prior to our current one; and they are round in shape, underscoring the circular nature of human evolution. Pamela Colorado in "Indigenous Science in the Modern World," (*Noetic Sciences Review,* Summer 1992) says all indigenous peoples of the Americas recorded and have passed on knowledge of four previous cycles, each ending in a destructive cataclysm. The clairvoyant, Edgar Cayce also spoke of four previous cycles.

I think I can identify those four cycles: The first would be our "First World," our entry into physicality, perhaps as Lemurians, when we were still conscious of our Oneness and spirituality and still used pure intelligence before taking on intellect. We were love and light, as were all beings on Earth, and we lived harmoniously and cooperatively together. The second age likely would have been the period of downward evolution for the first wave, our devolution, during the early Atlantean period, through which many of us humans lost our great intelligence—covering it with intellect—exchanged our spiritual senses for physical senses, and hid from ourselves our spirituality, our Oneness, and everything about Reality. Ours was a gradual degeneration of sorts. The third prior cycle might have been when, still as Atlanteans, the second wave began devolving and using intellect, started relying on technology which copied natural functions into unnatural form. We formed language and writing. Corruption and greed entered our consciousness and eventually caused the demise of Atlantis. The fourth age, one of darkness, I think began with ancient civilizations creating empires and aggressive warrior behavior, conflict, and war. And, like the later part of the Atlantean period, emphasis in the last hundred years or so has been on intellect and technology. But, the fourth age also included the wisdom of the masters and prophets, the writing of religious texts and the forming of institutional religions. Who knows what cataclysms might have occurred to end the first three ages? We are now on the upward arc of our cycle, in transition from the fourth cycle to the fifth, which will again be one of light, love, and spirituality like the Lemurian first age, only lived in even higher consciousness because of our experiences throughout the ages.

EARTH CHANGES

Earth changes from natural cataclysms have occurred throughout Earth's existence. Those above mentioned calendars, as well as most other aboriginal lore indicate that each prior age has ended in a natural disaster. And both the Lemurian and Atlantean civilizations are said to have been destroyed or dispersed when their lands were devastated by cataclysmic events. Many people believe that something will happen to us as we close out the fourth cycle. Prophesies of earth changes say that more and more frequent and severe earthquakes, hurricanes, tornados, and volcanic eruptions may culminate in a polar shift, causing major change to land and sea patterns of our Earth. Past psychics, such as Nostradamus and more recently Edgar Cayce, have foretold of such cataclysmic events, as does Revelation, the final book in the Christian Bible. Scientists agree that earthquakes of great magnitude are likely and a polar shift more than possible. Natural earth changes aren't strange or new; they have figured noticeably in humanity's recorded history, and scientists believe Earth has also undergone several polar shifts in her time.

There have always been Armageddon-type prophecies, but more often than not they don't come true, particularly at the time predicted. Is our world really coming to an end? Some people believe so and that it will be soon—but then people have thought that many times before. The Western religions all were based on salvation from an immanently expected devastating disaster. Some people suggest that such an apocalypse would be karma or punishment for our many evils. Others say that humanity is on a path of self-destruction and that God will take cataclysmic steps to prevent us from destroying the planet along with ourselves in a nuclear holocaust. They contend that God can be selective in his methods, leaving much of our Earth still inhabitable, and will enable some people to remain on Earth—or return to it—to rebuild and begin the new and glorious life, also foretold. The December solstice of 2012 was thought by many to be that auspicious time. Nothing happened! At least nothing obvious happened.

This sort of prophecy doesn't fit my philosophy, for two reasons.

First: We are God and whatever we do God is doing. We human actors are perfect, acting under divine guidance at all times. As in the Atlantean times, our current state of degradation and disharmony is part of our plan for Earth and for humanity, and is a background for our individual and group scenarios. If we are on an unalterable course toward self-destruction—which I doubt—that, too, is by design and perfect. There are loving reasons for our taking the current path as well as any disasters that occur all the time.

Second: Humanity is nearing a time in which enlightenment will help us to Shift our awareness to ever higher levels of consciousness. This will enable us to see our unity and true spirituality become our conscious reality, and with it brotherly love and harmony. Yes, it's true that the world is coming to an end, but only the world *as we have known it*. The old is ending to make way for the new. But, it's an attitudinal event not a physical one. Our old separating, self-absorbed materialist beliefs, attitudes, and behavior are being replaced with heart-based ones. Such a change would normally be slow, gradual, so something drastic *may* have to occur to bring about the change more quickly. If we don't voluntarily change, Mother Earth may force the issue.

WORLD CONDITIONS REFLECT OUR THINKING, BELIEFS, AND ATTITUDES

World conditions reflect our individual emotional conditions and attitudes, which have amassed into the collective unconsciousness. Wars reflect the composite of our individual internal conflicts; our intellect striving to maintain control by keeping intuition at bay; our male energy fighting our female nature and vice versa; our adult self inhibiting our inner child. Oppression, hunger, disease, and economic recessions result from individual poverty of spirit, lack of self-esteem, the victim stance many of us have assumed. Crime in our cities mirrors our own individual self-dishonesty. Homelessness comes from our confusion over who and what we are and what our real place is in this life. Pollution of air, water, and land stems from our pollution of our minds and the minds of our children with negative judgmental programs. So long as our individual energy is fragmented and negative, our collective unconsciousness—those old programs humanity has bought into—will prevail and cause destructive separation rather than positive, harmonious unity.

GAIA'S ATTENTION-GRABBING CHANGES

Mother Earth—or Gaia if you prefer—reacts to the energy of collective unconsciousness, and when that energy becomes oppressively heavy, stress builds up within Earth's bowels and must be vented before causing her to explode. She burps lava, ash, and steam through volcanic vents and shifts, and rumbles to ease gas pains. She enlists the aid of the physical atmospheric elements to pour water on her to cleanse physically and spiritually, like our taking a shower. Gaia sometimes asks the elements to perform abnormally, with heavier rain, snow, ice, wind, and greater cold than normal, or with higher humidity or more heat and less water. With these, along with her own eruptions and quakes, she shakes us up to disturb our constantly ongoing negative thought patterns and to redirect our focus.

HUMAN ATTENTION-GRABBING CHANGES

Humanity has its own attention-getting ways. Wars, genocide, airplane crashes, and skyjackings, other terrorist activities, serial killings, child abuse, and kidnapping, stock market crashes, oil spills, and arson fires, are some of our human means of changing our ongoing thought patterns. While appearing negative, the effects of all such events are purely positive. They draw our attention and elicit heartfelt emotions; causing us to individually lessen our devotion to our materialist way of life, and let loose of some of our material possessions. They temporarily move our focus off ourselves and whatever we think is our plight. They help us lighten collective unconsciousness, temporarily. They tug at our hearts, opening them, filling us with compassion, generosity, and kindness. They Shift our concerns from the material to humanitarian and cause us to pull together for everyone's good. In doing so, they illustrate the direction in which we're heading. They also provide a means for many beings to leave this life and return home.

HUMANITY'S CHANGE

Although enlightenment is escalating, wide-scale consciousness raising still appears slow. Some of us may need something to push us over the edge. It may well take disaster in such proportion that shock is unmistakable and change inescapable. We might need a human excuse to live harmoniously and let spirituality into our lives. The obviously drastic measures of mass destruction, inundation, and death provide us with such an excuse. At times of disaster we band together in ways we don't normally. Recent tsunamis, hurricanes, and earthquakes illustrate that in time of disaster we humans reach out to each other, accept help ourselves, or stop and rethink our values, priorities, and the direction of our lives. Although those devastating disasters have grabbed us and caused some attitudinal changes, when the dust has settled, most of us have gone right back to business as usual. And, many of us think of God only in our hour of need, seldom when things are going well for us. What will it take to make more permanent changes? It may seem horrible that we should require death and destruction to cause us to share love. But, in fact, it's what we planned for this time. Death isn't bad; it's a painless release to a more beautiful life, and that which is destroyed isn't real or of lasting value anyway.

Those Earth Angels described in the previous chapter are here to help humanity in general. For some, their Earthly mission is nearing completion and their stay here need not be prolonged. The earlier those extras in our play leave Earth life, the sooner they can get on with other aspects of their own spiritual journey. To prolong their misery would be unkind and a poor way to thank them for loving service to humanity. A mass exodus may be the final scene of their mission, shocking, and devastating survivors, leaving them vulnerable and empty, ready to refill with love, harmony, Oneness, spirituality.

It's obvious to many of us that humanity's attitude of greed and our indifference toward Earth and her other inhabitants must change. Earth's resources are being depleted and our environment devastated. With global warming, we too may be destroyed. The loving lifestyle projected for the new Aquarian age would benefit greatly from a cleansing of Earth's environment. Disasters can do that.

Can one segment of humanity convince the other segments to change their attitudes? Of course anything is possible, but are we all ready to make such a major change? Our existing ways are ingrained; it's human nature to be concerned with our own life in the present. Oh, we wonder what legacy we are creating for our children, and give lip service to resource-depletion and the effects of global warming. But is our concern for our children's future or even our own, enough to cause us to change our way of living now? Our prevailing philosophy is to let tomorrow take care of itself.

Our old materialist belief systems were perfect for us earlier, just what we needed for our experiences of earlier times. But now we want something different. We want spirituality. As I explained in my 2013 book *WAKE UP! Our old beliefs don't work anymore!*, if we awaken to the failures, falsities, and fallacies of current predominant belief systems, we can change our worldview from materialism to spirituality and raise our human awareness to higher levels of consciousness. We can transform nearly overnight, and obviate any need for disasters.

ATLANTIS AND LEMURIA

Great earth changes may well have taken place millions of years ago under circumstances similar to ours today. Earthquakes and flooding are said to have been instruments of destruction of the lost civilization of Atlantis. According to Edgar Cayce, the peoples of Atlantis toward their end suffered from wickedness, greed, and disharmony similar to our current experience. He contended that many of us living today are reincarnating from lives in Atlantis, and may have returned here now to continue unfinished business begun under similar conditions in Atlantis. Those Atlanteans were devolving, and now we are moving upward in consciousness toward greater spirituality, so I believe we won't need the cataclysms that ended previous ages. Or, if they occur, they won't be as severe and will serve loving purposes, as is always true. They will help us to Shift.

OUR CHOICE TO BE HERE

Each of us chose to incarnate at this particular time for our own reasons. We chose to participate in whatever events are planned to occur. Fearful mass dwelling on earth-change prophecies will only add negativity to collective unconsciousness, cause individual stress and worsen any suffering and grief in response to any disasters that do occur. If we look upon prophecies impersonally, with interest and optimism, then go about our business of Shifting and of becoming enlightened, we will benefit from their forewarning. Keep in mind that death is only a change in living conditions.

THE SHIFT

With potential earth changes in mind, we might rethink our approach to life. We might learn to take one day at a time, enjoying each moment, accepting people, conditions, and events as they are, and sharing ourselves with our loved ones. Let's either find some enjoyment in whatever we do or quit doing what we don't enjoy. Let's be a little self-indulgent, but not selfish. Let's be loving (nonjudgmentally accepting), and let's take ourselves and life in general less seriously. It's time to open to greater spirituality. Let's examine our beliefs about ourselves and life on Earth to be sure they aren't the self-engrossed, separating, conflict-oriented beliefs of materialism but are heart-based and unitive.

My book, *WAKE UP! Our old beliefs don't work anymore!* (Portal Center Press, 2013), thoroughly examines our materialistic beliefs, in both science and religion, and offers possible alternatives from our ancient ancestors, aboriginal cultures worldwide, and current spiritual metaphysical philosophers and teachers. It also puts my view of "creation" into story form. It could help you understand what those old beliefs are and why they need to change. *WAKE UP!* also helps us see our own individual responsibility in changing world conditions and explains our personal role in that change. It points out the success we can achieve with relatively little effort.

The Shift, as many of us see it progressing, is a two-fold one, the first part leading ultimately to the second part. The first is an attitudinal change, while the second is our ultimate transformation, our awakening. I believe that most of us in the first wave have already made the transformation necessary to the attitudinal Shift in consciousness without drastic cataclysmic measures. Now as One, we can further that part of the Shift for the second wave by encouraging a spiritual revolution. I call it a revolution because, like the cycles of human evolution, it's a *return* to spirituality. It's a case of not only remembering our spirit beingness but becoming more spiritual in our beliefs, thinking, and behavior, as we were in the Lemurian age.

A CRITICAL MASS

Once enough of us realize humanity's need for a Shift in conscious awareness, see that it's possible, and accept our individual responsibility for bringing it about, we will create the spiritual environment and change in our energy necessary to cause a quantum leap in human consciousness everywhere. Not all of us need to reach that realization for the Shift to occur. The effectiveness of a relatively small percentage can be phenomenal—it has been called the hundredth monkey effect. The power of the few with loving intentions will bring about the Shift in much of humanity.

What is referred to as the *hundredth monkey effect* came out of a 1950s anthropology study of behavior in groups of monkeys on the Japanese islands. Scientists reportedly found that as some monkeys on one island learned to wash their sand covered sweet potatoes before eating them, their new behavior attracted the attention of others in the group. Soon, many monkeys were doing the same thing. Suddenly, the scientists observed, when the number reached a critical mass (called the hundredth monkey), nearly all of the monkeys on that island began behaving the new way, and simultaneously, monkeys on other islands and the mainland began washing their food before eating it, without ever having seen it done. While there's some doubt that there were not, in fact, other monkeys that did this in the past, the story nicely illustrates what truly is possible.

CREATING OUR CRITICAL MASS

I *know* this critical-mass effect can work and that all we need do to change humanity is for those of us who have completed the attitudinal phase of the Shift to focus our intentions in a uniform direction. I encourage that direction to be spiritual or love—the same One thing. I mean for us to love everyone and everything unconditionally and to demonstrate spirituality to benefit others. No one needs to know we're doing anything; we don't have to be obvious and don't have to be organized. We just each need to be dedicated and sincere in our intent. A relative few of us can spread love and spirituality around the world. We are ONE, and what affects one of us affects all others to some degree.

Accept unconditionally every single person as part of God, the ONE, no matter how they look, talk, or behave. See Kosmic beauty in every situation. Have compassion for every human and animal apparently suffering in this life. This is the outpouring of spirituality in our culture. It will obviate the need for drastic measures.

Let's start with ourselves. Let's love—nonjudgmentally accept—ourselves just as we are. We can accept ourselves with whatever flaws we think we have. We each are an extension of a higher vibrating, more knowing, more loving intelligence, and we've been guided through life by that intelligence. Many of us are *consciously* guided by it now. We are each a shard of the hologram that is this Kosmos, so we are also that ONE. How can we be flawed? How can we be anything but perfect?

What we each do serves higher purposes than we know or can imagine. What others are and do aren't ours to know and certainly aren't ours to judge. Is anything stopping us from accepting all others—humans and non-humans alike—with unconditional love? The acceptance kind of love I'm talking about is purely an attitude we each can assume by choice and intent. We merely have to put our hearts and minds to it. *Be* love.

Earth and Human Vibrations

The powers that be of the Kosmos are also helping us. Earthly and human vibrations are increasing and speeding up not only time, but our thinking and experiencing processes. We are experiencing more and becoming more rapidly aware. We are recognizing synchronicity and symbiosis (cooperation between two or more organisms to their mutual benefit) in the goings-on of our life, and are seeing the hand of the divine everywhere we look. We are transcending human life, rising in awareness through ever higher levels of consciousness.

Spiritual Transformation

The time grows near for the spiritual transformation of humanity, as we move from a dark age into an age of light, beauty, and Oneness. Everything going on in our world today is helping a portion of humanity—the first wave—focus on the job to be done. The polarization we see today is making our choices clear, showing us what we don't want in our world, helping us be clear about what we do want. We are spreading love, compassion, and spirituality. We are creating the mass of energy that will rebalance the scales of spirituality/physicality, feminine/masculine, and separation/Oneness, and cleanse our collective unconsciousness.

Let's now take advantage of the stimulation that disasters have provided. We need only change ourselves to the extent our beliefs and attitudes are materialistic, selfish, and separating. Let's each of us focus on nonjudgmental acceptance, beginning right now. Let's each of us be more spiritual, now. Let's recognize our Oneness and *know* that we (humans, animals, and other creatures, rocks and elements, too) are all ONE in consciousness. Let's help others to realize their spirituality and their divinity. Let's gather with others of like heart to spread love. Let's create the critical mass needed to effect a spiritual revolution, then cataclysmic disasters won't be needed. Let's begin ... now.

By identifying with our God-Self and awakening to oneness with our Self, we individually empower our soul to create according to its ideas rather than our own limited ones. We, in effect, say, "Thy [Self's] will be done on Earth as it is in heaven [Reality]." We are returning Eden to Earth. It's an exciting time. I look forward to whatever is in store for us. It can't be anything but perfect, loving, and wonderful.

22

AWAKENING

As waves together shape Earth's seashores, we humans together shape the whole of our world. As each wave adds to the life of succeeding waves, we each contribute to the individual lives of others. And like waves, we too shall one day return to that larger, greater whole—the Oneness of the Kosmos that is God—in fully awakened consciousness.

In my understanding, the way to reach that Oneness is through our own individual conscious wholeness. It is to awaken from our facade of human beingness to the Reality of our oneness with our higher-vibrating, soul-Self. Only then will we truly experience our Oneness with all.

CHRIST CONSCIOUSNESS

Some Christian denominations,—particularly New Thought—see Christ as the spirit of God everywhere and within and as each of us, as this Bible quote implies: Christ *is* all, and in all (Colossians. 3:11). Christ is our inner, soul-Self, the consciousness of God expressing in each of us. Christ consciousness, therefore, is the state of conscious oneness with the Christ within, the perfect attunement of our inner and outer selves—our wholeness, or whole-I-ness (holiness)—as exemplified by Jesus. I believe that the New Testament Jesus, during the last few years of his life, was fully awake and consciously one with his soul-Self in Christ consciousness. He said:

I and my Father [Self] are one (John 10:30).

Believe me that I am in the Father, and the Father in me (John 14:11).

The words that I speak unto you, I speak not of myself; but the Father that dwelleth in me, He doeth the works (John 14:10).

In becoming consciously one with his Father (his soul-Self), Jesus awakened to Christ-consciousness. He was a revelation of God on Earth. Jesus never singled himself out as the only Christ. He instead said, come, follow me to the Father, do as I have done, follow my lead. That was the most significant part of his mission: to show humanity who/what we truly are and what is possible. Jesus called his soul "Father," while I call my soul "Self." And, to avoid religion's misinterpretations, instead of "Christ"-consciousness, I prefer to call this awakened state "Kosmic" consciousness.

SECOND COMING

Following Jesus' way, we too can awaken to Kosmic consciousness. Our awakening is our rebirth into the kingdom of God. We all lived in Kosmic consciousness (Reality) before we began Earth life. Our awakening and return to that state, therefore, is again, or the second coming of Christ for each of us.

BUDDHA CONSCIOUSNESS

Siddhartha Gautama also was a perfect example of an awakened human being. Five hundred years before the birth of Jesus, according to Huston Smith in *The Religions of Man*:

> He (Gautama) was asked, "Are you a god?"... "No," (he answered) "An angel? "No." "A Saint?" "No." "Then what are you?" Gautama answered, "I am awake."

He was called the Buddha, meaning "enlightened" or "Awakened One."

Jesus and Buddha are by no means the only awakened human beings; many before and since have united in consciousness with their soul-Self. Muhammad's Qur'an quotes him as saying: "He who knows his own self knows God." Once he accepted his role in the spirituality of his people, the Arabs, and began to recite to followers the beautiful wisdom he received from the voice he identified as the Arch Angel Gabriel, Muhammad, too, awakened to Kosmic consciousness. The same can be said of Lao Tsu and Confucius, and probably many others.

OUR RESURRECTION

When reunited in Kosmic consciousness with our Self, we, too, can be such a revelation of God. We can individually free ourselves from reincarnation (if we want) by attaining Kosmic consciousness in this life. Such would be our resurrection. When we pull the veil over our conscious awareness and join the human race, our Christ or inner, soul consciousness appears dead to us. When we awaken from human life and reunite with our soul in consciousness, Christ is resurrected, alive in physical form. Resurrection is not an overcoming of death, but is awakening while in human life. It's symbolic of our atonement, or at-one-ment. Human conditioning and attachments have been put aside, the old has been put off and we have awakened anew, possibly seen as have been "born again."

PREPARE FOR AWAKENING

To awaken from our veiled state into union with our soul is not, however, something we can decide we want, then do. As humans, we aren't in a position to know when the time is right for our awakening. We don't know when we've experienced all we've set out to or when we are sufficiently prepared. Also, our awakening may be an experience for others or may need to mesh in some way with others' awakening or their enlightenment. Only our soul, can know these things and reunite us. It's up to us, though, to be duly prepared, which means being completely receptive to and eager for reunion of self with Self.

PUT OFF THE OLD

The necessary preparation includes choosing a path and making a decision to give up our commitment to Earthly material attachments and our old beliefs and way of life: the limited, negative judgments and programming of our intellect and of the collective unconsciousness. We can't achieve Kosmic consciousness and express from our all-knowing intelligence while expressing from our limited outer intellect and engrossed in material human existence.

> Therefore, if any man be in Christ, he is a new creature; old things are passed away.
>
> ~2 Corinthians 5:17

We convert from the old to the new.

The ultimate goal of our human experience has always been to—eventually, when we are ready—uncover and remember our spirituality and unite with our Self in Kosmic consciousness. We've never lost it; we've just temporarily hidden it from ourselves. We have veiled it from our awareness with human existence. The more thoroughly we become embroiled in our human condition and the more we accept, live by, and dwell on human emotions, the more deeply we keep Christ trapped within. So long as we see our human self as separate and apart from our spiritual Self, we perpetuate our separateness and can't accept Oneness.

We need to separate ourselves from Earthly attachments—what devastating natural and man-made disasters often help us do, especially stock market crashes. People devoted to material splendor are shown the transience of their idol. Also, the more thoroughly we stay attached to either of the materialist belief systems—fundamentalist religions and classical science—we deny our spirituality and our Oneness, as they do. We can't awaken to Reality and unity while stuck in those old beliefs.

We each also need to give up attachment to the results of our actions and words, prayers, and desires. We need to get out of the way and let our Self be and do according to its wisdom, its purposes, its will. We don't have to concern ourselves with either control or results; we can trust our Self to create what is in our best interests. When we give up our attachment to and our reliance on external things, pleasures, and people for our happiness, we take back the power we've given our human condition. We prepare for awakening by setting aside anything that might obstruct our view of Reality or impair our ability to hear our inner voice. By that I don't mean to quit smoking and drinking alcohol, eating meat and meat by-products, or any other "shall not." Those are all expressions of God, too, and serve loving purposes in our life. The life and death of cattle, chickens, and other abused animals for the greed associated with the supply of human food are parts of the natural food chain, modified to help us develop compassion and general concern for other species. It's part of our awareness expansion and enlightenment, part of our shift to higher levels of consciousness. We open our eyes with nonjudgmental awareness and turn within to our source of Truth, Love, Beauty, Serenity, Joy, and Creativity.

GET PAST THE HUMAN FACADE

I think that to *know* Kosmic consciousness we have to get past the physical facade and see only God in, as, and through everyone and everything. We have to realize our Oneness. The Latin word, "persona," from which our word "personality" comes, according to *Brewer's Dictionary of Phrase and Fable*, "...originally meant a mask worn by actors and later transferred to the character or personage represented by the actors." The people whom we love, dislike, our friends, our enemies are all actors with personae, donned in our world for our mutual benefit. Beyond that, they are temporal and insignificant and needn't be held in high regard. We are all heroes; no one is any more special than anyone else.

PUT ON THE NEW

Jesus said: "Except ye be converted and become as little children, ye shall not enter unto the kingdom of heaven" (Matthew 18:3). Not yet indoctrinated into the negative world of humanity, at birth children are closer to their spiritual Selves than they are apt to be again for a long time. They haven't yet had the veil pulled over their awareness by a judging and emotional intellect. They haven't yet put on "the old man." Without a well-trained intellect, thinking they have to make things happen in their lives, children are more apt to bow to the will of their own Self, their God.

Also, we are born curious; that's how we learn as we grow. All children go through a stage when they ask why about everything. To me that's an indication they innately know there is purpose to everything. Many of us have long forgotten how thrilling learning can be. Most of us have focused our learning toward the judgmental programs of outer human living and materialism. We've forgotten to ask those spiritual why questions. If we are to be enlightened in preparation for awakening, we would benefit from regaining that curiosity and begin again to ask why. This time, though, our focus might better be on the inner and the spiritual.

I think all children are aware of spirit. Their consciousness has only recently left home in Reality and hasn't yet become enmeshed in the programs of human life. While some people have buried that awareness so deeply it may have no chance to surface in this life, many others retain some spiritual awareness. How deeply we've hidden or how near the surface our memories are of Reality and our Oneness is by choice in our design for this life. It is part of our life's scenario and depends also on our other missions and goals. Rest assured, though, when the time is right, each of us will awaken to the full memory of our spirituality and we'll experience Oneness.

OUR ONENESS

Between incarnations and throughout most sleeping hours our Oneness is obvious. During those times, we're separated, instead, from our human role and physical body. They're unable to distract us from Oneness, nor is the veil of collective unconsciousness able to obscure our vision of Reality. To realize our goal of awakening in human consciousness, we will need to consciously rise above those distractions and dispel that obscurity.

Raising Our Vibrations

Everything is alive with vibrations and is individualized by differing rates or frequencies. Everything in material form has been made to appear solid by slowing the rate at which it vibrates. Once both inner and outer consciousness are joined in communion, the rate of our vibrations becomes more rapid than while we're engrossed in three-dimensional Earth life. Our inner consciousness doesn't slow down to our human level, but our Self raises our vibrations and our human awareness to ever higher levels of consciousness. These vibrations are not the same ones we use in our various states of human consciousness. The latter go in the opposite direction. When we meditate, for instance, rather than increasing our human rate of vibration, we lower the rate. That is, our normal conscious state throughout our day is what is called "beta." Meditation or communion slows our vibrational rate to alpha or theta. The more relaxed our body and the more quiet our intellect the slower our human consciousness vibrations. When we slow those self vibrations they can more easily attune with our soul-Self vibrations until we become consciously one. Then our soul pulls us up to our natural level of vibration, its own level, where our awareness rises to ever higher-vibrating levels of consciousness, and we awaken.

By rising to higher levels we are able to see, hear, and know truths at those levels. Just as air is thinner at higher elevations, in the faster vibration at more lofty levels of consciousness the veil of collective unconsciousness appears more transparent. The higher we go, the less effective the veil is and the more we can see with greater clarity. The faster we vibrate, the lighter we are and the higher we can go. The higher we go, the higher we're able to go. Rather like an airplane, which by air flow over and around its wings creates a lightness (vacuum) in the air above the wing, into which it climbs, we create a lightness at the next higher level into which we rise. Like the airplane, we climb ever higher as our energy vibrates faster and the air above lightens.

In the awakening process, as one of us rises to a higher level, the way is made easier for all others. Not only do we show others the way, but we lighten the energy surrounding humanity. Also, because we all are ONE, each of us experiences Oneness, everyone else, perhaps deep in their being, gets a tiny glimpse of the wonders of that experience. The more of us who consciously experience unity, the more of those unconscious glimpses amass in the energy of all others. This creates and strengthens a longing in the depths of every human being, a longing that will eventually surface. We will each become a consciously whole being. We must; it's the final step in our material human experience. Our world's energy, too, is lightening and increasing in vibration, aiding in the whole process.

OUR WHOLE BEING: "FULL SELF"

> The ocean transformed, through the action of clouds, into the form of rivers, etc., ceases to be itself; so indeed hast thou forgotten thyself through the power of conditions. Oh friend! Remember thy full Self, THOU ART THE REAL SELF....
>
> ~ The Upanishads, Svarajyasiddhi

Our whole being, or "full Self," consists of both our outer human awareness—the actor in our play—and the inner soul-Self. We won't be consciously whole until we make our wholeness real by automatically thinking directly from our whole Self, as our self, without hesitation, translation, or interpretation. Many of us have learned to know and to communicate with our Self; still we do so as if we are talking with someone else, a separate being. Translation was only a beginning point. So long as we consciously translate into human terms what we hear from the voice within before speaking or acting, we maintain separateness. As long as we hold separateness in our human consciousness, we deny the whole being we are and separation persists.

Jesus said to his disciples:

> Be not anxious how or what ye shall speak; for it shall be given you in that hour what ye shall speak. For it is not ye that speak, but the Spirit of your Father who speaketh in you (Matthew 10:19-20).

Once our inner and outer selves think and act as one, we'll be able to consciously speak Godly words to help our fellow human beings. When we can trust our inner guidance and are willing to subdue our beloved ego, we'll no longer hesitate. When we feel an urge to speak, we'll open our mouth and speak from our heart, not knowing or judging what comes out.

OUR PATH TO AWAKENING

Contrary to how we might think of our life on Earth, it isn't a popularity contest nor is it intended to be a bed of roses, nor at this time Utopia. I believe its ultimate purpose now is to lead us to awakening back to Reality with greatly expanded awareness. It doesn't matter how we get there.

Whether we achieve this goal through misery, loneliness, ill health, and poverty or through happiness, love, and spirituality is of no consequence. We may achieve it through being "born again" in Christianity, by way of devoted service to God and humanity, through the meditation, exercise, and discipline of a Hindu yogi, or the silence of a monk, or we may get it through enlightenment (my choice, as it was for Siddhartha). We may be surrounded by people or exist in solitude. Regardless, each of us has our own path to follow, as ill-defined as it may be.

We needn't follow rigid rules, nor name our path. It's what we make it and is personal to us individually. Choosing a path is allowing ourself to be guided from within, following where our loving inner Self leads. All paths lead ultimately to awakening to conscious Oneness with our soul, everyone and everything. And the most enjoyable part of our journey towards awakening is consciously taking our own path.

ACCEPTANCE

Why hesitate? What's so wonderful about your personal identity, intellect, and human emotions that you aren't willing to give them up for conscious Oneness and the wonders of omniscience and undying universal love? Your persona and intellect are yours only for this life. They, like the human roles of your loved ones and material possessions, are only vehicles for Earth experience. While you can learn through them, you won't be taking them with you. You insist on having, doing, thinking for yourself. Why, because you're afraid to let go the familiar? What will happen if you stop clinging to what you think you have and what you think you are? Are you afraid you'll lose everything—your precious worldly possessions, the companionship and love of those who are dear to you? You don't want to lose your identity, your self-esteem, your free will, your freedom of choice. You don't want to set aside your ability to judge or to reason. You want to continue to like or dislike, to feel happiness, pain, or sorrow, because it's easier to continue the familiar. Are you unwilling to make the supreme sacrifice of your intellect to achieve the unknown wonders of your true intelligence and your Oneness with all?

You can make intellect a partner in your awakening; then you won't have to sacrifice anything. You can keep all of the above. You don't have to give up anything; you just have to experience it from a less material, more spiritual vantage point. Spirituality is not a losing or giving up of anything but is an expanding and a remembering of who and what you truly are. You merely have to be willing to change, willing to give it up; in other words, no longer be driven or guided by a devotion to anything material.

What's so great about freedom of choice when there's always an opposite to fear? You seek wealth but never lose your fear of poverty. You choose good but see bad all around. You opt for status but fear the loss of it. You look for happiness but find it illusive, always outside of you or ahead in your dreams or in your past experience. You choose youth but expect to age. You select good health but suffer ill health brought on by fears, judgments, expectations, and anxieties. You want love but, because you don't know how to love yourself and give of yourself freely, you block the very love you desire. You seek excitement but depend on others to provide it, so live in unhappiness and boredom. Whatever you choose, you'll either witness its opposite or suffer from the fear of experiencing it. You swing from exaltation to depression as your choices meet or fall short of your expectations. Many of the things about which you humanly make choices aren't yours (human self's) to decide. They are facets of your pre-chosen scenario and will follow the outline or script through to its conclusion. Your human choices, made in ignorance, do not always lead to your highest good, so are apt to bring frustration instead of contentment.

You may say you prefer to wait and meet your maker (be one with your Self) after you've finished this life. What makes you think that will work? It's your human awareness you're trying to awaken. Until you achieve its awakening during a life on Earth, you will probably want to reincarnate until you do. You may then have to live a life in which you have nothing at all to lose before you're willing to give it up. Jesus was a poor carpenter. Perhaps you must reach a time when you think you have so much to lose that to give it all up is the greatest gift you could give to God, to yourself, and to humanity. Siddhartha's father was a king and he a prince, ideally married to a beautiful princess who bore him a handsome son. He was heir to his father's throne and fortune. He chose enlightenment for himself and devotion to humanity's enlightenment.

Most importantly, the decision is one of acceptance rather than denial. You give up or lose nothing. You recognize that all separation and all fear is of your imagination and has no basis in Reality. You accept that you are God. You accept the will of God. You don't have to quit your job, leave your home, family and friends and run off into the wilderness to spend a solitary life in communion with Self, God—although, that too might work. You might sever your connections to Earthly human conditions and achieve Oneness. You might awaken in solitude, but you have the opportunity to accomplish much more by staying put and letting your world see and reflect your awakening. Your goal is not a solitary one. Your own awakening is important and the only one over which you have conscious influence, but you are also part of a total awakening of humanity. Much of what you do in this life is helping others toward that end. You can help others by being part of their experience, by being available to them when their need arises, perhaps showing them the way.

Other people may need to hear a word or phrase from God through you. Maybe to feel your warmth, your nonjudgmental love, would help them. They may need to see serenity made manifest in another human being, someone not very different from themselves. You are where you are and with whom for good reason. You can best show others the way through your example. Your attitude will have changed, and when you're at home in your own environment, the change will be evident to the people who know you. They can't help benefitting from your transformation.

THE KINGDOM OF GOD

Jesus said: "...seek ye first the kingdom of God and all these things shall be added unto you" (Luke 12:31). This instruction, I believe, is the third most important lesson to learn as a human—the first being that we are all ONE in consciousness, God, and the second is to go within to *know* ourselves as God. The kingdom of God is the ONE consciousness within each of us, accessible to us humans through communion with our individualized soul-Self. By going within to know both your self and your Self, you are seeking the kingdom of God, Kosmic consciousness. Once you are on that seeking path, everything about Earth life gets easier. Your wants are fewer and those you have are abundantly supplied. With your body, mind, and spirit held steadfastly on realizing the kingdom of God, all things are automatically added unto you. There's no other way it can be.

When you awaken (to the kingdom of God), you are filled with love for everyone with whom you come in contact, and that love is recognizable. Loving energy flows smoothly throughout your body in balance and harmony, aligning your energy and providing good health, vitality, and strength. Serenity shines through your eyes and gives your face a youthful glow. You are actually younger—not in years but in body, mind, and spirit. Your love automatically attracts those around you. Your example to them is the greatest gift you could give them, for it causes them to want to experience for themselves such a transformation.

So, you see, it isn't an active, physical separation you make but a passive change in the way you view everything, a spiritual *knowing*. It's a change in attitude, being a natural open (new, child-like) channel for the flow of love. Your awakening is in awareness, raising you to ever higher levels of consciousness. It is allowing your Kosmic Self to express naturally, without interference from your intellect. It is honestly saying "nevertheless, not mine but thy will be done."

Freedom

Everything is just as intended and isn't yours with which to agree or disagree, like or dislike. Each of us is doing what will help us toward our goal. Each has to experience and learn on our own, and at our own pace. What we're going through and doing is perfect. Seeing that as truth sets us free. Seeing others as the actors and loving them adds to our freedom.

To keep us on track, we're given glimpses of Oneness along the way. For instance, sometimes while petting a beloved cat or dog, or as a parent caressing our child, or in a rare moment of intimacy with someone very dear, we're filled to overflowing with love, nearly overcome with joy. When you allow yourself to express love honestly and openly, you literally *bare your soul* and express as One. Someday soon that feeling will pervade your being and dominate your life. When it does, you'll know you're free and one with your soul in human consciousness. You will recognize it, but only because you've experienced human contrasts without it.

BE YOUR SELF

Once you've made the all-important change in attitude and perspective and are firmly entrenched on your spiritual path, there's little else to do but let go and let God. You are an aspect of God and everything you do is being done by the God that is truly you, your Self. Stop believing that you, the human being, are separate and apart from God.

Center yourself in God, your true soul Self. Be your Self. Let the child in you surface: the real, unconditional, unlimited, questioning Self you've learned to hide. Let your love and enthusiasm show. Don't be afraid to be natural. Rid yourself of inhibitions. Let your wonder at everything beautiful around you show.

Remember that not only is the goal of awakening important, but the journey to it is just as important, and truly the most enjoyable. As you come closer to unity with your soul-Self, you find your life changing enormously, wonderfully. You see all life differently, feeling nothing but love for all beings and all events. You accept, if not recognize, the perfection in everyone and everything. You have no need for affliction or heartache. Life is easier and more clearly synchronous. You realize your spirituality and see it everywhere. You *know* that everything is ONE, and that nothing can be separate from you or what you truly are: the Kosmos, God, Consciousness.

You chose to read this book for your own reasons. It may be that you are searching for some words to show you the way. If that's the case, you don't need more words; your own longing from within is enough. You're on the brink of your discovery. Your own inner-Self will show you the way. Go within; let your Self raise your awareness to ever higher levels.

A PRAYER

Our God, who art our winged Self, it is thy will in us that willeth.

It is thy desire in us that desireth.

It is thy urge in us that would turn our nights, which are thine, into days which are thine also.

We cannot ask thee for aught, for thou knowest our needs before they are born in us: Thou art our need; and in giving us more of thyself thou givest us all.

~ Kahlil Gibran

AFTERWORD

Soon humanity will live in harmony, dedicated to spiritual living, brotherly love, cooperation, peace, and sharing. We'll live with love in our hearts for one and all, and we'll know and be serene in our spirituality. We'll enjoy the fruits of our own creativity, and understand the meaning of life and our role in it. We'll no longer be slaves to the judgments of our intellects, the ups and downs of the teeter-totter of choice, and the sufferings of our emotions. We will be free. We'll fully appreciate the perfection and beauty that are ours, thanks to our human experiences.

THE WONDERS OF AWAKENING

No words in a human language describe the wonders of awakening. I'm convinced that our joy will be far greater than any happiness or pleasure we've ever felt. The beauty—brilliance of light, vividness of color, lilting harmony of sound, and savory aromas and tastes—of everything will far exceed our wildest imagination. We'll know complete serenity and total freedom. Our love will be all consuming, all encompassing, and stronger and deeper than we can now imagine.

Our love for mate, family, and friends won't cease, but will no longer control us or them. Our love will actually deepen and increase, flowing freely to everyone in an accepting, unconditional way. Our soul's freedom to choose will be ours to enjoy; we'll find no conflict where choice is necessary, and will automatically do according to our Self's will. We won't need language, but will communicate more truly by telepathy and feelings. No longer needing words to express, we'll implant thoughts into others' minds and receive their thoughts by our focus. Not limited by words and their dubious interpretation, we'll always *know* exactly the intent, meaning, and feeling of another's thoughts. Without judgment, our thoughts will be loving and happily shared.

Ultimately, those of us who wish to enjoy physical human life on Earth will do so using only our one whole soul consciousness. Thinking only with pure intelligence and tapping the record of all knowledge and experience, we'll know everything. We'll live in physicality as briefly or as long as we wish. Travel again will be simple, vehicles minimally used; thought transference will be our primary mode of transportation. When we wish to travel, we'll think ourselves there and be there. We can opt to go in consciousness only if we prefer, leaving our form temporarily behind, and pick it up and transform it later as we choose. Like some of us did when building the pyramids and other megalithic structures, we'll think matter into a different vibration to dissolve it in one spot then reform it in another. Eventually we will no longer use form, unless we want to for some loving experiential reason. We won't need food for nourishment but will be able to create a delicious feast in seconds if we wish. We'll need or want nothing. We'll know the abundance that has always been available to us, tapping it for our enjoyment.

We'll no longer teach our children to pull the veil of human unconsciousness over their true, beautiful, divine Selves. Each member of all kingdoms will be a fully conscious participant in what we call life, and that life will be abundantly harmonious and fulfilling and unbelievably joyful. There will be no need for illness, physical or mental challenge, or injury, no affliction of any sort. Coming and going at will, we will no longer want such experiences nor will we need them to enable us to transcend human life (die).

We lived like this for hundreds of millions of human years in the first cycle, when we originally created Earth and physicality. Of course, it wasn't millions of our current years to us then, for we hadn't yet slowed down to the time frame with which we are accustomed. Then we could only guess at the limitations and dualistic opposites we were finally to create on Earth and experience for ourselves. What did we call that cycle, Lemuria? The Garden of Eden? Humanity is closing its circle, awakening and returning to the consciously loving, spirit beings we were in our beginning. Our new Earth cycle will be wonderful. What shall we call it, Heaven?

MY WAY

All of the foregoing has been my way of helping others to see themselves and the world we live in differently than what the materialist view offers. It has been to demonstrate our spirituality and help others remember the truths of Reality: our loving spirituality and our Oneness.

I believe that the single most important thing to always keep in mind is that there is only ONE, and that Kosmic ONE is Good. That ONE is Omnipresent, Omnipotent, and Omniscient. It is spirit, energy, light, consciousness. It is Love, Harmony, Serenity, Joy, Beauty, and Creativity.

It is Everything that lives; and since everything lives, nothing can be excluded; nothing can be apart from us. We are the ONE and we are the individualized multitude of possibilities and intelligences that are the physical faces and viewpoints of the singularity of the ONE. We are the shards of the holographic ONE. There can be nothing else, nothing outside the ONE, no other power and no other truth but Love.

SPIRITUAL PERSPECTIVE

This book has been about our Earthly human life, from mostly the human perspective as we bring spirituality into view. But there's much more to the story than can be seen from that view. Let's take a peek at Earth life from the perspective of the spirit being off-stage. Then we'll leave that big picture's whole story for another book.

When awake the actor sees only ONE in consciousness everywhere, and only love, peace, harmony, joy, intelligence, creativity, good health, and well being for and as everyone. The actor sees prosperity, enough of everything for each and every being. There is happiness galore, with animals and humans harmoniously co-existing, companionably sharing Earth life. Everyone is healthy, strong, whole, and youthful. Life is wonderful, beautiful, and abundantly good. Spirit knows that as ONE there can truly be only these conditions, this Good. In fact, nothing else is possible. Anything other than this good is purely illusion. It is in the human mind, and can be wiped away in an instant.

Once we've awakened to the Omnipresent, Omniscient, Omnipotent Love, we can set all else aside and never again get caught up in the dualistic programs of the human condition unless we want to. We can accept the world of Good as it truly is and never again accept anything less or different. We can choose Love, and allow the ONE to be our only experience.

We all are spirit beings and the ONE consciousness; there is nothing else to be. We are all Love; there is nothing else to be. We are all in good health, harmony, peace, joy, and general well being; there is no other condition or state in which to be. Awaken to Reality, and see for yourself.

You are the ONE; there is nothing else, nothing outside you, no power or truth apart from your Power, your Truth.

You are, I AM, The ONE!

WE ARE ONE!

Are you AWAKENING to that understanding?

The foregoing has been offered with a great deal of love.
Andrée (Dee) Cuenod

APPENDIX

A SUMMARY OF WHAT I WANT PEOPLE TO KNOW

We all—everything and everyone together—are ONE, in the interconnected unity of everything.

Consciousness is what everything in the Kosmos is and is what we call God.

Objective consciousness—on a higher level—is what thought the universe or cosmos into being, the First Cause, the "Creator." We humans, the spirit beings who have come to Earth, are that consciousness.

Everything, all of the Kosmos, is alive, each entity vibrating at a different rate, or frequency. Material things are merely consciousness with vibrations slowed to create form.

We are eternal immortal spirit beings having a physical human experience.

We all—each and every one of us—whether human, animal, fish, reptile, insect, rock, plant, tree, or Earth herself, are consciousness, so are what we often call God; there is no other.

This Earthly human life is illusion of our own making, in the form of plays on the Earth theater stage. Each of us has a role to play in many others' lives, and are needed by them in that role.

Human life is about relationships, change, and emotions brought on by our beliefs and attitudes. We each have created our world (experience, reality) by our choices of beliefs, attitudes, and emotions.

Our beliefs about ourselves, all other beings, God, and our world create our reality—what we see and respond to in our world. Our attitudes determine how we respond or react.

Everything that ever occurs or that anyone does in Earth life has love as its cause (on a higher consciousness level). There are no accidents, no coincidences, no mistakes or errors, no victims or villains, no evil, and no death, only Love, Harmony, Joy, Creativity, and Beauty.

We humans are enacting plays to help us *know* and appreciate our true selves/Selves and our spirit Reality through contrasting experience.

Dualistic contrasts of negative and positive are needed in Earthly human life to define and help us know and love ourselves and appreciate our spirit Reality.

Our relationships help us mutually experience both the contrasts of negativity and the love of positivity that are our growth experiences, expanding our awareness.

Go within. Your individual inner God—your higher soul-Self—will answer all your questions and lead you to what you personally need to get to a higher level of understanding, if you let it.

Our Earthly journey is circular/spiral in nature, beginning with us as fully spiritual, then devolving to what has seemed fully material, and finally evolving gradually back to full awareness of our spirituality and Oneness, having risen to ever higher levels of consciousness: our destiny.

Everything is perfect as it is, in its time.

The cosmos is a quantum hologram, an illusion, and everything in it is a unique aspect of the ONE.

Many of these statements have been proven by quantum science.

BIBLIOGRAPHY

AUDIO/VIDEO PRESENTATIONS
Braden, Gregg, *The Science of Miracles, the Quantum Language of Healing, Peace*, Feeling, and Belief. Hay House, Inc., 2009
Dyer, Wayne, *Excuses Begone*. Hay House, Inc., 2009
Goswami, Amit, *The Quantum Activist*. Quantum Activations, 2010
Lipton, Bruce & Rob Williams, *The Biology of Perception & The Psychology of Change*. Spirit 2000, Inc.
Zukav, Gary, *Soul to Soul*. Sound Ideas, 2007

BOOKS
Alexander, Eben, *Proof of Heaven*, Simon & Schuster, 2012
Allen, James, *As a Man Thinketh*. Self-published, 1912 (see *As We Think So We Are* by Ruth L. Miller, Atria/Simon & Schuster, 2013
Anonymous, *Impersonal Life, The*. C.A. Willing, Publisher, 1969
Braden, Gregg, *The God Code*. Hay House, Inc., 2006
_____, *The Divine Matrix, Bridging Time, Space, Miracles, and Belief*. Hay House, Inc., 2007
_____, *The Spontaneous Healing of Belief, Shattering the Paradigm of False Limits*. Hay House, Inc., 2008
Dyer, Wayne, *Excuses Begone*. Hay House, Inc., 2009
Ford, Arthur, *Unknown But Known*. Harper & Row, Publishers, Inc., 1968
_____, *Life Beyond Death, The*, Berkley Publishing Corp., 1971
Gawain, Shakti, *Creative Visualization*. New World Library, 1978
Goswami, Amit, *The Self-Aware Universe, how consciousness creates the material world*. Tarcher/Putnam, 1993
_____, *The Visionary Window*. Quest Books, Theosophical Publishing House, 2000
_____, *Creative Evolution, A Physicist's Resolution between Darwinism and Intelligent Design*. Quest Books, Theosophical Publishing House, 2008
_____, *How Quantum Activism Can Save Civilization*. Hampton Roads Publishing, 2011
Hall, Manly P., *The Secret Teachings of All Ages*. Tarcher/Penguin, 2003

Joseph, Frank, *Edgar Cayce's Atlantis and Lemuria*. A.R.E., 2001

_____, *Atlantis and 2012*, Bear & Company, 2010

Kubler-Ross, Elizabeth, *On Death and Dying*. Macmillan Publishing Company, 1969

_____, *Death, The Final Stage of Growth*. Prentice-Hall, Inc., 1975

Lamsa, George M., *Gems of Wisdom*. Unity School of Christianity, 1966

Lipton, Bruce, *The Biology of Belief, unleashing the Power of consciousness, matter, and miracles*. Mountain of Love/Elite Books, 2005

_____, and Steve Bhaerman, *Spontaneous Evolution, Our Positive Future*. Hay House, Inc., 2009

Miller, Ruth, *Unveiling Your Hidden Power, Emma Curtis Hopkins' Metaphysics for the 21st Century*. Wise Woman Press, 2005

_____, *Mary's Power: Embracing the Divine Feminine as the Age of Invasion and Empire Ends*. Portal Center Press, 2010

_____, *Make The World Go Away, The Gift of 2012*. Portal Center Press, 2011

Moody, Raymond A., Jr., *Life After Life*, Bantam Books, 1975

_____, *Reflections On Life After Life*. Bantam Books, 1977

Ruggles, Michael, *Quantum Conversations, How Thoughts, Feelings, and Beliefs Shape and Create Your Reality*. Fast Pencil, Inc., 2011

Samuel, William, *A Guide to AWARENESS and TRANQUILITY*. Seed Center, 1976

Schlitz, Marilyn, Cassandra Vieten, Tina Amorak, *Living Deeply, the Art and Science of Transforming Everyday Life*. New Harbinger Publications, Inc., 2007

Smith, Huston, *The Religions of Man*. New York: Harper & Row, Publishers, Inc., 1958

Spalding, Baird T. *Life and Teachings of the Master of Far East, Vols I-VI*. DeVorss & Company, 1924-1935

Walsch, Neale Donald, *Conversations with God, Book One*. Putnam, 1995

_____, *Conversations with God, Books Two and Three*. Hampton Roads Publishing Company, Inc., 1997 and 1998

_____, *Tomorrow's God*. Atria Books, 2004

Waters, Owen, *The Shift, the Revolution in Human Consciousness*. Infinite Being Publishing LLC, 2006

Zukav, Gary, *The Seat of the Soul*. A Fireside Book, by Simon & Schuster, 1990

ACKNOWLEDGMENTS

I thank my Self for giving me these insightful "truths," and for helping me share them with others. I am especially grateful to Terri, Bev, and Dea for their perfect presence in my life at the perfect time and their perfect teachings which aided me so greatly in the early stages of my quest for enlightenment. I appreciate Ishvara for helping me refine my truths, and for leading and showing the way. I also express my sincere love and appreciation to those people who helped me at various stages along my early writing journey. To Nancy, Dixie, Liane, and Janice for giving of their time to read the original edition in draft form, and for offering thoughtful comments. To Jane, Mara, and Valik who, as members of my writing support group, helped me get so many of the words right, and gave me love and support beyond imagination. To Bobbi, Lori, Waneta, and especially Carol, for typing various early versions of the manuscript, BC—before computer. To Carol W., Sharon C., and Linda D., members of my more recent spiritual discussion group and very dear friends, for their reading of and comments on many later versions of my writing and for their general spiritual support of me in my endeavors to share with others my spiritual insights. To my dear friend Mauri for her help in reading (many times) and commenting, and for her extraordinary words of wisdom and encouragement. And most of all for her ever loving understanding and support of me throughout this endeavor. The help these wonderful people gave me was invaluable.

A special thanks to a wonderful editor, Elizabeth, and also to a later editor, Julie, both for helping me get it right, and in the process teaching me to write. Finally, thank you Barbara, for your editing of this version and your expert words of wisdom and encouragement.

I love you all.

I also greatly appreciate the following for giving me permission to quote from their work:

Harper & Row, Publishers, New York, for: Arthur Ford's, *Unknown But Known, my adventure into the meditative,* 1968.

Raymond A. Moody, Jr., M.D., *Life After Life.* New York: Bantam Books, Inc., 1975.

Also, an interview with John White, *Science of Mind* magazine, March, 1986. Los Angeles, CA: Science of Mind Publications.

William Samuel, *A Guide To AWARENESS and TRANQUILITY.* Palo Alto, CA: Seed Center, 1976.

Huston Smith, *The Religions of Man.* New York: Harper & Row Publishers, Inc., 1958.

All Biblical references are from *The New Scofield Reference Bible,* C.I. Scofield, D.D., Editor. Oxford: Oxford University Press, 1945.

Other quotes used in this book, and not otherwise identified, were taken from:

Bartlett's Familiar Quotations, Originated by John Bartlett. Boston, MA: Little, Brown and Company, 1980.

Dimensions of Man's Spirit, an anthology of metaphysical prose and poetry, Edited by Virginia W. Bass. Los Angeles, CA: Science of Mind Publications, 1975.

Great Quotations, The, compiled by George Selde. Secaucus, NJ: The Citadel Press, 1983.

New Dictionary of Thought, The, originally compiled by Tryon Edwards, D.D., revised and enlarged by C. N. Catrevas, A.B., Jonathan Edwards, A.M. and Ralph Emerson Browns, A.M.. Standard Book Company, 1964.

Oxford Dictionary of Quotations, The, Third edition. Oxford: Oxford University Press, 1979.

Spirit Of The Upanishads, The, or the aphorisms of the wise, compiled and adopted by Yogi Ramacharaka. Chicago, IL: Yogi Publication Society.

INDEX

adversity 33, 73, 92, 127, 128, 136, 151, 267
   adversities 9, 80, 81, 91, 127, 132, 136, 261

beliefs 7-10, 15, 18, 44, 72, 76, 83, 85, 89-91, 97, 117, 121, 138, 153, 154, 158, 210, 215, 217, 219, 220, 227, 229, 230, 233, 239, 242, 243, 259, 272, 275-279, 283, 284, 297, 305, 313

blame 90-92, 125, 147, 174, 203, 208, 235

cancer 13, 14, 62, 153, 156, 157

children 5, 31, 32, 68, 70, 78, 85, 108, 116, 118, 119, 128-133, 142, 145, 157, 160, 165, 174, 177, 178, 193, 194, 205-208, 242, 264, 273, 275, 285, 294

choices 5, 57, 68, 71, 82, 91, 93, 103, 104, 127, 208, 229, 233, 234, 238, 239, 245, 267, 279, 289, 297

communion 3, 25, 27, 29, 40, 69, 74, 109, 243, 249, 250, 251, 252, 253, 254, 286, 290

contrast 55, 61, 64, 66, 73, 79, 81, 89, 103, 115, 137, 194, 264, 267

creation 1, 6, 10, 42, 50, 57, 63, 64, 66, 75-77, 99, 101, 228, 229, 245, 276

death 2, 9, 25, 29-31, 45, 65, 68, 73, 80, 97, 99, 108, 118, 130, 133, 146, 147, 156, 161, 162, 165-179, 238, 265, 274, 276, 282, 284, 298

Eastern traditions 9, 15, 62, 85, 88

enlightenment 3, 5, 7, 9, 10, 21, 23-25, 29, 35, 38, 39, 42, 43-45, 49, 78, 85, 93, 99, 109, 110, 135, 145, 241-244, 252, 261, 262, 266, 267, 272, 274, 283, 284, 288, 289, 303, 305

evolution 2, 3, 9, 40-42, 57, 66, 70, 71, 79, 84, 86, 93, 100, 134, 185, 197, 242, 260, 262, 265, 267, 269, 270, 277

fundamentalists 1, 4, 6-8, 50, 176

future 1, 9, 70, 86, 87, 105, 107, 129, 161, 162, 184, 217-220, 227, 275

healing 9, 115, 151, 154-159, 161-163, 180, 199

health 9, 90, 132, 138, 139, 140, 148, 151, 152, 154, 161, 162, 175, 217, 226-229, 259, 263, 288, 289, 291, 295

heaven 59, 72, 191, 279, 285

Hebrew Scriptures 1, 50, 266

human self 30, 31, 40, 78, 122, 170, 215, 230, 283, 289

illusion 18, 31, 53, 56, 64, 71, 75, 77, 101, 106, 107, 109, 110, 111, 125, 131, 136, 208, 224, 239, 295, 297, 298

infirmity .138, 141, 142, 146, 171

interconnectedness 8, 74, 117
intuition 28, 31, 40, 43, 45, 52, 67, 69, 79, 82, 94, 187, 206, 244-249, 262, 272
Jubal 27, 35, 36, 37, 38
judgment 9, 21, 38, 40, 51, 57- 59, 73, 87, 90, 95, 96, 97, 99, 127, 130, 141, 147, 176, 183-191, 196, 198, 201, 205, 207, 212, 216, 217, 220, 230, 246, 259, 293
karma 33, 39, 85, 86, 88, 89, 237, 272
Kosmos 8, 49, 55, 60, 61, 66, 84, 101, 224, 262, 278, 281, 292, 297
lack 57, 98, 101, 119, 123, 142, 176, 194, 195, 204, 205, 225, 226, 239, 242, 262, 273
materialism 8, 169, 272, 273, 275, 284, 294, 305
meditation 24-26, 33, 38, 40, 159, 241, 288
medium 27, 37
metaphysics 15, 25, 42
Mysteries 50, 78, 109, 267
mystics 9, 50, 246
natural selection 2, 41
New Age 51, 84, 89, 241
Oregon coast 23, 29, 35, 219
pain 75, 82, 92, 100, 103, 127, 131-137, 140-144, 147, 149, 151, 152, 156-158, 161, 163, 166, 168-170, 178, 210, 212, 216, 263, 288
plays 47, 65-69, 74, 75, 77, 79-88, 95, 96, 98, 99, 104, 106-109, 117, 119-122, 125, 130, 138, 179, 190, 260, 263, 297, 298
prayer 151, 152, 225, 226, 229
quantum hologram 56, 298
reincarnation 31, 32, 33, 39, 67, 70, 80, 84, 85, 108, 282, 289
relationship 1, 9, 14, 17, 33, 79, 80, 87, 90, 104, 132, 137, 201, 202, 203, 204, 205, 213, 228, 229, 236, 253, 297
relaxation 17, 20, 21, 26, 175
Religion 2, 6, 260
responsibility 38, 59, 90, 92, 147, 176, 197, 220, 235, 276, 277
Science 2, 15, 16, 49, 140, 172, 176, 270, 299, 301, 304
separation 51, 53, 61, 109, 124, 175, 179, 183, 201, 245, 261, 267, 273, 279, 287, 289, 291
Shift 5, 9, 72, 74, 93, 110, 191, 242, 243, 248, 260, 266, 268, 272-277, 301
spirit beings 3, 8, 9, 36, 56, 63, 64, 66, 68, 73, 77, 78, 81, 89, 100, 101, 111, 117, 122, 124, 148, 173, 178, 185, 243, 244, 294, 295, 297
spirit guides 3, 25, 31
spirit life . 2, 17, 89, 116, 118, 135
Truth 1, 5, 7, 244, 284, 295
truths 3-7, 9, 10, 18, 28-30, 33, 39, 42-45, 49, 50, 68, 91, 93, 110, 136, 148, 183, 188, 243, 245, 250, 251, 254, 256, 261, 266, 268, 286, 294, 303
Upanishads 1, 6, 197, 219, 243, 246, 266, 287, 304

vibration 37, 56, 57, 66, 73, 74, 107, 109, 110, 286, 287, 294

visualization 157, 158, 299
Wisdom 14, 113, 248, 300

ABOUT THE AUTHOR

After receiving UCLA's MBA at for women executives, Dee Cuenod left her management career in the space industry and became Associate Director of Planning at UCLA, responsible for coordinating campus-wide academic planning. She later headed UCLA's Administrative Data Processing and Information Systems, and instigated a change in the way that processing and those systems were handled at all nine campuses of the University of California.

No longer comfortable with her materialist way of life in Los Angeles, Cuenod left academia and, settling in Oregon, pursued spiritual enlightenment. She learned to commune with her higher-vibrating, soul-Self, and got answers to all of her numerous and deep questions about life on Earth and in spiritual dimensions.

So happy and content with her life now, she seeks to help others see life on Earth differently than what we've been taught, so they too might better understand their life, find it easier to cope with, and actually enjoy it. A self-taught spiritual metaphysical philosopher, she is on a life-mission to help humanity evolve to higher consciousness. As a spiritual teacher and mentor, she teaches classes in spirituality and privately counsels individuals and groups in person, by e-mail and over the phone.

Cuenod is author of *WAKE UP! Our old beliefs don't work anymore!* (Portal Center Press, 2013) and *AWAKENING, a journey of enlightenment* (Northwest Publishing, Inc., 1995). This is an updated and expanded second edition of that book.

Portal Center Press

Other Titles from Portal Center Press

Kat's 9 Lives, moving passion into action for a "feel good" life, by Kat Cunningham

Kindred Spirits: the quest for love and friendship, by Bob Czimbal & Maggie Zadikov

Language of Life, answers to modern issues in an ancient way of speaking, by Milt Markewitz, Ruth L. Miller and Batya Podos

Make the World Go Away, the gift of 2012, by Ruth L. Miller

Mary's Power: Embracing the Divine Feminine as the Age of Empire Ends, by Ruth L Miller

Miracles through Music. Odyssey of a Music Healer, by Joel Andrews

Views from the Pew, moving beyond religion & discovering Truth within, by J C Pedigo and friends

Wake Up! Our old beliefs don't work anymore! by Andrée L. Cuenod

www.portalcenterpress.com • 541-351-8461

CPSIA information can be obtained at www.ICGtesting.com
Printed in the USA
BVOW08s1457140415

396091BV00004B/8/P